The Utopian Mind and Other Papers

The Utopian Mind and Other Papers: A Critical Study in Moral and Political Philosophy

AUREL KOLNAI

Edited by Francis Dunlop

Unfinished at the time of Kolnai's death, *The Utopian Mind* will be widely welcomed by students of moral and political philosophy. It provides a powerful critique of the 'Utopian' mode of valuation. Kolnai locates utopian thinking in Totalitarian systems of the Right and Left and as an unspoken background to much liberal thought and to many of the best known theories of moral philosophy.

The book carries an Introduction by Professor Pierre Manent of the Centre de Recherches Politiques Raymond Aron, Paris, and a Preface by David Wiggins, Wyckham Professor of Logic in the University of Oxford.

Aurel Kolnai lectured in Ethics at Bedford College, University of London, from 1959 until his death in 1973. His earlier collection of papers is *Ethics, Values and Reality* (Athlone, 1977) edited by Bernard Williams and David Wiggins.

Dr Dunlop was a pupil of Aurel Kolnai. An Honorary Research Fellow of the University of East Anglia, his previous publications include *The Education of Feeling and Emotion* (1984) and *Scheler* (1991).

Also published by Athlone

Ethics, Value and Reality
Selected Philosophical Papers of Aurel Kolnai
'Recommended to all students of ethics' D.Z. Phillips, *Philosophical Quarterly*
0 485 11169 1   hb

AUREL KOLNAI

The Utopian Mind and Other Papers

A Critical Study in Moral and Political Philosophy

Edited by Francis Dunlop

ATHLONE
London and Atlantic Highlands, NJ

First published 1995 by
THE ATHLONE PRESS
1 Park Drive, London NW11 7SG
and 165 First Avenue,
Atlantic Highlands, NJ 07716

© Francis Dunlop 1995
Introduction © Pierre Manent 1995

British Library Cataloguing in Publication Data
A catalogue record for this book is available
from the British Library

ISBN 0 485 11232 9

Library of Congress Cataloging-in-Publication Data

Kolnai, Aurel.
    The utopian mind and other papers : a critical study in moral
and political philosophy / Aurel Kolnai.
        p.   cm.
    Includes bibliographical references and index.
    ISBN 0-485-11232-9 (hard)
    1. Utopias--Moral and ethical aspects.   2. Political ethics.
I. Title.
HX807.K65   1995
321'.07--dc20   94-23954
                                                            CIP

Typeset by
Bibloset

Printed and bound in Great Britain by
The University Press, Cambridge

Contents

Foreword

This volume contains Aurel Kolnai's hitherto unpublished draft for *The Utopian Mind: A Critical Study in Moral and Political Philosophy*. The original work was never finished, however, and the *Other Papers* referred to in the title of the present volume include both published and unpublished work, selected to try and make good what seem to have been Kolnai's intentions.

The best indication of the nature of *The Utopian Mind*, which was actually begun in 1956, is probably afforded by Kolnai's own 'synopsis' (I have reversed the order of the paragraphs):

> The gist of my theme, put in a nutshell, is about this. There is a 'Utopian' mode of valuation almost, but not quite, as deeply rooted in the human mind as its opposite, which I might call the Commonsensical mode of valuation. Utopianism is a perversion of our sense and concept of Values, its supreme stigma being perhaps the confusion of value-categories and intolerance of distinction they embody. It is ineliminable and perhaps not without some useful function but accessible to argumentative essential criticism. It necessarily involves typical self-contradictions of a quite different nature from the incongruities, incertitudes and opacities of Common Sense. On the social and political plane, it is the vital core of Totalitarianism.
>
> In a very broad sense, devoid of any 'school' allegiance, I might describe my frame of mind as Aristotelian. As a student of philosophy, I was most directly influenced by modern German neo-objectivism and phenomenology (Franz Brentano, Edmund Husserl, Max Scheler, Dietrich von Hildebrand), and some kindred English and Spanish thinkers such as G.E. Moore and C.D. Broad, and Ramiro de Maeztu. Later, my philosophical thinking came to be stimulated also by some aspects of scholasticism (Aquinas, Duns Scotus, Luis de Molina) on the one hand, contemporary British logical empiricism on the other. My political outlook has been moulded, as concerns direct and

indirect literary influences, by such older classics as Vittoria, Richard Hooker, John Locke, Samuel Johnson, Edmund Burke, Tocqueville, Lord Acton and Jacob Burckhardt, and by more recent writers like Irving Babbitt, Sir Ernest Barker, Hermann Heller, Clive Bell, Wilhelm Röpke, Alfred Cobban, José Ortega y Gasset, F.A. Voigt, Christopher Hollis, C.A. Macartney, Claude Sutton and others. Particularly would I mention, in the context of the present subject matter, Karl Mannheim (*Ideology and Utopia; Diagnosis of our Time*), Raymond Ruyer (*L'Utopie et les utopies*), and K.R. Popper (*The Open Society and its Enemies*).

(12 July 1966)

As *The Utopian Mind* was still unfinished when Kolnai died in 1973, the question inevitably suggests itself: why publish it now? The Preface, by Professor David Wiggins, undertakes to answer this, with reference both to the state of contemporary philosophy and to that of world politics. The Introduction, by Pierre Manent, Professor at the Ecole des Hautes Etudes en Sciences Sociales, fills out the skeletal 'synopsis' printed above. As well as enlarging on the link with totalitarianism, Manent shows the intrinsic connection between Kolnai's analyses of utopian thinking, his concept of conservatism and his interpretation of phenomenology as a systematic working out of our 'world-experience'. In a final section he addresses himself to the question why utopian thinking should be so rampant in our own times. My own Editor's Introduction contains a history of Kolnai's project, a short description of the material on Utopia Kolnai left at his death, and an account of how the selection of supplementary material was made.

Francis Dunlop

Preface

This volume contains Kolnai's hitherto unpublished draft for *The Utopian Mind*. In order to supplement this material in its partly fragmentary state, it also reprints two related papers, namely 'The Moral Theme in Political Division' (*Philosophy*, XXXV, 1960, pp. 234–54) and a translation of 'La Mentalité Utopienne' (*La Table Ronde*, 153, September 1960, pp. 62–84), together with some other unpublished material.

Kolnai's interest in the idea of Utopia, and his suspicion of it, were implicit in his earliest writings on the subject of value, and implicit in his once celebrated diagnosis of the psychical and philosophical impulsions that sustained Nazism, namely his *War Against the West* (Victor Gollancz, 1938). His explicit interest, according to his own account, dated from 1946–8:

> I conceived this project when still well below the turn of life, about 1946–48 in Quebec; later, during the years 1955–59, I consumed three research grants relating to it. By 1961 I had collected an immense store of literary material, extracts with copious notes of my own, which I could not now hope to cast into a readable book – even in five times the allotted space and even if I were in my seventeenth instead of in my seventieth year. At the same time, a good many things relevant to the theme have remained unfamiliar to me – and now there are again emerging some important recent symptoms of the disease, [e.g.] the 'New Left' and the sham-scientific, allegedly 'anti-humanist' and 'meta-marxian' new brand of Utopianism of the Althusser sect in Paris. Even Raymond Aron's superb intelligence and caustic sarcasm have not quite succeeded in making this not wholly meaningless trash intelligible.

> Surely I told you, either here at Bedford College or later at Swansea, that Raymond Ruyer's masterpiece, *L'Utopie et les utopies* (1950), which I had discovered when spending the summer of 1952 in Europe, had exercised upon my mind an enormously stimulating but also, in the long run, a paralysing

impact. . . . I have long been wondering whether there is much point at all in expounding the subject once more after that somehow 'definitive' work (which surprisingly enough doesn't seem to have achieved world fame and is unknown in the English-speaking sphere). Nevertheless, I could not honestly say either that my own points of view have all been borrowed from Ruyer's book [or] that whatever I have written about Utopianism consists exclusively of embroideries upon it.
(Letter dated 2 February 1970 to D.Z. Phillips)

Kolnai's ideas about Utopia are explained with sympathy and brilliant understanding in Pierre Manent's Introduction. The connection of these ideas with the rest of Kolnai's work and with his life is set out in short compass in Bernard Williams's and my Introduction to *Ethics, Value & Reality*, edited by Francis Dunlop and Brian Klug. In a larger compass, it is set out by Kolnai himself in *Twentieth Century Memoirs*.

Kolnai died twenty years ago, leaving his book unfinished. What is to be gained now by giving it to the public in its present condition? What does his book add to the present stock of understanding?

The question might be considered under two heads: (a) current philosophical understanding; (b) general understanding of the realities of world politics, especially of the collapse of the communist regimes of Eastern Europe (from which so many different morals are so effortlessly drawn by so many different political practitioners).

Under (a), the following extract from Thomas Nagel's recent book *Equality and Partiality* is a representative (far better than representative) sample of present-day understanding.

A theory is utopian in the pejorative sense if it describes a form of collective life that humans, or most humans, could not lead and could not come to be able to lead through any feasible process of social and mental development. It may have value as a possibility for a few people, or as an admirable but unattainable ideal for others. But it cannot be offered as a general solution to the main question of political theory: How should we live together in society?
    Worse still, when what is described is not in fact motivationally

possible, the illusion of its possibility may motivate people never-theless to try to institute it, with results that are quite different. Societies are constantly trying to beat people into shape because they stubbornly fail to conform to some preconceived pattern of human possibility. Political theory is in this sense an empirical dis-cipline whose hypotheses give hostages to the future, and whose experiments can be very costly. (As Hannah Arendt once said, 'It is true that you can't make an omelet without breaking eggs; but you can break a great many eggs without making an omelet.')

But while the avoidance of utopianism is important, it is no more important than the avoidance of hard-nosed realism, its diametrical opposite. To be sure, a theory that offers new possibilities must be aware of the danger that they may be purely imaginary. The real nature of humans and human motivation always has to be an essential part of the subject. Pessimism is always in order, and we have been given ample reason to fear human nature. But we shouldn't be too tied down by limits derived from the baseness of actual motives or by excessive pes-simism about the possibility of human improvement. It is impor-tant to try to imagine the next step, even before we have come close to implementing the best conceptions already available.

What Kolnai's work adds to these sensible observations is a phenomenological diagnosis of the utopian impulse itself, a diagnosis drawn from the philosophical study of value as such, and a searching examination of the contradictions within it. These contradictions make Utopia not only unrealizable but unthinkable and inconceivable. Kolnai's diagnosis furnishes an explanation – one deriving from the human understanding of the structure of human and non-human values themselves and emphasizing their diversity and their mutual non-reducibility – of why it is that, when the reforming spirit turns from urgent piecemeal improvement to the pursuit of Utopia, it must inevitably desecrate value itself.

Under (b), one speculates that, having rejoiced in the cessation of Communist terror, the author of the pieces printed in this book could not possibly have gone on to find the last decade of this century to be a good period for conservative thought, in any philosophically or politically interesting sense of 'conservative'. Kolnai defined the difference between Right and Left in various ways, both by reference to attitudes towards the idea of the organic state and, more pointedly perhaps, by reference to the question of orientation towards the *Is/Ought* distinction. According to Kolnai, a true conservative's understanding of what ought to be must be conditioned by his understanding, valuation and appreciation of what contingently is. This relation between *is* and *ought* is constitutive of conservative thought. Of non-conservative thinking there is no such expectation. To judge by these and the other marks that Kolnai mentions, conservatism as Kolnai understood it has almost disappeared (except as a residual attitude of mind among conservatives displaced from all power or influence). Conservatism as a political creed has been swallowed up by what might be called simplistic Economism, where Economism itself shows telltale signs of Utopianism. By finding ways to appeal as much to egalitarian envy (formerly the perquisite of the Left) as to greed (formerly the perquisite of the Right), the new Economism bid fair to swallow up not only conservatism and Conservatism but Socialism as well.

I speculate here that the moralizing monetarism of the 1980s and the more recently institutionalized replacement of all other modes of judgement by the real or (shadow) prices of a real (or notional) market might have put Kolnai in mind of Oakeshott's remark about Hayek: 'A plan to resist all planning may be better than its opposite, but it belongs to the same style of politics' – to wit, the utopian. Even as Utopianism is sent forth from the front it returns by the back door, promising exactly the same conceptual and practical mischief.

One of the many achievements of Pierre Manent's admirable Introduction is to show how, even now, Utopianism as Kolnai castigated it still undermines the capacity to pay attention either to reality or to value. Manent's account of Kolnai also helps one to notice how far current reactions to the stirring events that the world has recently seen must leave us from any positive restitution of our relation to values – how starved such reactions leave us of any political thinking ('personalist' thinking, as I think Kolnai would have said) that could sustain a genuinely pluralistic response to the vast variety of objects, problems and situations that confront us as objects of individual or collective concern.

David Wiggins
University of Oxford

Introduction

Aurel Kolnai: A Political Philosopher Confronts the Scourge of Our Epoch

As early as the middle of the eighteenth century, it was possible for Adam Ferguson to write that we had entered 'the age of separations'.[1] Ferguson's is one of the first and most striking formulations of an idea that has become a commonplace to us, and conveys as much satisfaction as disquiet – satisfaction at the advance of knowledge, which makes possible the division of labour, especially intellectual labour; disquiet at the impossibility of a synoptic grasp of the scattered elements of human learning. There are many separations. If there is any that arouses more disquiet than satisfaction, it is the long-standing division between political and moral philosophy.

A political philosopher – or a *political scientist*, as we now have to call him – who describes shrewdly the workings of the body politic, or issues judicious suggestions for the improvements of these workings, will habitually do this without concerning himself with the question of the kind of human being who inhabits or will inhabit it. Such a theorist is anxious not to let a value judgement escape him, lest it spoil the scientific nature of his work. The moral philosopher, on the other hand, examines minutely the perplexities of the moral agent, but normally without attending to the fact that these perplexities may be intimately bound up with the political regime in which the moral action unfolds. His fear is of obscuring or sullying the specificity and the purity of his field of enquiry.

Among the reasons for this remarkable divorce between moral and political philosophy, there is one we should mention immediately. Over the last two centuries, at points widely separated on the political spectrum and on the basis of divergent and even contradictory analyses of the nature of modern society, there has emerged a single conception of political action. This conception rests on the assumption that as soon as a certain rational arrangement of our institutions has been achieved, the whole human problem will be essentially solved – or that whatever remains problematical in human affairs will not affect the essential and definitive validity of the political structure. The happy contemplation of a certain institutional automatism, the servo-mechanism that is supposed to guide the body politic on its way to being what it ought to be, excludes all fundamental questioning about the motives of man in society or about the ambiguities and tensions that characterize the relation between man and citizen. This idea of an ultimately infallible 'political mechanism' may be given a liberal or a socialist content, and it can prompt initiatives with very different practical consequences. But it retains one single essential characteristic – that of being *utopian*.

Aurel Kolnai is one of the philosophers of the twentieth century who have given most attention to the growing power of the utopian mind, the spirit which both expresses and aggravates the loss of meaning in human action – our loss of any relation to values. Kolnai belongs also among thinkers who have given most attention to the 'ideologizing' of modern politics. From the moment when the conviction grows – however justifiably within certain limits – that man can and ought to change society by making it conform to his ideal, there looms the risk that, paradoxically, the content of the ideal will become less and less desirable as its form – its *ideal* character – is embraced with increasing zeal. There is the risk that in the name of Utopia the legitimate search for social improvement will be perverted into an exercise in destruction. Thus the seductive power of Utopia is owed not so much to its value-content – the social, moral and philosophical ideas which give it an intelligible outline, or the passions and aspirations which first attract its zealots and enthusiasts – as to its promise of a certain formal perfection, which will infallibly and definitively reconcile *reality* and *value*, reconcile the *is* and the *ought*. Kolnai's study of modern society and politics convinced him that the utopian mind is an object *sui generis*, quite distinct from the political stances or sociological ideas that it will engage as its ministers. The utopian mind deserves philosophical study on its own.

At this point two caveats suggest themselves. The first caveat is this. It may well be true that the utopian mind works more spontaneously in the social and political ideas of the Left; yet, as Kolnai himself remarks, the utopian mind has no analytically necessary

connection with ideas of the Left. For the same leftist sociological
ideas (the idea which sees the emancipation of the working class
as a central requirement of modern society, for instance) are just
as susceptible of common-sense presentation (reformist, moderate)
as of utopian. In the second place, we must note the existence of
what could be called 'rightist' Utopias. There are the moderate
Utopias of the moderate Right. Economic liberalism, for instance,
according to which market mechanisms can by themselves solve
the problems of social man, has an incontestably utopian stamp. But
there are also the extreme Utopias of the extreme Right. These
come in two kinds: (1) reactionary Utopias, common on the Con-
tinent until quite recent times, which see a glorified *ancien régime*
as the natural order of human society, or as the order required
by Christianity; (2) subversive Utopias, like Nazism, which attract
those whom they attract by a particularly murderous vision of racial
purity. In short, if Aurel Kolnai's approach in this book may be
called conservative – in a sense we shall have to clarify – it would
be a grievous error to see in his critical analysis of the utopian mind
a conservative attack on, let us say, socialism or democracy.

The second caveat to be entered here concerns the impression
of excessive generality created by the idea of the utopian mind.
The idea of Utopia is much more determinate than the idea of
'modernity', for example. Yet the idea of modernity has long
had the freedom of the philosophers' city, if only by virtue of
the flamboyant criticism that was directed at the modern world
and modern ideas by such writers as Nietzsche and Heidegger.
The idea of the utopian mind is still less imprecise than the idea
of political rationalism, the target of Michael Oakeshott's sharp
– if not mortal – barbs.[2] Above all, we should not charge the
analyst with the abstraction that is apparent in the *object* of his
study. It is not in Kolnai but in Marx that one comes across ideas
as abstract, emphatic and vague as that of the 'reconciliation of man
with man and with nature'. The extreme generality of the idea of
the utopian mind is not something with which one might justly
reproach Kolnai. Excessive generality is the reproach that Kolnai
himself wants to make against utopian thinking.

It appears that what first drove Kolnai to his study of the spirit of
Utopia was his dissatisfaction with the usual criticism of Utopias:

that they are 'unrealizable', 'too beautiful' ever to exist in this world. Such criticism is obviously true in one sense. The state of complete human satisfaction envisaged by Utopia is indeed unrealizable. But such criticism is superficial, because it leaves out what is special about Utopia. It is precisely its unrealizable character, or the particular nature of its unrealizability, that provides the motive power for attempts to realize Utopia, and is responsible for the peculiarly destructive effects of these attempts.

Utopia is not unrealizable in the way that a barefoot ascent of Everest is unrealizable. It is impossible in empirical fact for the human body to harden itself to the point where it could surmount those icy slopes barefoot, but no essential contradiction of human nature, or of the laws of gravitation, is to be found here. Kolnai emphasizes that what singles out the utopian project is precisely its being unrealizable *a priori* – that is, its being *contradictory*, or *unthinkable*. The reproach one can and ought to make against the political utopian is not that of wanting to realize what is not realizable, but that of wanting to realize – or at least, claiming to want to realize, and acting as if he truly wanted to realize – what is not even thinkable, what neither he nor anyone else can completely think out without contradiction. The man who gives himself unrealizable but thinkable objectives, such as climbing Everest barefoot or conquering the world, incurs ridicule; or, like Alexander the Great, he commands the admiration that we will accord to one who fails nobly because he has undertaken too much. One who gives himself objectives which are unrealizable *because* they are unthinkable destroys or corrupts, both in himself and in those he seduces or subdues, the natural relationship between ideas, motives and values on the one hand, and human action on the other. What he attacks is the internal constitution of the human world.

In Kolnai's eyes this 'unthinkable' or 'contradictory' character of the utopian project is immediately apparent from its claim that the new order of humanity must be attained by the conscious and deliberate actions of an enlightened group that is in full command of the direction in which they are headed, fully aware of each stage on the way, *even as* the new order itself nevertheless represents perfect spontaneity or total freedom. On the one hand there is the artificial, the self-conscious, the preconceived; on the other, there is the natural, the spontaneous, the unforeseen. These will mingle, support or hinder each other, yet be inextricably entangled in ordinary society; in the utopian project they are at the same time violently divorced and totally confounded. During the phase of 'constructing' the new order they will be violently divorced. But then it seems they will be totally confounded in the new order that is realized. The distinction between two phases – of before and after the institution of the new order – does not remove the contradiction. For even during the phase of construction, the utopian group or sect *simultaneously* desires sovereign mastery over nature or history *and* docile servitude under it.

This contradiction is especially characteristic of totalitarian Utopias. In the Bolshevist project, for example, the organization and action of the Party are kept rigorously apart from civil society and even apart from the working class that they are thought to represent. Yet at the same time, this organization and action are identical with the irresistible spontaneity of the historical movement for which society provides the location and the instrument. (That is the basis of their legitimacy.) The emphasis differs in the project of National Socialism. Here, deliberate political action is the servant not so much of history – though Nazism did itself claim to be borne along by the wave of history – as of nature, the nature which precedes and transcends every human project, a purely biological or animal nature, lacking all specific human characteristics. The superhuman is claimed and constructed in the name of the subhuman. Though it uses the language and the disguise of a distorted 'biological science', it represents the same, familiar utopian contradiction. In every case the totalitarian project simultaneously affirms the absolute sovereignty of man – his triumph over necessity through his own efforts and his ushering in of the reign of liberty, or else his creation of the superman – and his absolute enslavement, either to historical necessity or to blood and race.

Kolnai's analysis, of which I have here been able to give merely the bare bones, has the considerable merit of defining clearly the concept of totalitarianism. This idea once attracted considerable attention, largely as a result of Hannah Arendt's work,[3] but today it has fallen somewhat out of favour, at least in Anglo-Saxon countries. But whatever totalitarian regimes may have in common with dictatorships and despotisms, their specific characteristic – the one that most markedly affects their functioning and their impact on the societies enslaved by them – is their utopian logic. It is in this utopian kernel that the explanation is to be found of the strange yet absolutely central role of terror in these regimes. The totalitarian organization or Party must not only show that it is still the only victor in the political struggle, the one and only sovereign; it must also make people understand and feel that a new reality has replaced yesterday's shabby and corrupted world. Yet, according to the theory, this new reality will be realized only when the totalitarian organization has withered away and the new man has been left to his spontaneity. To get over this contradiction, the regime compels society – that is, the old society now overturned through its violence – to *say* that it *is* the new reality, the new world transported with happiness; it compels it to acclaim its total subjection as a complete liberation. Thus it is the office of terror both to affirm and to deny the distance between the surreal world of Utopia and the real world.[4]

The reason why there is such a temptation to consider totalitarianism as simply an extreme version of ordinary or perpetual despotism is, as we have just seen, precisely the element of unthinkability that resides in its specific project or proper essence. How, then, can the unthinkable be thought? The analyst or interpreter must force himself, let us say, to think objectively somehow what cannot be thought subjectively. If he wants to render the temptation harmless, he must show how this subjectively unthinkable, contradictory end is none the less objectively possible. The better he can show how the utopian project helps man to escape from his condition, the more he is obliged to show how such an aberration is possible, how it has its origins and the conditions of its possibility in the shared human situation.

On this point, Kolnai establishes, with a great wealth of psychological analyses, the continuity of the utopian mind, even in the extreme form of totalitarianism, with mental attitudes that are commonly encountered among ordinary people and in ordinary society. He carefully distinguishes the different varieties and gradations of perfectionism, and of what could be called the utopian mind in its moderate form. This is responsible for what Kolnai calls departmental Utopias, which relate to a limited sphere of human life. Above all he shows how the utopian mind is born of a perversion – something which, if not natural, is at least intelligible – of our relation to values. It is natural to desire the incarnation, or realization, of positive values. In this sense, for every significant theme of human action and for every value, it is natural to desire a coincidence between the *is* and the *ought*. But in ordinary, non-utopian life, everyone is aware, despite this desire, not only of his own inadequacies and of human inadequacy in general, but also of the tension between different positive values (not to speak of the ambiguity and indetermination of every one of them), of the way in which urgency can shift value-priority, of the weight of necessity and the role of contingency. Departmental Utopianism, then, selects a *single* value, and claims that its realization will lead infallibly to the realization of all other values, or at least the main ones. For example, it is supposed that morality will bring prosperity, health and happiness. But extreme or totalitarian Utopianism – that is, Utopianism *par excellence* – allows itself to become obsessed with, or infatuated by, the evident desirability not just of a particular value, or even all of them together, but of the coincidence of *is* and *ought* as such. It will experience a burning desire for resolute action – so that this coincidence may be effectively guaranteed. By a subtle but decisive displacement, the idea of 'evidence' is transported from the intellectual to the volitional sphere. Since it is far from evident to the intellect what would count as such a coincidence of *is* and *ought*, the will takes its place and conceives the desire for that which it cannot conceive – while making the intellect believe that it conceives it. But then, in reaction, there is an inevitable rebound, and the feeling of contingency and freedom emigrates from the volitional to the intellectual sphere. Cut off by the will's decision from all authentic contact with the real world, the intellect feels an intoxicating licence to justify and motivate whatever actions the utopian will dictates. Thus the respective places in the human economy of theory and practice, intellect and will, are interchanged.

To see these diagnoses of Utopianism as metaphysical subtleties would be a great mistake. As Kolnai deploys them, they make a powerful contribution to our understanding of certain particularly strange features of totalitarian action. Take Bolshevism. This is characterized by an astonishing formal rigidity of ideological framework, coupled with an almost incredible arbitrariness in the ideas that form the immediate accompaniment of action. (Thus, simultaneously, the Party is always right: yet, between one day and the next, such and such a hero of the Revolution becomes an inveterate enemy of the people.) The rigidity of the ideological framework certifies the absolute legitimacy of the totalitarian organization and the self-evident desirability of its action. Since the will is thus guaranteed and strengthened in its self-evidence, revolutionary action enjoys absolute freedom in its choice of means and measures, and in their justification. And, whereas the ideology affirms that 'socialism is achieved', action – that is to say, terror – is justified by the claim that many individuals, even within the Party, even among the companions of the supreme leader, are busy day and night in the work of re-establishing capitalism. Thus, the ideas which constitute or go to formulate the utopian project are not there to create a bond between the agent and values, to guide his action or inform his will; on the contrary, their function is to liberate the will from all rules, from any mental content whatsoever, and to protect the agents of Utopia from all spontaneous and personal contact with values.

For all its intrinsic aberrancy, and the destructiveness of its practical implications, this inversion of the roles of theory and practice has been, if not directly caused, then made possible at least by an intellectual development which seems quite innocent and even salutary – it is one with which we are, in any case, perfectly familiar – namely, the virtual disappearance of 'practical reason' from the political thought of the last three centuries. It is a commonplace that political philosophy has traditionally been conceived, largely under Aristotle's influence, as a practical science. But now it has tended to become pure theory. (The almost complete substitution of the idea of political theory or science for that of political philosophy is the linguistic expression of this noteworthy fact.) The social or political scientist tends to regard the body politic as a 'system' or 'structure' whose functioning he endeavours to describe, while so far as possible ignoring the motives or ends that lead men to act in this structure or system. That is to say, he refuses to take account, as philosophy once did, of what links

him, the observer or thinker, to the object of his study. He refuses
to take account of what makes both of these human. For the most
part he is content to rely on what is a virtual tautology – that men
act in accordance with what he calls their interest. Since 'interest'
is defined here as what the agent himself thinks it is, the political
scientist's assumption amounts to this – that men act as they desire
to act, or desire to act as they act.

The rationale of a development such as this seems to me to
be the following. An Aristotelian analysis of human conduct in
terms of motives or ends – in terms, that is, of *our* motives or
our ends – seemed to lead almost inevitably to a *ranking* of these
motives and ends, and the subsequent elaboration of a dogmatic
philosophy of human nature or human good. This conception
of human nature and human good leads to the conception and
promotion of a political regime 'in conformity with the nature'
of man. But this in its turn seems to endanger the liberal idea of
a political power which is neutral between various conceptions of
human life or between various world-views. It is clear that the
transformation of political philosophy and its practical knowledge
into a political science which is *value-free* is closely bound up with
the development of liberal and representative political regimes.
Thus, in so far as it rests on the dwindling of ideas of practical reason
and the hypertrophy of theory or science, the utopian or totalitarian
temptation is bound up with an intellectual development that is
inseparable from the progress of our civilization. How, then, can
we triumph over this temptation without reintroducing a dogmatic
idea of human nature which would conflict with our liberalism,
besides being heavy with the threat of reactionary Utopia? It is as
an answer to this question that Aurel Kolnai's conservatism is so
important.

We are not obliged in ordinary life, or in the political arena, to
act in the light of any clearly defined image of human nature – any
thick concept of human nature. To do so would involve us once
again in those arguments I have just mentioned over the definition
of the 'highest good', from which our fathers escaped with such difficulty when they conceived of a State which would confine itself
to guaranteeing the external conditions of free action and abandon
any pretension to tell us what our good is. We are born in and act
in a world *already* structured by institutions, models, achievements,

traditions – by traditions, moreover, which do not force us to be 'traditionalists', precisely because we have the good fortune to be heirs to the tradition of rationally criticizing traditions. We do not have to construct an alternative world, an alternative society, as the utopian mind supposes – a construction for which we should find ourselves forced to borrow features of the world and society that we already have. (Separated from other features that complete and correct them, these would lose their value and even their meaning.) Rather, our task is quite different. It is to explore our world phenomenologically, and thence to derive our concepts and motives. Any legitimate reason for transforming the world will arise from the world as it reveals itself to this kind of enquiry. I have just alluded to the phenomenological outlook. Although Kolnai hardly mentions phenomenology in this work, he was a student of Husserl, and his fundamental inspiration certainly came from that quarter. It is perfectly possible to 'bracket' the ultimate categories once beloved by metaphysics and their claim to capture all that there is of nature or history. A scrupulous description of the framework of thought through which we express our humanity is enough, if not to guide all our actions, at least to provide a sound orientation for our thinking and living.

In order to define this 'phenomenological conservatism' more clearly, it is well worth comparing it with the conceptions of two writers to whom Kolnai thought himself closely allied: Karl Popper and Michael Oakeshott. Like Popper, he believes that reforming activity presupposes a fixed – hence traditional – framework without which the reform cannot even be thought or appraised. In order to assess what changes, we must have something which does not change.[5] Like Oakeshott, he holds that the human world is structured by 'idioms of conduct', and that human life, as Europe has come to savour it, finds its mainspring and its happiness in an attentive fidelity to the immanent meaning – and thus, for the most part, to the traditional procedures – of each of these idioms, whether culinary, scientific or political.[6] But in fact Kolnai also sets himself firmly apart from these two authors. He thinks that Popper's conservatism is too exclusively epistemological, too much concentrated in the value of a traditional frame of reference for the progress of knowledge and the appraisal of reforms: that Popper is not sensible enough of the *intrinsic* merits, both moral and vital, of a conservative attitude. In the last analysis, Popper puts too much faith in the reformatory ideas of the age. As for Oakeshott, Kolnai thinks he goes too far in his criticism of 'rationalism', and puts reason itself in jeopardy; that he exaggerates the virtues of 'immanence', of 'habitual' and 'unreflective' absorption in a traditional 'idiom of conduct'; that he failed to see both the necessity and the possibility of the mind's acknowledgement of objective rules, formulable in universal terms, such as moral laws; and even of its striving, within certain limits, to define something resembling a human nature, albeit in sketchy and tentative fashion. If Popper's political philosophy is tainted with 'progressivism', Oakeshott's is tainted with 'obscurantism' with the conviction that it is possible to be a conservative and nothing else.[7]

A second and fundamental objection Kolnai makes against Oakeshott's moral philosophy is that it gives no place to *conscience*, through which a human being is able to bring his conduct into living contact with the universal rules of morality; nor to that splitness, that interior dialogue, by which one is reminded of the irreducible distance between what one does and what one ought to do, what one is and what one ought to be. This is one of the main objections Kolnai makes to the utopian mind too. According to Oakeshott's extreme conservatism, morality consists in spontaneous conformity to the moral idiom of our civilization and to the habits it has developed – or ought to have developed – if it had not been in part overlaid by reflexive and abstract conceptions of morality. But the utopian mind empties conscience even more radically. In its contemplation of a future state of humanity in which reality and value, *is* and *ought*, coincide, it contemplates a human condition in which conscience will have no function and no meaning. The man of the future, man *par excellence*, is a being without conscience. It follows that what is given to us as conscience in our present state is, in the Utopian's eyes, merely social man's dissatisfaction with our actual and provisional condition, a dissatisfaction which will naturally come to an end when Utopia is realized.

Thus, whereas Kolnai judges Oakeshott to display a kind of aestheticizing extremism in his striving to be a conservative and nothing else, the distinctive mark of Kolnai's own conservatism could be said to be its giving so large a place to conscience, understood as the capacity and the duty of every person to judge situations, actions and human beings (himself included) not only in the light of the idioms of conduct implicit in our civilization, but also in the light of explicit and universal rules. Certainly conscience, as such, is not conservative. On the contrary, since it judges – wisely or unwisely – in the name of a moral absolute, it can easily become the principle of a revolutionary attitude if it is left to run on its own. That is why, in practice, totalitarian undertakings find so ready a support among sincerely conscientious people who are indignant at the misery of the poor, say, or at national humiliation – moving them to place their moral energy in the service of a conception which destroys the very idea of conscience. But this is the point. It is because there is a natural and necessary tension between the conscientious and the conservative attitudes that the prudent man has to learn how to combine them, to learn that the relative weight of each depends on circumstances and on the agent's ability to compose and harmonize, judiciously and even stylishly, the various legitimate themes of free conduct. A conscience with a lively sensitivity to universal moral demands, but also well aware of political constraints, of ambiguities and conflicts of values and the uncertainties attending action; a conscience which, when it is at odds with the world, does not hurry to condemn the world, but takes time to weigh the adversary's reasons; in short a conscience informed and armed with a conservative political philosophy – here, says Kolnai, is the rock on which the totalitarian temptation, and the more general utopian temptation, will founder.

Kolnai's criticism of the utopian mind is pertinent and convincing and his phenomenology of the social world contains a wealth of suggestions. Nevertheless, it seems to me that there is an important question that he largely ignores: what is it that has brought about the devastating spread of the utopian spirit in modern times, especially the twentieth century? As I have already pointed out, one can only admire Kolnai's demonstration of how the utopian illusion rests so naturally on the human relation to values and to the desirable, yet goes on to falsify and pervert it. But is this psychological genealogy enough? The real theme of Kolnai's investigation is not so much the utopian mind as such, which is always possible and present to some degree in every age. It is the modern, extreme, form of the utopian mind: namely, totalitarianism. Kolnai does show that there is a legitimate place for a study of the social, political and spiritual circumstances which have favoured the development of totalitarianism, and among these it would seem that he accorded central importance to the mechanisms of mass society. But he does not enquire more deeply into them.[8]

Certainly the utopian mind displays more than enough striking and clearly defined characteristics for it to be treated as a kind of essence. The fruitfulness of Kolnai's analysis amply justifies singling out this mentality for study. Not only that — there is even a danger of blurring the sharp outline of totalitarianism by concentrating on an enumeration, however erudite and discerning, of the circumstances which have favoured its development. But between the uniqueness and solidity of the essence on the one hand, and the multiplicity of circumstances to which the analyst seems free to refer or not as he sees fit on the other, there seems to be too great a hiatus. Something is still wanting in the analysis. I am led to think that the missing link we are looking for, between the essence and the circumstances, can be found only in the study of ideas. Is the utopian mind an ever-present possibility for the human relation to values as it is actualized under particular circumstances? Perhaps this is so, but if these circumstances are to set in motion such a radically new historical phenomenon, with the consequence that this natural possibility should be realized and stabilized in an essence as prodigiously effective as that of totalitarianism, then the explanation has to lie in the working of some intellectual system that can make what is in fact unthinkable apparently thinkable, or present a contradictory project of the will as a positive scientific theory. From time to time Kolnai does recall the theories that seem to him to be particularly suggestive of the contradictions of the utopian mind, especially the theory of Rousseau. But it seems to me that Kolnai is insufficiently attentive to the actual workings of intellectual mechanisms and systems of ideas — not only in what makes all sorts of totalitarian projects possible but also in the development of modern politics more generally.

In my discussion of the dwindling of practical reason and the enlargement of the theoretical point of view, I have already pointed to what seems to me to be one of the intellectual preconditions for the existence of the totalitarian attitude. To this as it were negative condition, I should like to add a positive one.

Let us remember that Kolnai sees the central contradiction of the utopian project in the fact that man is given two strictly contradictory roles. The Utopian wants man to be responsible for a radically new social world, yet thinks of him as the passive product of the society which precedes him. He is thus at the same time the omnipotent master of society or history, and its raw material or docile creation. He is both sovereign maker or sovereign artificer, and mere matter. How can one avoid thinking here of Thomas Hobbes who, in his *Leviathan*, presents us with social man in precisely this double role, described in these very terms?[9] Certainly Hobbesian absolutism has hardly anything in common with modern totalitarianism. But I would like to suggest that certain fundamental categories of the modern politics whose framework Hobbes did so much to determine – especially the categories of 'sovereignty', of 'representation', of the 'artificial' body politic – are pregnant with the possibility of the development or dialectic whose study might shed a strong light upon the genesis of totalitarianism. In this way – thanks to our making room for this third term, which is the workings of a system of ideas – might one not articulate more completely and adequately the study of particular historical circumstances with the general phenomenology of the human world?

This is only a suggestion. Whether or not there is the need that I suppose there to be, this does not in the least impair the essential validity and importance of Kolnai's study of these matters. After all, we have plenty of judicious historians of modern political philosophy. Only very rarely do we come across thinkers like Kolnai, with the nerve to link political reflection with a phenomenology of the human world, to meet a historical emergency with their gaze fastened on the invariants of the human condition, with the nerve and the capacity to assume the role of a political philosopher.

Pierre Manent
Ecole des Hautes Etudes en Sciences Sociales, Paris
October 1993
(Translated by Francis Dunlop and David Wiggins)

Editor's Introduction

1 HISTORY OF KOLNAI'S PROJECT

(a) 'Prehistory'

If the present volume convincingly shows the existence of a 'utopian mind', Kolnai's writings, from the time when his distinctive 'voice' begins to make itself heard, show that his own mind was, at least in important respects, anti-utopian, or 'commonsensical'. He himself was accustomed to refer back to parts of his doctoral thesis *Ethical Value and Reality*,[1] and to the two papers, respectively on the 'Ideology' and the 'Critique' of 'Social Progress', which he wrote in 1927 for the *German Economist*,[2] as evidence of his enduring interest in fighting Utopia. But this is also embryonically evident in such things as his lifelong fascination with 'the Mystical', as witness the paper of that title published in 1921 in the Psychoanalytical Association's journal.[3] One of the marks of the utopian mind is its longing for a new and 'cleaner' reality where everything will be fully perspicuous and controllable; Kolnai was a champion of 'given reality', where things have 'mystical' aspects that we can never totally master, cognitively or practically.[4] This is part of what he means by 'the world', a frequently recurring motif in his writings.[5]

After four years' experience of life in the USA the anti-utopianism becomes much more emphatic, as can be seen, for example, in the 1944 paper 'The Humanitarian versus the Religious Attitude'.[6]

(b) 1955 onwards

Kolnai and his wife moved to London from Canada in the summer of 1955. The anti-utopian concern had gone on growing during his time as a lecturer at Laval University, Quebec, and culminated in *Notes sur l'Utopie Réactionnaire*.[7] Here he identifies the corrupt Quebec regime of Duplessis (1944–59) as a manifestation of rightist, or reactionary, Utopia.

His removal to London was made possible by a Nuffield Foundation travel grant, to run for one year from September, which gave him access to the 'libraries of the British Museum and of the School of Economics and Social Sciences'. His memoirs tell us that he had been preparing this study for many years. But when he travelled to Spain in May of the following year (1956) to lecture on his findings, he had still only completed the first chapter. The grant, without which he felt it would be difficult, if not impossible, to continue, was unfortunately not renewable, though the Kolnais were now fixed in London.

There was more lecturing, and some illness, in early 1957 in Spain, where he gave a short course of four talks on 'the Hungarian Revolution and the crisis of political Utopia'. In December he sent in an application to the Canada Council for a *Bourse Spéciale*, supported by Professor H.A. Acton and many of his former colleagues, to enable him to go on with *The Utopian Mind*. A year's grant was awarded. By this time he had also applied for a British Academy grant to work on a book on Morality and Practice, a topic 'neatly distinct from the Utopia theme but closely connected with it'. The summer of 1958 saw the composition of 'The Moral Theme in Political Division',[8] which is reprinted in this volume. At this time he intended to use the paper for Chapter IV of his book.

The *Bourse Spéciale* took effect from September, and it seems that he had completed Chapter II of *The Utopian Mind* before taking off the following March (1959) for another Spanish lecturing tour (and more illness), during which his subject was 'the political aspects of contemporary British philosophy'. On his return in May he applied for a research fellowship at Nuffield College, Oxford, stating that he hoped to be able to finish chapters III and V by the end of October, and VI and VII by October 1960. He was unsuccessful in his application.

In the autumn he therefore applied for a grant from the Rockefeller Foundation, which was awarded for the following spring and summer (1960). Meanwhile, an unsolicited approach from the Librairie Plon in Paris stimulated Kolnai into composing and publishing 'La Mentalité utopienne',[9] a translation of which is also included here. The Rockefeller grant enabled him to begin the last (unfinished) chapter of *The Utopian Mind* as we have it.

The grant was renewed for a time in 1962, and in the same year Kolnai was able to take up the British Academy grant, already awarded in principle, to begin *Morality and Practice*. Two chapters of this were eventually completed.[10] But he had also been having 'second thoughts' about *The Utopian Mind*, and the solicitations of two United States university presses (alerted by announcements of the Rockefeller award) eventually had to be rejected.

The last important event in this story came in 1966, when a possibility arose of having *The Utopian Mind* published in the series edited for Routledge & Kegan Paul by D.Z. Phillips: 'Studies in Ethics and the Philosophy of Religion'. Kolnai was awarded a travel grant to do some more research in continental libraries, but the fresh impetus this imparted soon ran out of steam, and the project was abandoned.

2 THE STATE OF THE MANUSCRIPT, AND NATURE OF ADDITIONAL MATERIAL ON UTOPIA

The typescripts which look like original versions of the different chapters of *The Utopian Mind*, especially the later sections, were not altered very much by Kolnai, except for the addition of some extra passages and footnotes (sometimes substantial). He was relatively new to England when he wrote the first chapter, though he had long had a very fair command of the English language, and it is inferior to the later chapters in facility of expression, as of organization. I have pruned Kolnai's total text of some 2,300 words, and made small alterations where the sense was not entirely clear, the phrasing unduly awkward, or where there were definite linguistic errors.

The two previously published papers in this volume, 'The Moral Theme in Political Division' and 'La Mentalité utopienne', are reprinted virtually as published, except for the fact that the latter is a translation. Their origins have been indicated above. The short book, or long pamphlet, published in Spanish as *Crítica de las Utopías Políticas* (the substance of his 1956 lectures) was described by Kolnai as a condensed version of Chapter I of *The Utopian Mind*. 'Notes sur l'Utopie réactionnaire', already referred to above, was published in Spanish translation in 1956. It contains some interesting material on tradition and progress. Kolnai's review article on Michael Oakeshott's *Rationalism in Politics*,[11] and his review of J.L. Talmon's *Political Messianism: the Romantic Phase*,[12] also contain material on Utopia. All this is, of course, apart from the many incidental references or the treatment of allied themes in other published work.

Kolnai left quite a lot of unpublished material relating to his project. The self-contained paper 'Utopia and Alienation', which we publish here for the first time, needed only a very little editorial polishing. A French counterpart, 'Éloge d'Aliénation' (In Praise of Alienation), largely overlapping in content with the English paper, may even have been submitted (unsuccessfully) for publication. There is also a short complete paper called 'The Utopian Mind', probably written for delivery at a society meeting or seminar. This is essentially a summary paper of the book's first chapter.

Perhaps the most interesting items in the 'utopian' *Nachlaß* are two indexed notebooks, much of whose contents concerns Utopia, Morality and Practice, and closely related topics. The first, which he refers to as 'Copybook I', seems to have been written between 1951 and perhaps 1953, and consists of about 250 pages of almost continuous discussion of utopian, and especially anti-utopian, themes. It includes a very interesting section on his anti-utopian, or common-sense, conception of philosophy. The second notebook, 'Copybook II', entitled 'Morality and Practice' and composed between late 1956 and 1961 or later, contains rather more material on allied themes. The relatively self-contained section 'The Utopian Negation of Fundamental and Ineliminable Distinctions' is published here as an independent paper. This, especially the first section, needed a fair amount of editorial attention, as did 'Some Formal Principles of the Anti-Utopian Attitude', which I have also taken from 'Copybook II' to form the first part of 'Life without Utopia'. Both these extracts probably date from 1956. Two other Utopia notebooks contain extracts from and comments on some of the many books Kolnai read for his project.

Apart from the notebooks, there are about thirty small papers, ranging in length from one to twenty pages, some containing no more than lists of headings (one of which I have added as an editorial note to Chapter III of *The Utopian Mind*), others being the copies of Utopia grant applications, and yet others constituting the basis (usually in note form) of several short articles. I translated the second part of 'Life without Utopia', entitled 'How can we live without Utopia?', from a two-page paper in French, dating probably from late 1959 to early 1960. Another half a dozen or so of these items are of considerable interest, and exhibit the wide variety of directions in which the Utopia theme can be taken. The short note on 'wanting' is appended to *The Utopian Mind* as a footnote.

3 HOW THE ADDITIONAL MATERIAL WAS CHOSEN

It would, of course, have been possible to publish *The Utopian Mind* in its unfinished state, without any additional Kolnaian work. But this would have deprived the reader of much valuable material and many further suggestions of the wide-ranging importance of the utopian theme. So on what basis was the selection of supplementary matter to be made?

Had Kolnai left behind a firm statement of intent, the basis would have been obvious. But it is all too clear that he frequently changed his mind about the book. At least twenty lists of topics, or chapters, often subdivided into sections, remain, and these cannot be easily collated with a view to working out a kind of 'average' scheme. Even a rough page entitled 'running notes' for the third (and unfinished) chapter is surprisingly uninformative, though an effort has been made to try to cover what can be covered, where this is clear. Some of the projected material from the many schemes never seems to have been tackled by him at all.

The problem is made worse by the fact that the very 'centre of gravity' of the theme kept shifting. Was it to be ethics, politics or metaphysics? Was Utopia to be treated historically, religiously, or purely philosophically? What sort of mixture would be best? As first envisaged in the 'frozen wastes' of Canadian 'reactionary Utopia', the analysis of the logic of Utopia was to lead on to the logic of non-utopian reform, and a philosophy of conservatism. The philosophical emphasis was on the confusion between morality and practice. In England, in about 1958, the emphasis shifted to the logic of perfection values. When the possibility arose of hiving off the philosophical issues surrounding morality and practice to a separate book, the political emphasis reasserted itself once more, only to die down again with the possibility of *The Utopian Mind* taking its place in the Routledge series on Ethics and the Philosophy of Religion. But this, perhaps, is to impart too clear-cut an impression. The fact is that Kolnai could not make up his own mind. Even in 1956 he could write to his Spanish friend Don Salvador Pons: 'I am rendered sick, tired and paralytic by my endless sorry attempts to find a solid base to work from.'[13] By 1970 he wrote to D.Z. Phillips that if he decided *not* to encourage Kolnai to 'submit a shortened, tidied up, version' of *The Utopian Mind* as we have it, 'it [would] make it easier for me to abandon the thing with a sigh of relief'.[14] Phillips, of course, encouraged him to continue, but shortly afterwards the scheme seems nevertheless to have run into the sand.

It has, therefore, proved impossible to work out any clear 'logic' for the selection of additional material. No doubt the insistence on doing so would itself have been utopian. So I have tried to work, more intuitively than systematically, with the following rather vague principles in mind: respect for Kolnai's predominant intentions, respect for later rather than earlier intentions, avoidance of too much overlap (though not at the price of painful dismemberment), attempt to give a glimpse of further ramifications of the subject.

'The Moral Theme in Political Division' could hardly be left out, though its utopian relevance may not seem obvious except towards the end of the paper, and though Kolnai himself did not invariably include it in his post-1959 schemes. But if it is read as a contribution to the utopian theme, the paper shows various ways in which the perfectionist fallacy, and other utopian motifs, take effect in a familiar department of practice. 'La Mentalité utopienne' (here 'The Utopian Mentality') goes rather further into the important sub-theme of Social Utopia than *The Utopian Mind*, and is in any case a concise and comparatively late summary of the main ideas, with some suggestive hints about their further development. 'Utopia and Alienation' seems definitely to be mentioned in the 'running notes' referred to above; it opens up a new and fruitful approach to human existence in reaction to a prominent utopian theme.[15] 'The Utopian Negation of Fundamental and Ineliminable Distinctions' goes further into the attack on conscience and into the denial of the estimative rather than calculatory nature of practice than the book as we have it, and also illustrates the historical background of utopian thinking in ethics. Finally, the two short fragments on 'Life without Utopia' represent, first a political, and second an ethical, approach towards the topic that almost invariably forms the last section of his book in its numerous schematic projections.

4 WHY THE UTOPIAN MIND WAS NEVER FINISHED
I think there are three main reasons:

(a)   Outward circumstances. Throughout their married life the Kolnais had been poor. As refugees in the United States they regularly received money from a relative and had for a time accepted Catholic charity, until Mrs Kolnai (who had an artistic training) got work in a factory sewing buttons on military uniforms, while Kolnai earned his mite as occasional journalist and translator. Even when he was the recipient of a regular salary at Laval University, Quebec, Kolnai's income was pitifully small. When he came to England he meant virtually to live off his grant, though the small monthly allowance he received for many years from two other relatives may have started before this time. When the grant came to an end he had perforce to look about for other sources of income. Already fifty-six, and in wretched health, he applied unsuccessfully for many jobs, both academic and journalistic (for instance, in the Hungarian Department of the BBC), and took on miscellaneous translating and editorial work that would bring in at least *something*. But he never got a full-time post, and even when it was understood that his 'Visiting Lectureship' at Bedford College was 'permanent', he still feared the possibility of having to resign on health grounds. His various chronic complaints compelled him to husband his strength, especially during the winter months.[16] All this meant that his work on *The Utopian Mind* was continually jeopardized by what he calls 'the urgent pressure of material cares'.

(b)   The nature of the project. I have already drawn attention to Kolnai's difficulties in deciding exactly what that was to be. The bulk of *The Utopian Mind* as we have it consists largely of philosophical analysis, but in his own mind there was a vast historical and political literature to be studied before he could write the long projected ('original') Chapter III, 'which would have been devoted to the historical ambit of Utopianism and to Historicism as well as to Millenarism', and perhaps other chapters requiring much quotation from contemporary documents or citation of historical and social facts.

But even in philosophical terms the project seemed to burst whatever confines he tried to place around it, until it threatened to engulf life itself. Nearly all his work in ethics, social and political philosophy from the 1950s onwards *relates* to Utopia, or to 'Morality and Practice' (this 'neatly distinct' theme was continually trying to coalesce once more with the utopian one), as we can gather both from its content and from the fact that the Utopia notebooks contain the beginnings (in draft or notes) of several of his papers. Again and again Kolnai seems to have felt himself faced with the task – too great for his declining strength – of having to write a systematic treatise of conservative moral, social and political thought, based on common sense, with a history of all conceivable aberrations and their utopian roots thrown in! When Kolnai wrote that all practice is virtually utopian, he must have been only too conscious of his own project.

(c)   Psychological. It is noteworthy how much of Kolnai's writing was solicited by editors, publishers, secretaries of learned societies, and so on. This is no doubt common enough in the academic world, but it was, I think, especially important in Kolnai's case. He badly needed encouragement, as can readily be seen in the extract from the letter to D.Z. Phillips which is quoted in the Preface to this volume.[17] The 'paralysing impact' of Raymond Ruyer's *Utopie et les utopies* is a frequent theme in almost all Kolnai's letters and other papers in which he describes his project. When he did receive indubitable encouragement, and some definite plan was, as a result, temporarily substituted for the amorphous and unbounded one, his own 'perfectionist' attitude to *The Utopian Mind* could be overcome, and he could produce excellent papers to order, such as 'La Mentalité utopienne'. But Kolnai's cast of mind always favoured the detailed analysis of confined themes rather than the synoptic treatise. In his last years he was inclined to regard the vastness of 'Utopia', as he had sometimes envisaged it, as a temptation he would have been wiser to resist. We have to accept that he was (at least in his fifties) psychologically unsuited for the task he had set himself in *The Utopian Mind*. We can only be glad that such worthwhile fragments of the uncertainly projected whole survive.

Acknowledgements

I should like to thank Sarah Lumley-Smith for her preparatory work on the text of Kolnai's *The Utopian Mind*; also David Wiggins for help in translating Pierre Manent's Introduction, and for general advice and help throughout the period of my work on this volume.

Acknowledgements are also due to the Librairie Plon, for permission to translate 'La Mentalité utopienne', and to Cambridge University Press, for permission to reprint 'The Moral Theme in Political Division' from *Philosophy* (July 1960), XXXV, pp. 234–54.

Francis Dunlop

THE UTOPIAN MIND

1
Critique of Utopia

1 THE NEED FOR A CRITIQUE OF UTOPIA

Why criticize utopias – or Utopia, if it should be true, as I believe it is, that 'Utopias' have an essential content, drift or coinage in common? Is it not enough to say that Utopias, by their nature, are unrealizable, irrelevant to what actually happens or is going to happen in society, and therefore devoid of any serious interest, much as they may aesthetically amuse some and perhaps disgust others? Again, so far as we are inclined to hazard a moral appraisal of utopian thought or imagination, it might seem that our first impulse should be not to criticize but to admire it for the 'generosity', 'idealism' and yearning for 'perfection' it displays. True, we may be no less naturally disposed to blame in it the 'excess' of these noble emotions, which, after all, is likely to cause some harm owing to the disillusionment it invites and the inevitable failure of such practical experiments it may inspire. But a mere 'excess of good' will hardly deserve censure; the blame it evokes is no more than a qualification of the praise it is entitled to. A 'Critique of Utopia', then, would at first sight appear to lack point.

To this plausible initial objection, I retort that the unrealistic character of utopias – that is to say, the anti-realism of their *content* – in no wise determines their reality as a mental and historical fact. If a paranoiac kills his putative persecutor, his delusion is certainly not validated thereby; he has acted on unreal suppositions, but the death of his victim is not a whit less real for that. Similarly, from the assumption that Utopias are unrealizable it can by no means be inferred that political action informed by utopian conceptions is unable to exercise a strong and perhaps pernicious impact on the actual life of society. Whatever its other roots and conditioning factors, totalitarian tyranny – the paramount scourge of our epoch – is underlain, as few will deny, by utopian visions. But if most advocates of totalitarian tyranny would regard this statement as nothing but a truism, many of them might still hesitate to admit that the historical connection between Utopia and tyranny warrants an *intrinsic* examination and criticism of utopian aims, conceptions and presuppositions. Totalitarianism is no doubt erected on utopian foundations; but – seeing that its workings are utterly repulsive, while the utopian pictures of bliss are, by definition, attractive – should we not conclude that tyranny expresses Utopia 'gone wrong', perhaps betrayed and forsaken – or, in other words, that totalitarianism is utopianism *misapplied*? If, as it appears, mankind is not 'good enough' or not 'mature enough' for Utopia, the fault lies not with Utopia as such, but with Utopians who are forgetful of this human weakness: to our criticism of totalitarian tyranny itself we might, not unprofitably, append Pascal's warning *Qui veut faire l'ange fait le bête* [He who would make an angel will make a beast]; but still, why proceed to a destruction of the utopian hopes of mankind? Can it ever live hopefully and aspiringly if it is deprived of the utopian vision of an altogether different and entrancing future?

Thus shaded off, the objection appears more convincing and is less open to immediate disproof. For the moment, the common-sense answer may suffice that utopian conceptions have been 'misapplied' on too vast a scale, too consistently and with effects too deleterious to allow for the glib excuse of 'misapplication' owing to accidental vices in agents or defects in circumstances, and to disarm the suspicion that there must be something deeply wrong with the *basic attitude* at the core of political utopianism. I suggest that both the thesis of the 'unrealizableness' and that of the 'attractiveness' of Utopia are ambiguous and problematic. The satisfying heavenliness of Utopia *is* radically unrealizable, but the material details of utopian visions and – what is a great deal worse – the assumption of political power by utopian visionaries are largely realizable. Again, presenting itself as a promise of heaven on earth, the utopian vision is inevitably adorned with a number of obviously attractive traits; but on closer examination, its attractiveness is likely to prove illusory – resulting from the seductive suasion of its formal *concept* of 'perfection' rather than inherent in the constitutive principles of the kind of world it offers. To put it differently, I suggest that Utopia is 'real' enough, considering its evil fruit in the shape of totalitarian tyranny, to demand earnest enquiry into its nature; and that whatever the possibility of putting it into practice and the risks attending the attempt to do so, the utopian conception *taken in itself* can be shown to be logically untenable and an absolutely unfit object of human endeavour. Only by a critique such as this can we strike at the root of totalitarian tyranny; so long as the utopian idea remains sacrosanct and inviolable, it will provide a spiritual shield and justification for the totalitarian programme and the tyrannical practices devoted to the aim of realizing it, no matter how we may resent this 'misapplication'. If we do not understand that Utopia cannot be 'applied' otherwise than by being 'misapplied', we will continue, for the sake of the alleged 'goodness' of Utopia, to condone the 'blunders' of those who, for the time being, 'misapply' it.

From a philosophical point of view, especially as regards some fundamental problems in ethics, an analysis of the concept of Utopia and of the utopian type of mind appears to me of the highest interest; it is often by such detours, arising from more or less urgent practical concerns, that new or freshly experienced points of view are injected into the sphere of standard philosophical reflection. Thus, I would attempt to throw some additional light, in the perspective of a 'critique of Utopia', on the problems of the relation between Value and Reality and between Morality and Practice.

2 REFERENCES AND CRITICISMS

Although, perhaps, this work is the first to offer a 'critique of Utopia' with full thematic emphasis, I am by no means the first to have realized either the problematic value and predominant disvalue or the practical importance of Utopia. Indeed, as I shall presently show by a selection of references, I can rely on authority.

Here, first, is Nicholas Berdiayev, whose words have been rendered famous by their adoption as the motto of Aldous Huxley's *Brave New World*, that brilliant presentation of the utopian 'heaven' in the colours of hell:

Les utopies apparaissent comme bien *plus réalisables qu'on ne le croyait autrefois*. Et nous nous trouvons actuellement devant une question bien autrement angoissante: *comment éviter leur réalisation définitive?* ... Les utopies sont réalisables. La vie marche vers les utopies. Et peut-être un siècle nouveau commence-t-il, un siècle où les intellectuels et la classe cultivée rêveront aux moyens d'éviter les utopies et de retourner à une société *non utopique, moins 'parfaite'* et plus libre.

[Utopias seem far *more realizable than people used to think*. And we now find ourselves confronted with a question which disturbs us in quite a new sense: *how to prevent them being permanently realized?* . . . Utopias are realizable. Life moves towards Utopia. And perhaps a new era is beginning, an era in which thoughtful and cultivated people will dream of ways of escaping from Utopia and returning to a society which is *non-utopian, less 'perfect'* and more free.]

In his foreword to M.L. Berneri's *Journey through Utopia*, George Woodcock writes:

It is significant that not only are those writers who are conscious of present-day social evils writing anti-Utopias to warn people of the dangers of going further in the direction of a regimented life, but these very books have the same kind of popularity which the smug visions of a socialist paradise enjoyed before 1914....[Berneri's book warns] us, from various points of view, of the doom that awaits those who are foolish enough to put their trust in an ordered and regimented world.

I would not labour the point now, but I think it is necessary to express even at this stage my view that Marxian Communism, the standard form of totalitarian tyranny, is so far the most important – thought not, perhaps, the most typical – manifestation of the utopian mind and will. Miss Berneri, in G. Woodcock's words,

has ... pointed out the fact that, although the Marxists have always claimed to be 'scientific' as opposed to utopian socialists, their actual social experiments have in practice tended to take on the generally rigid structures of the classic Utopias.

H.B. Acton comes to a similar conclusion in *The Illusion of the Epoch*:

> It is difficult to see how any attentive reader of their works could have taken at their face value the Marxists' profession of being scientific socialists rather than Utopians....Marxism is Utopianism with the Communist Party as a visible and authoritative interpreter of the doctrine striving to obtain supreme power.

My meaning is not, of course, that instead of fighting Communism on multiple planes of action we should concentrate on making fun of the scurrilous fancies displayed by the classic literary Utopias from Plato to Renan and from Thomas More or Campanella to Shaw or Wells, but that, on the spiritual plane, we do not fight Communism effectively unless we fight it with an eye on its utopian soul; and that for this as well as for other – more broadly political and more purely intellectual – reasons, the critique of Utopia as such constitutes a worthwhile task.

That totalitarian tyranny, inspired by and seeking its justification in utopian delusion, is peculiarly congenial to the mode of life of 'mass society', and is to a certain extent 'invited' by the functional exigencies of machine civilization, is a widely known truth I would not dream of denying; that it is an invention of our age or an inevitable product of the 'objective data' of industrial society, representing no autonomous spiritual and political force which in its turn *acts upon* the destinies of that society, is a palsying fallacy whose uprooting is among the prime tasks of those who are anxious to help preserve a modicum of our freedoms and our intellectual level of life. I concur wholeheartedly with J.L. Talmon's words in the conclusion of his *Origins of Totalitarian Democracy*:

> Liberty is less threatened by objective developments taking place as it were by themselves, and without any context of a salvationist creed, than by *an exclusive Messianic religion which sees in these developments a solemn fulfilment.* Even if the process of economic centralization (with social security as its only mitigating feature) is inevitable, *it is important that there should be social analysts to make men aware of the dangers.* This may *temper the effect of the objective developments.* [emphasis added][1]

I must, however, disagree with another formulation of Talmon's, which echoes a widespread misjudgement: 'This is the curse of salvationist creeds: to be born out of the noblest impulses of man, and to degenerate into weapons of tyranny.'[2] The 'salvationist creeds' (i.e. the 'secular religions' of Utopia) are born not 'out of the noblest impulses of man' but out of a highly strung spiritual perversion which, not being at all in the nature of material greed or even of a trivial lust for power or renown, bears a deceptive resemblance to 'the noblest impulses', and may easily be mistaken for them. They do not 'degenerate into instruments of tyranny' by historical mishap or the deplorable cussedness of things, but portend tyranny by logical implication, for in their very essence they are antithetic to the order of reality, to the truthful acceptance of the human condition, to man's genuine sense of values and to common morality.

From Raymond Ruyer's masterly, profound and comprehensive book *L'Utopie et les utopies* I cannot, within the limits of this introductory chapter, give any literal quotation, but I would point to it in support of my own outlook and enterprise. Ruyer's greatest merit, I think, consists in his perception of the mental substance of Utopia common to the great manifoldness of single (and in some ways, greatly divergent) Utopias; but though his intention is more obviously directed to phenomenological description than to criticism proper, and though he also appears to assign some positive value to the *grandes anticipations* [great anticipations] of the forgers of modern Utopias, he not only discerns the practical dangers of utopian politics but fully sees through the intrinsic illiberality, inhumanity, amorality and inanity of the utopian worlds *as envisioned* by their creators. His comments on the vast material exposed in the second half of his book, no less than the general characterization of the utopian mind which fills the first, entirely bear out my contention that the nexus between Utopia and totalitarian tyranny is by no means merely historical or merely a matter of *a priori* probability but strictly essential, not to say analytic: that the oppression practised by utopian holders of power is but a translation into political reality of the inherent 'oppressiveness' of Utopia as conceived by the speculative dreamer.

In Karl Popper's *The Open Society and its Enemies*, and the essay 'Towards a Rational Theory of Tradition', we behold a social philosopher of leftist (that is, rationalist, progressive and democratic) origins and feelings, whose thought nevertheless consistently reveals a definite and sharp edge against utopianism. The following words, which I quote from the paper on tradition, adumbrate (as I read them) a fundamental criticism of Utopia, conceived on purely logical grounds:

> . . . the idea of canvas-cleaning . . . is impossible, because if the rationalist cleans the social canvas and sweeps away the tradition, he necessarily sweeps away with it himself and all his blueprints of the future. The blueprints have no meaning in an empty social world, in a social vacuum. They have no meaning except on the basis of traditions and institutions – such as myths, poetry and values – which all emerge from the social world in which we live. They have no meaning at all outside it. Therefore, the very incentive and the very desire to build a new world must disappear once we have destroyed the traditions of the old world.

I would conclude this preliminary survey of opinions with an impressive passage from the *Memoirs* of Pio Baroja, the great Spanish writer who might perhaps be called a Conservative Anarchist:

> Laws, I believe, are in general bad, because man has not enough discernment, and allows himself to be carried away by specious and empty formulae. As an old man, I have come to regard revolutions as harmful, and to believe that whatever is systematic is stupid and calamitous. So far as it is not *vitiated by evident injustice*, experience – routine, if you will – is best....[We see around us] *the utopias driving men to crime, without any possible freedom of dissent.* [emphasis added]

(I have emphasized the reservation about 'evident injustice', indicating as it does the most important non-utopian motive of Reform.)

3 DEFINITIONS: 'MAN AS EMANCIPATED FROM PLACE'

Apart from special cases of terminological innovation (which have to be clearly marked and accounted for), our use of a term should conform to its accustomed lexicographical meaning, or at least to one of its principal established meanings; if, as often happens, the etymology of the word reveals a symbolic force, it may help us to keep it in view and to turn to it for initial guidance in our analysis of the thing it is meant to denote.

The *Encyclopaedia Britannica* defines Utopia as 'An ideal commonwealth whose inhabitants exist under perfect conditions'. 'Ideal' and 'perfect' express, of course, the note of wishful speculation and of a sharp contrast with reality as we know it. But 'commonwealth' is also essential inasmuch as it hints at an ideal 'world', an all-round *state* of perfection – by contraposition to an ideal action or character, a perfect accomplishment, or the fully satisfactory solution of one problem. The phrasing 'perfect *conditions*' even more aptly emphasizes the utopian postulate of a given, inherent and comprehensive perfection of 'things', no longer supposed to depend on the right choice, the virtuous conduct and the practical wisdom of the men who live in that world. Utopian thought means not simply a *bold aspiration* to realize the good and to cure or prevent evil but a craving for the *automatic* operation of the good, the *a priori* coincidence of Value and Reality, and a tentative belief in the possibility of eliminating the *presence* of evil from man's field of consciousness.

The *Dictionnaire Larousse* submits 'Système ou plan qui paraît d'une réalisation impossible'; the concepts of 'system' and 'plan' are relevant enough but convey no suggestion of a utopian 'world' or 'mode of existence', while 'appears impossible of realization' brings in the trivial use of the word in which we indulge when we say, for example, that so far the cure for cancer seems to be a utopian aim.[3]

The *Shorter Oxford English Dictionary* judiciously sets out four definitions, the first of which refers to the narrower meaning of the term in the sense of its origin in literary history, and the last to its extension in more or less trivial usage. The second version is of interest only in marking the transition to the third, which is the one that principally belongs in our context.

1. An imaginary island, depicted by Sir Thomas More as enjoying a perfect social, legal and political system. b. *transf.* Any imaginary or indefinitely remote region, country or locality 1610. 2. A *place, state or condition ideally perfect* in respect of politics, laws, *customs, and conditions* 1613. b. An impossibly ideal scheme, especially for social improvement 1734. [emphasis added]

'Customs and conditions', indeed: not merely a new code of law or political programme but a condition of man new in its totality; a refashioned ambit of man, the creation of a new world and a new human nature, as it were. And *place* aligns with *state or condition* to the effect of reinforcing the suggestion that what is meant here by a new 'state or condition' is not a mere determinate set of stipulations, reforms or satisfactions but something like an ideal 'world', a 'realm' of perfection, a 'kingdom' of heaven on earth.

Sir Thomas More coined the Greek word Οὐτοπία as a title for his not particularly subversive vision of a perfect world – a literary extravagance rather in keeping with the Renaissance mood of progressive spiritualism and optimism – simply to hallmark it as a flight of fancy. His happy island is 'nowhere', occupies 'no place', and its description need imply no reference to actual earthly reality. Nevertheless – and this may have helped the word to prosper as it has done – there hangs about the concept of ou-topia a slightly different, more essential second meaning: the meaning of 'placelessness', beyond that of a place which merely happens to be 'nowhere'. Utopia connotes a type of life that is not only 'so far non-existent' (like, for instance, a house that is being planned today but not yet being built, and thus is 'nowhere' so far except 'in the minds' of the planners) but is meant to be *toto caelo* different in quality from the life we have known so far: not subject to the laws of 'space', with the *limitations* and *contingency* implied therein; not constituting 'a place' among other places or a place in which the men who embody it 'are placed'. The men of the utopian world are meant to live on a plan devised purely in accordance with their needs, wills and well-being as envisioned and underwritten by the utopian mind. They are not meant to live in any adaptation to the 'topical' exigencies of the spatial and temporal context in which they find themselves incorporated – a world of given things – nor in a world of their own desiring and making, which surrounds, confronts and permeates them. They are to be free from the concrete determinations of place and the ballast of traditions, including the psychic landscape of their own dispositional heritage and haphazard biases; they are called to incarnate the sovereign self-determination of Man universal, Man pure and simple, cleansed from all that is particular, limiting, fortuitous and adventitious in the being of men.[4]

4 THE DISSOLUTION OF PLACE AND INVERSION OF ORDER

Here are a few symbols, in utopian literature, of 'placelessness', also of 'timelessness' (for which the analogous term 'Uchronia'[5] has sometimes been used).

In Campanella's *City of the Sun* – inspired by More's *Utopia*, but much bolder – everyone must occupy the lodgings which the magistrates assign to him, and these *must be changed every six months*. A man's local 'space of behaviour', as I would interpret this rule, must not grow on him so as to become part of his personality; the abstract concept of 'perfection' is hostile to 'local patriotism'. Goethe – not primarily a Utopian but obviously bitten, here and there, by the utopian spirit – describes in his novel *Wilhelm Meister's Years of Travel* a kind of Masonic Order (much in the style of the eighteenth-century Utopias of Reason and Virtue) called the 'Society of the Tower', whose adepts are subject to three principal rules: they must (i) not stay longer than three consecutive days under the same roof (a good deal stricter than Campanella's six-month limit!); (ii) never complain (all utopian conceptions, in their widest compass, aim at excluding suffering, discontent and the sense of disorder or incongruity, and their non-expression is one aspect of this suppression); (iii) never speak either of the past or of the future, but only of the present (Utopia tends to reduce time to the plenitude of the moment). In Etienne Cabet's *Icarie*, the spatial ambit of man is modified by some strange reforms: pieces of furniture have no sharp angles or edges, so that children may run into them without being hurt; everyone wears uniforms supplied by the state (though varying according to circumstances) which are not made to measure yet always and automatically fit, for they are manufactured from a peculiarly elastic cloth. Man has become, if I may so put it, 'his own Providence'; as a Collective, he has made for himself a material environment in which he may indulge his impulses in full 'spontaneity', without coming up against anything hard or rigid, and without needing (or, for that matter, wishing) to mould his personal environment, by his own thought, effort and selective taste, into suitable shape. (Let it be added that all principal meals are communal, but that the Republic is thoughtful enough to supply Sunday excursionists with cold provisions for the day.)

Dissolution or inversion of what we experience as the more or less 'natural' order of things, even though it is not linked specifically to a sense of pain or want, is a frequent theme of utopian imagination. In Plato's *Republic* – notwithstanding the rightist rather than leftist, hierarchical rather than egalitarian sign of this Utopia – children are trained for a strictly equal use of their right and left hands, which carries the suggestion of a more abstract structure of space. Among Cyrano de Bergerac's 'Men in the Moon' the old treat the young with deference – not in the sense of Juvenal's beautiful words *Maxima debetur puero reverentia* [It is the child to whom most reverence is due] but in the grossly inverted sense that fathers obey their grown-up children and, if recalcitrant, are liable to the whip. In the eighteenth-century Utopia *Aventures de Jacques Sadeur*, by Gabriel Foigny, the happy inhabitants of the 'Austral Land', who ignore the difference between mine and thine and hoard nothing for the next day, also represent Perfection or Completeness in that they are hermaphrodites – they walk abroad naked, admiring the beauty of their two-sexed bodies. But despite their meekness and tolerance in general, they would mercilessly kill foreign monsters or half-men (that is, one-sexed persons). In Bulwer Lytton's *The Coming Race*, a society in which work is rendered unnecessary by the disposable energy (called *Vril*) and 'everybody is omnipotent', woman is the wooer and man the coy and reluctant partner.[6] Again, in Samuel Butler's *Erewhon*, illness is considered to imply guilt, is concealed by the sufferer so far as possible, and exposes him to disrepute and condemnation, while crime and moral disorders are freely talked about and treated in clinics.[7] Finally, under Karl Marx's 'dialectical dispensation', the proletariat, embodying man in his purely negative condition - denudation and deprivation – is *eo ipso* invested with the mission of restoring man to the perfection of his being. It is not the consciousness of men that determines their being but, on the contrary, their being (that is, their material needs and the apparatus of ensuring their gratification) is what determines their consciousness. Pre-Marxian 'philosophy', which contented itself with the modest task of 'interpreting' the world, is to be superseded by a higher type of thought which is ordained to the object of changing it.

Modern Utopias (Renan, Shaw, Haldane, Stapledon and others) have shown an increasing tendency to tamper with the order of *time*. The optics of 'uchronia' are symbolized by references to such dates as 31,920 or, more generously still, 17,846,151. The background to this itch of anticipation is not only the modern experience of technological progress with its promise of unlimited extension, but a bold concern – 'meta-socialist', as I would venture to call it – with refashioning the *biological* nature of man. Moreover, the very structure of time is called into question in some speculations, implying that the utterly changed Mind of the future – no longer 'human', though deriving from human progress – will actually change the past, that is, refashion the long-past history of its ancestor, mankind.[8] The well-known Communist technique of substituting in various matters a different 'truth' for the Communist truth of yesterday, as caricatured in Orwell's *Nineteen Eighty-four*, conveys a not insignificant innuendo of this high-pitched utopian pretension.

I do not, in either philosophy or the pursuit of 'essential' knowledge, believe in neat definitions; it is by approaching an object, intuitively and discursively, from many sides, and by groping round its contours carefully and with a sustained readiness for self-correction, that we may best hope to penetrate its mystery. With this proviso in mind, I would now suggest as a working definition of Utopia – to guide our next enquiry – something like 'the conception of a perfect condition, envisioned as real, of men (or of a superhuman kind of beings evolved from men), which is free from painful tensions and from the awareness of any presence of evil'. In Marx's Hegelian language, bent to the service of a mind aflame with secular messianism, this 'tensionless condition' is intimated by the phrasing 'a society without contradictions'. In Christian language, we may describe Utopia as the state of mankind restored to its condition before the Fall, or risen to a consciousness no longer tinged with the memory or the delusion of that Fall – with the rift in his nature healed. Rousseau's dream of the *volonté générale* [general will] – Man's 'true' will, which is necessarily *toujours droit* [always right], found at the cost of every citizen 'wholly alienating' his 'private' will in favour of the indivisible community – is merely a graphic political version of the same pattern of thought.

5 THE UTOPIAN AND THE PERFECTIONAL EMPHASIS

Before prying further into the concept of Utopia as outlined here, I would emphasize the necessity of guarding against certain possible misunderstandings, both in the sense of extending and in the sense of restricting its range unduly: the first error would make the 'critique of Utopia' pointless or preposterous, causing it to miss the distinctive core of its object; the second would render such a critique comparatively trivial or idle, reducing it, as it were, to an exercise in literary criticism.[9]

A The perfectionist pretension of Utopia must not self-evidently or unreservedly be attributed (a) to the concept of social reforms as such; (b) to moral endeavour as such; (c) to the attitude of the political Left as such; (d) to the religious outlook as such. To distinguish the utopian spirit from each of these things, examining its aspects of kinship and its possible fusion but also its antithetic relations with each of them, will indeed be no mean part of our business. As regards reforms and improvements, their difference from utopian aspirations is, I think, one of emphasis rather than mere degree: non–utopian emphasis bears upon determinate goods which, in context, appear particularly worthy and susceptible of pursuit, and determinate evils whose elimination similarly presses into the centre of practical attention; whereas utopian emphasis is fixed upon the formal idea, in some concrete manifestation, of a self-contained and all-pervading state of man, not warped by any sense of limitation, division and frustration or beset by any evil. Again, the main difference between the religious and the utopian outlook lies in the affirmation of a supernatural, radically other than human, Reality, and of Man's dependence upon it: this affirmation holds the primary place in religion, whereas it is, at most, accidental and merely instrumental to Utopia. Therefore, religion does *not* visualize human or creaturely perfection in the same self-subsistent, consummate and logically 'closed' sense as does Utopia; properly religious and properly utopian ideals of perfection will be found to differ *intrinsically* in atmosphere and content.

B Notwithstanding the utopian reference to a perfect condition of man taken in its *totality*, the workings of the utopian temper far outstrip the sphere of total visions or all-comprehensive pictures of a perfect existence. Single departments of life and limited fields of problems *can* be treated in a utopian fashion, without the explicit complement of a utopian philosophy of existence as a whole. In this subdued sense of the term, private as well as public life is not infrequently tinged with illusions which sound a utopian note. What I have in mind here is not excessive love of a thing or excessive striving for an object; nor, again, bold hopes or hazardous ventures. These types of attitude and conduct, whatever their drawbacks and dangers, need have nothing utopian about them. Rather, I allude to utopian *presuppositions*, beliefs, interpretations and ostensibly 'evident' axioms at the back of many a human purpose or conception which, so far as its proper content goes, may be fairly sensible and in keeping with reality. Thus, both the case for private ownership and the case for state ownership, or at least for a relative predominance of either, can be supported with rational arguments. But the belief in an 'ideal' economic system – 'individualist' or 'socialist' – preferable in every respect, superior in itself (regardless of social and historical circumstances) and guaranteeing universal 'welfare' or even 'the good life of man', obviously savours of Utopia. Bentham's 'calculus of pleasure and pain' is eminently utopian inasmuch as it deflects man's genuine pursuit of value – which must keep aware of the order of values and the possibility of a rational choice between them, but also of their manifoldness and mutual irreducibility – to the perfectionist mirage of a 'maximum possession' of value. But similarly utopian are such fancies as that a 'return to religion' would of itself bring about the 'solution' to all the problems and difficulties of the age; or again, that morality is necessarily conducive to health and happiness, or that flourishing health and a 'natural' way of life would guarantee morality or make it superfluous. Briefly, all unilinear concepts of 'perfection', even though they are limited in their particular scope of objects, are instinctively utopian in spirit. The very belief that a 'perfect' management of life is conceivable on neatly 'departmental' lines reflects the utopian illusion that there must exist some ultimate 'key' to the puzzle of practice whose discovery and application would make everything 'fall into place', and henceforth pervade the life of mankind with a unitary tone of evident success and justification 'without remainder'.

From these considerations emerge such classic problems in the 'critique of Utopia' as 'How exactly can we distinguish between the proper pursuit of the good and its perfectionist aberration?'; 'What motives underlie the utopian degeneration of man's natural and generous yearning for perfection?'; and 'Is the thought of cleansing life from Utopia itself utopian?' I must reserve these queries, of course, for later discussion.[10]

Perhaps, however, it has become clearer even by now how such a thing as a 'rightist' or 'traditionalist' Utopia is possible, and in what sense we may speak thereof. No doubt, Utopia in its full character has a natural affinity with the Left; its rejection of 'given' reality and suggestion of a reality issuing from a preconceived norm of perfection is in basic accord with the leftist critique of traditional society on the basis of abstract moral and rational postulates. But the correspondence is not unequivocal. The dualism of a social reality and its critical examination as a permanent mode of life suits the leftist mind as such, but is distasteful to the utopian mind as such, attached as that is to the dream of a *consummate* identity between that which is and that which is 'all good'. Hence the possibility for it of a 'second choice': a 'toned-down' utopianism which, instead of envisioning an altogether new reality, an epitome of human perfection 'created' to standard, alights upon a historical model – present or past – of social order, *interpreting* it, illusively, as an embodiment of perfection - every departure from which must mean ruin and degradation, return to which accordingly means the high road to salvation.

Reactionary Utopia, riveted to an actual and contingent (although, of course, arbitrarily construed) form of reality and obliged to explain away, to cover up, to minimize or to embellish its ill-reputed and disturbing features, necessarily falls short of Utopia at its height, which is essentially subversive of all reality known as reality (except, in a sense, for the reality of 'revolution in permanence': the dictatorship of proven and fanatical utopians). Nevertheless, the ideal glorification of one determined regime and tradition, with the branding of all criticism of it as sacrilegious, offers one possible outlet for the utopian urge to force a total fusion, or at least to insinuate a massive unity, between Being and Value. Indeed, the literature of political Utopia begins with Plato's *Republic*, a vision that is certainly not 'conservative' in any way recalling Samuel Johnson's terse common-sense Toryism or even Burke's philosophy of Tradition, but still restorative rather than revolutionary, tribalist rather than universalist, and more of an artistic (or aestheticistic) reconstruction than a subversive appeal measuring up to the full stature of Utopia.[11]

6 THE IDOL OF UNITY AND IDENTITY

Once more, Utopia means a tensionless world from which the standard divisions intrinsic to the human condition have been cleared away; a world no longer properly a '*world*' in which man is placed but a supra-mundane creation or expansion of man entirely 'at one' with himself. It means, then, a wholeness of unbroken identity; accordingly, a complete rupture of identity with 'present' and 'past' – more exactly, with the world of man so far known. Lamartine's poem *Utopie*, though it is suffused with a benign mood of progressive idealism and expresses a distrust of revolutionary impatience and anger, is fairly, if verbosely, illustrative of the concept:

Matter has been conquered; work, henceforth, is thought. To thought and the light of human knowledge, no limits are set. Religious doubt has been swept away together with traditional religions and denominations. Temples, idols and dogmas are no more; but prayer, worship and spiritual belief are universal and identical. Faith and rational knowledge 'in the mirror of nature' are one. Mankind is united in a single cult and a single love. The divisions that separated the sons of the father into a diversity of kingdoms and nations are broken. So are the thrones of yore; no-one is a slave, everyone a king. War – that is 'murder' recognized as 'suicide', seeing that all men are brethren – has passed out of existence. So have errors and vices; and thus, starved of fuel, 'factitious passions' such as greed and lust for power have died out. Man serves his fellows for the asking and his well-doing is his treasure. Cursing the narrow egoism – 'hatred for all' and worship of self – in which he was formerly imprisoned, he now shares the common happiness, expands his soul to the point of being not only 'immense' but coextensive with humanity, and, still enlarging, stretches his universal life throughout the Indivisible Unity. He lives in the Deity and bears everything within him like the supreme Mind, fusing his own self into universal oneness.

The utopian principle of fusion and indivision works out along all classic dimensions – although, of course, in the single Utopias the distribution of stress may differ. What is doomed to disappear is the division – not necessarily the conceptual or descriptive distinction, but at least any division implying a sense of tension, limitation, pressure and impenetrable 'otherness' of opposition – between God and Man; between Mind and Body; between man and his cosmic environment, or again, Nature and Civilization; between order and contingency; among individuals and among social groups; between different planes or modalities of value; finally – most important, perhaps – between Value or the Good as such and Reality or Being as such: in particular, between moral value (virtue, obligation and conscience) and man's nature, character and conduct as they actually are. As the anti-utopian poet John Betjeman concludes his nightmare vision of the Socialist State: 'No right, no wrong: all's perfect, evermore.'

Admittedly, the emphasis may vary not only in respect of the particular distinction or antithesis that appears peculiarly obnoxious to this, that or other utopian thinker, but in respect also of the sign his monism will take: for example, pantheistic and suggestive of a Romantic pietism, or strictly atheistic; spiritualistic or materialist; individualist (on the assumption of a 'natural harmony' of selfish interests, which may be brought to fruition by the right kind of code) or Communist (implying that men may be conditioned directly to will on behalf of the community, irrespective of any self-regarding motives);[12] moralistic and super-puritanical or immoralistic (a 'perfect nature' being capable of interpretation as 'all moral' or as needing no moral restraints, or even tests), and so forth. The preference of emphasis as between the severe *postulate* of perfection and the ecstatic picture of its happy *manifestations* may also be a mixed one, and sometimes the distinction would appear merely verbal: at the peak of its artificial conditioning and re-creation, man's nature is meant to recover its unbroken spontaneity, resplendent with all hues of effortless perfection. Utopia is neither an exhortation of man to obey a proposed code of rules nor an encouragement of him to yield to his impulses and do what he likes, it is the conception and portrayal of him in a state of *non posse peccare* [not being able to sin] – which at the same time means a state of saturation with every kind of value, and of undisturbed correspondence with his environment. Along with being 'good' (or 'beyond good and evil' taken in a conventional sense), the citizens of utopian worlds are also happy, vigorous, long-lived and beautiful – supposing, as is mostly the case, that they are embodied at all, not pure spirits as in the visions of Renan's and Shaw's old age – and in enjoyment of a complacent cosmic scenery.

In William Morris's *News from Nowhere*, an idyllic Utopia of small-scale communities at peace with one another – no laws, no government, no parliament, no formal family ties, no property and no jealousy; everything bathed in 'love and affection' – all persons and all things are handsome, and the weather is always fine and warm ... in England. Fourier goes one better with his more formally and scientifically organized *phalanstères*:[13] here, beyond the mere regulation of climates, the ensured harmony of society is seen to pervade the universe and beget a more harmonious order of the solar system as well as of the animal and vegetable realms. But the utopian details are by no means always preposterous, unrealizable or *a priori* impossible. The *differentia* of Utopia lies not in these – symbolic as they may be in their sickly-sweetish philistinism, jejune vastness, or defiant eccentricity – but in the basic structural contrast between Utopia and reality.

In the real world, we experience a manifold interpenetration of Value and Being, but also an ineliminable tension between them: things may be good, but they may also be bad; they can often be improved, but in general only at the cost of accepting *some* drawbacks; and even a good thing *might* be different and better. In Utopia, what is is *eo ipso* good, and what is desired as good *eo ipso* is or comes about: *ens simpliciter bonum ut ens* [a being which is good simply as that (kind of) being], as some theologians have predicated of God. Moreover, in the real world we also experience – rooted in the tension between Value and Being – a diversity, in many ways discordant, *among values*. A thing is better than an alternative thing in one respect but worse in another; and the pursuit of one kind of value is liable to render others less accessible. In the utopian concept, however, this 'law of scarcity' no longer obtains: all forms of value invariably belong together, and automatically pledge one another; an 'evidently just' order of society also 'means' a maximum of welfare, of physical beauty, of creative art, of a satisfied and satisfactory private life. One central value entails or guarantees all others; or rather, every value aspect only reveals and irradiates the selfsame perfection of being. This is what Ruyer has aptly called *la confusion des normativités* [the confusion of normative categories], in which he sees the prime ground for the 'oppressiveness' of the utopian atmosphere: from such a world, all *personal choice* between incompatible – or, at any rate, competing – values appears to be excluded.[14]

7 THE UTOPIAN FALLACY OF CONTENTMENT

I have – unpardonably, perhaps – used above the sleek phrasing 'a satisfied and satisfactory private life'. No doubt the pair of words 'satisfied and satisfactory' is bristling with fundamental problems of ethics – or, to put it more clumsily, of the logic of moral appraisals. But the cast-iron identity of the two terms belongs to the very core of utopian perfectionism. The men or demigods of Utopia are meant to be absolutely satisfied with their lot, but also with themselves and, again, with their neighbours – the three, anyhow, being part and parcel of one another. What thus totally satisfies must indeed be objectively satisfactory; and, inversely, such a state of full satisfaction must itself appear as the goal of human endeavour. Its envisioned existence must satisfy *our* yearning and imagination. Utopian conditions *are* perfect; they are *experienced* as perfect; and their being so experienced is one aspect of their perfection. The split between subjective content and objective value has vanished – along with the split between what is and what ought to be, between desire and fulfilment, between self and community, and between man and his ambient world. The *volonté générale* [general will] is always right; and right is what the *volonté générale* wills.

Conditions are so fashioned as to be altogether fit to satisfy men: which they could not be unless *men* were conditioned to fall in wholly with the scheme of perfection they represent. The two aspects are inseparable; accordingly, viewed from a standpoint *outside* Utopia, the conception is saddled with a basic ambiguity. Granted the initial assumption that in the society of Utopia some *evils* we know are non-existent, some imperfections ironed out, some obvious and incontestable advantages secured: how do we assess the spiritual stature of men who are uncritically appreciative of the world they live in, lacking the desire to imagine and discuss conditions other and better than theirs; how do we gauge the moral level of men who are satisfied with their morality, exhibiting certain virtues and the absence of certain vices but, by definition, amoral in the formal sense of the word: that is, living without a *conscience*?

By one and the same act, the utopian conception of man would appear to soar above the loftiest and to descend beneath the nethermost conceivable plane of human existence; perhaps we should say that our categories cease to be applicable to life designed in its terms. In a humbler – more prosaic and psychological – form, however, the same ambiguity is revealed in a witty and substantial dictum by Shaw: 'Get what you like, or else you'll grow to like what you get.' The point of this admonition is incontestably activistic and, as it were, favourable to rugged self-help and sober reason, hostile to illusion and uncritical acceptance. The emphasis is not on being satisfied as such but on *obtaining* what *is* satisfactory. Yet on closer scrutiny, the argument seems to be underlain by a very poor view of man. Unless he actually succeeds in 'getting what he likes', he is (on that view) *doomed* to 'grow to like what he gets'. That is to say, to like whatever *inferior* things he may get; for in *both* cases he is supposed to like – 'eventually' at any rate, but ineluctably – what he gets. Whereas in fact, it is inherent in the spiritual dignity of man not only to *distinguish* – and to persevere in distinguishing – between that which is and that which satisfies him, even though the two may coincide in many respects, and though he may exert himself to extend the range of that coincidence by changing things. Utopia conjures up the dubious bliss of a humanity that *has* actually 'got' whatever it 'likes' – or, perhaps, some such things, and others which it is constructively supposed or, again, told, to like – and thus abandons itself, without reserve or limit, to the attitude of 'liking what it gets'.

The 'perfect condition of man', then, dialectically cuts both ways. On the one hand, it seems to imply perfect men; on the other, it carries a suggestion to the effect that there is no longer any need – or even room, perhaps – for *personal* perfection in men. On the one side, we have Plato's 'philosopher-kings', the conventional orgies of 'idealism' and 'altruism' (as in Lamartine's *Utopie*), the various kinds of 'supermen' of the later Utopias down to Shaw's disembodied 'purely rational' spirits, or to Stapledon's 'Neptunians' who form, as it were, a *corpus mysticum* [mystical body], one individual experiencing the bodies of the rest as one single body that is 'all his', seeing with the eyes of all and sharing their sensations. On the other side, we have such para-utopian constructions as the pure self-seeking of individuals concerted by the 'hidden hand' to make the guarantee of universal happiness (Adam Smith; in a more pointed and cynical form, Mandeville's 'Private vices, public benefits'; or again, Bentham's reflective egoism of each as the foundation of the happiness of all, supposing that it can be properly actualized and organized). And, further, a significant trait in More's *Utopia*: its happy inhabitants, Epicurean in temper, are sufficiently well served – once they are in possession of their perfect institutions – by a 'moderate virtue'; they have no use for a 'heroic morality'. This was to be put more elaborately in Condorcet's *Esquisse d'un tableau des progrès de l'esprit humain.* True morality and statecraft are to make 'great' virtues *superfluous*; the more advanced a civilization is, the less it needs them. Moreover, the progress and diffusion of science render genius similarly useless. Knowledge and its fruits will be at the disposal even of mediocre intelligences – the sovereignty of the button-pushing 'common man', that paramount ideal of our world of technology and the 'mass' mode of life, anticipated at the threshold of the industrial age.

Again, part of the utopian perfection may consist simply in an *abolition of moral 'prejudices'*. Obviously, a tensionless mental state of man – the entelechy of his attained or fully developed immanent perfection – may be pursued either by eliminating from the tissue of reality what is resistant to moral demands or by eliminating moral demands that meet with resistance. The latter is the easier way (though, in fact, it is less easy than it might seem). It is not that utopian thought predominantly tends to decide for this alternative but that its logic points this way, seeing that its principal emphasis lies on an experience of 'flawless perfection' rather than on the intrinsic tests of perfection; on virtue identified with the whole nature of man rather than on a prevalence of virtue as a 'second nature' of man; and not on man's capacity to *cope* with evil but on the absence of evil. Thus, in Morelly's *Basiliade*, there are no laws bearing on the relations between the sexes. Love, including incestuous ties, is completely free; modesty (pudeur) is unknown. Hence, such ugly things as adultery and prostitution are non-existent, just as greed and theft are non-existent owing to the absence of private property. (The strand of this 'sublime' immoralism recurs, of course, frequently in the weft of later literature, utopian or not strictly so. It is never without a utopian tint, for moral taboos concerning sex, though not in themselves weighted with direct and painful immanent sanctions in a way comparable to the elementary rules of justice, are as inherent in the constitution of man as are the temptations to transgress them.)

8 THE SUBVERSIVE INTERPRETATION OF 'VIRTUE'

In the realm of utopian thought, and sometimes even within the pales of *one* utopian world – between Plato's *Republic* and his *Laws*; between Rousseau's *Emile* and his *Contrat Social* – we may observe contradictions and oscillations; but the focal concept of a tensionless, self-contained and closed sphere of perfection remains immutable. What matters is neither moral austerity nor sensual hedonism as such; neither sophistication nor simplicity as such; neither abundance nor Spartan sobriety as such. It is, rather, that there should be *no discrepancy* but pre-established congruence and consummate identity between the moral experience and standards of men and their actual moral achievement, between what they appreciate and what they are, between what they wish for and what they possess. When the radical ideologists of the French Revolution (Robespierre and Saint-Just, with their literary precursors Rousseau, Morelly and Mably, and their unsuccessful communist disciple Babeuf) speak of 'virtue', they have in mind something that is not wholly dissociated, as regards content, from the ordinary meaning of 'virtue', but stands in a sharp structural contrast to it.

In the traditional perspective of ethics, man 'should' be 'virtuous', and some men *are* so, which is a good thing for society as a whole and should be encouraged by various means. But the 'virtue' of the revolutionists is not an excellence or a distinctive moral prowess some men happen to display, however appreciated and encouraged by the state – it is a quality proper to men as such by right, a quality that they are all destined to possess and *will* possess once restored, by the artificial action of revolutionary power, to the integrity of their 'nature'. Virtue will then *mean* their own 'true' will: the 'general will' so far latent in the souls of the people, though as yet non-existent and in need of being evoked and brought to the fore – indeed, imposed – by organization and force. The value and destiny of men must *not* depend on whether they, as unpredictable individuals, are or are not 'virtuous'. Perfection must lie beyond privilege and incertitude; beyond limitations and contingency. As Morelly wrote in *Code de la Nature*, 'Providence could not have delivered humanity to eternal chaos and hazard':[15] which means that man, through his own rational construction and revolutionary effort, must be released from his haphazard dependence on his own free will. In order to be no longer morally (and otherwise) unsafe, he must cease to be a 'moral' being – that is to say, to be governed or acted upon by his personal conscience. 'L'idée particulière que chacun se fait de la liberté, selon son interêt, produit l'esclavage de tous' [When everyone forms his own particular conception of freedom, basing it on his own interest, the result is universal enslavement] – Saint-Just.[16]

In Talmon's summing up, 'Man and people have to be brought to choose freedom, and if necessary to be forced to be free. Human egotism must be rooted out, and *human nature changed.*' [emphasis added].[17]

> Liberté sacrée! [exclaims Saint-Just] Tu serais peu de chose parmi les hommes si tu ne les rendais qu'heureux, mais tu les rappelles à leur origine et les rends à la vertu.[18]

> [Oh sacred liberty! . . . You would be a poor thing among men if you merely made them happy; but you recall them to their origins and restore them to virtue.]

Rousseau's position, in the throes of the dialectics of 'perfection', is excellently condensed by Talmon:

> Man wavering between his inclinations and his duties, neither quite man nor quite citizen, no good to himself nor to others, because never in accord with himself....The only salvation from this agony, if a return to the untroubled state of nature was impossible, was either a complete self-abandonment to the elemental impulses or to 'denature (*dénaturer*) man' altogether.[19]

Thus freedom, for Rousseau, means

> not to enable men *as they are* to express themselves as freely and as fully as possible, to assert their uniqueness. It is to create the right objective conditions and to educate men so that they would fit into the pattern of the virtuous society.[20]

I shall return later to the utopian distortion of the meaning of moral words like 'virtue' and 'justice' as applied to *social conditions*. To round off our reflections in the present context, I would only recall Mably's plea, more forcefully echoed by Babeuf, for economic and also for intellectual and cultural 'mediocrity'. Outdoing in purity the Bolshevist regime, which saw itself compelled to make up for the natural advantages of capitalist economy by the *Ersatz* device of 'socialist competition' and to condemn 'mechanical equality',[21] Babeuf would forbid all competition, and brands all higher rewards for talent as a crime; in general, he inveighs against 'la folie meurtrière des distinctions de valeur' [the murderous folly of distinctions of value]. Justly so, for the utopian emphasis on 'perfection' is directed, not to a maximization of wealth but to a distribution of it that leaves everyone with the feeling of being a co-owner of 'total' wealth; and, above all, not to the bringing forth of abundant and high values but to the undivided oneness of their experience and possession.

No doubt the machine age and the dissolution of the remnants of puritanical Christianity will divert the utopian emphasis towards the fetish of 'plenty' and the mirage of 'culture for all',[22] but the contempt for quality, less tersely expressed, will have advanced in depth rather than vanished here. If the very word 'virtue' has passed out of currency, the utopian substitution for morality proper of the automatism of a 'perfect society' prevails all the more. Indoctrinating man with the ideal of 'getting what he likes' and conditioning him to 'like what he gets' are inseparable facets of the selfsame entity. The second is no less relevant to our theme than the first, and it is still worthwhile contemplating Mably's reply to the objection that economic regimentation may *engourdir les hommes* (benumb men and dull their minds):

> C'est que je souhaite, si par cet engourdissement on entend l'habitude qu'ils contracteront de ne rien désirer au-delà de ce que la Loi leur permet de posséder.[23]

> [This is what I wish for, if we understand by this numbness the habit they will form of never desiring anything which the law will not allow them to possess.]

That this ideology, following in Rousseau's wake, breathes the authentic spirit of Utopia rather than a spirit of parsonical moralism or of narrow schoolmaster's exhortations; and that the 'virtuous society' means something quite different from a society in which good men are numerous or govern the state – namely, a society that has *surmounted the scission* in man's nature and enchanted away the distinction between values and facts – is borne out clearly enough by Babeuf's ecstatic vision of the order to come:

> Let that government make disappear all frontiers, fences, walls, locks on the doors, all disputes, trials, all theft, murder, all crime;

all tribunals, prisons, gallows, torture, jealousy, insatiability, pride, deceit, duplicity: finally all the vices.... Guarantee to every one of society's members a state of stable felicity, the satisfaction of the needs of all, a sufficiency inalterable, independent of the ineptitude, immorality or ill-will of those in power.[24]

Total goodness, then, should repose not on awareness of evil and discrimination in favour of the good, not on focusing men's attention on the polarity of right and wrong, but on hammering society into an apparatus of 'infallible' perfection, in whose orbit no personal imperfection can appear – or if it does, it makes no difference and withers harmlessly away, irrelevant to the point of being unworthy of notice. How do we set about achieving such a state of things? The obvious answer involves the unlimited and omnipotent dictatorship of a conspiratorial sect committed to its realization: Babeuf, a diehard radical of Jacobinism on the down-grade, is at the same time an inspired forerunner of Bolshevism. But the point is not so much the exorbitance of the utopian aim and the price its serious pursuit will demand as the perverseness of its meaning. It is inconsistent not only with the lower and cruder states of man's nature but, more particularly, with his morality in the context of his nature. Shakespeare's Ulysses in his famous speech exposing the destructive and suicidal action of egalitarian anarchy ('O when degree is shaked' ... to 'Appetite, an universal wolf'), also strikes what must be the keynote of an essential critique of Utopia:

> Force should be right; or, rather, right and wrong,
> Between whose endless jar justice resides,
> Should lose their names, and so should justice too.[25]

9 THE UTOPIAN PERVERSION OF THE SENSE OF VALUES

From the ethical point of view, utopian perfection may be described as a completely moralized state of man, in which men are not bothered with moral preoccupations. Such an aim is unattainable; for whatever else in so-called human nature and in the conditions of human existence may be liable to change, imperfection – without and within – remains an invariable aspect thereof, and so does awareness of imperfection, together with the need to rectify or circumscribe it wherever the task appears to be urgent, feasible and fruitful. Political action informed by the utopian vision will not create either a community of saints or a society of happy savages with their moral sense amputated, but it will tend at the same time to enforce arbitrary demands of a preconceived sectarian code, outside the range of the actual moral sense of men, and to suppress spontaneous moral criticism genuinely arising from the clash between the moral sense of men and the vital and social framework of their lives. It is obviously necessary to appreciate the threat of collectivist tyranny, inseparable from the appeal of utopian speculations. It is no less necessary, however, to see through the *intrinsic* absurdity of the utopian concept of perfection, which lies at the root of that danger: for the blind alley of extreme tyranny and revolution in permanence is the direct manifestation of the attempt to subject reality to a schema of inherent unreality, destined to veil the impossibility of the aim and to maintain the illusion that it has been or is being achieved.

We have nothing like a standard, measure, model or applicable definition of 'perfection' *except in the context of reality*, with its manifoldness of good and bad, more and less perfect, thriving and failing things.[26] If we get out of that context, the very idea of perfection becomes as meaningless as, for example, the idea of a 'perfect food', neither meat nor fruit nor corn, uniting the mutually inconsistent advantages of all these but free of all their drawbacks. The usual tangible tokens of utopian 'perfection' – such as a conspicuous equality and uniformity, or the planned regularity of life – are not (to say the least) unmixed goods according to the taste of men in general, but arbitrary symbols of the empty *idea* of all-round perfection. More particularly, although the moral valuations and concerns of men are by no means infallible or invariably coherent, nor, as a rule, perfectly balanced, we have no valid criterion – or, indeed, definition – of a 'moral life' except in the context of the actual moral experiences and consciences of men.

Although a man's life is not moral (that is, 'morally good') in so far as it is saturated with moral reflection or responsive to other men's moral reflections, men cannot in any sense lead a 'moral life' in disjunction from their explicit moral preoccupations. It is doubtless arguable – and, in my view, certain – that an action approved by one's conscience may yet be gravely evil (for perversions of conscience occur, and conformity to conscience does not define Right and Wrong); but a life from which the control of conscience has been extruded is of necessity an amoral life, some of whose contents may be objectively good rather than evil, but whose spiritual tone is subhuman and whose protection against the influx of actual evil is accidental to the point of being non-existent. It is 'between the endless jar of right and wrong' that 'justice resides'; and perfection no longer felt to be in tension with imperfection[27] is a meaningless sham, reminiscent of the ubiquitous gold of the fable which starved Midas to death instead of enriching him to satiation.

The ethical paradox of Utopia may also be expressed in terms of a fictitious relationship between Morality and Practice, linked to the essential discontinuity between the mind of the utopian 'planner' and the mind of utopian man he proposes to 'condition'. Man in reality is imperfect but capable of perfective thoughts and efforts, inclined to evil but appreciative of good, endowed with a moral sense but easily slipping from its control. He is made to live in awareness of moral demands but is by no means a creature of morality. His conduct is primarily determined by non-moral vital concerns, and confronted with morality primarily in the form of 'taboos', interdicts, restrictive rules and onerous obligations. The new mankind of Utopia, on the contrary, is to be the product of a moral abstraction, 'born of' an ideal pretending to embody 'pure' or 'absolute' morality. It is to be a mankind redeemed from the sting of conscientious morality, performing its vital practice undisturbed by that 'alien and imperious voice within us'; for that Practice, sprung from the once-and-for-all fulfilment of a key postulate of Morality, is presumed to be of immanent perfection and *a priori* good. It does not grow out of *our* vital practice, in the mode of transition and gradual innovation; but neither, of course, is that future mankind meant to supersede us by means of a blind historical upheaval, as a race of victorious conquerors would take the place of the vanquished. On the one hand, we are supposed to exist merely for its own sake, with no present purpose of our own, as a condition of its coming; on the other hand, however, we are to 'create' existence on a plan conceived by, or at any rate ratified by, our own present mind – a plan in which we are called to 'believe' to the sacrifice of our other interests, but by dint of which we are still to be the forgers and conditioners of that future mankind predestined to unalloyed goodness and bliss. We do not, since we are wholly unidentical and discontinuous with it, know the actual 'taste' or 'feel' of that future 'perfection', nor that we should in fact experience it as perfection; but we are to envision and to create it *qua* perfect. We are not in any way of that world, but we are at the same time both the mere raw material for its construction *and* its sovereign makers. Again, the demigods of the utopian world – self-sufficiently 'good'; 'supermen', incommensurable with our drab humanity which is disfigured with blemishes, thwarted by limitations, rent with divisions and stamped with the seal of suffering – are at the same time homuncules manufactured by ourselves, incapable of understanding or imagining a world other than theirs, and ignorant of good and evil.

10 THE UTOPIAN MISUSE OF ABSTRACTION

Utopia means a mirage incapable of being translated into reality (though not of impinging upon reality), incapable even of being *thought out*. The attempt to think it out collapses in irrationality: it rests on a valuational delusion, on a type of valuation afflicted with the vice of overreaching itself. The utopian vision of perfection is out of focus, removed from the perspective in which the concept of perfection alone is meaningful, detached from mankind's horizon of values and conspectus of concerns; a prey to monomania and to abstraction running riot.

Abstraction itself is not, of course, an aberration but a natural and indispensable tool of all knowledge, thought and practice. We know concrete, 'singular' things just in themselves, without abstraction, as little as we know the alleged 'essences' of things without experiencing them in their concrete individuality. Nor can we estimate them or give them a place in our plans of conduct unless we apply to them general categories, rules and standards of value. Again, in dealing with an object or province of objects it is often convenient, or even of decisive help, to raise our level of abstraction, to generalize further, and to broaden our perspective. But here lies the temptation to *substitute* abstraction for the actual experience (theoretical and valuational) of concrete things, and to imagine mistakenly that we know and judge things more 'completely' and 'exhaustively' the more we account for them in increasingly abstract terms. This, however, means a tendency to *abandon* (rather than enlarge) *our perspective vision of them*, for the sake of universal formulae which we credit with the virtue of explaining, at one stroke, a vast number of problems, with 'ultimate validity' and 'without remainder'.

Utopian thought is dominated by this fallacious hope of getting hold of an 'open sesame' to the solution of vital problems and the secret of perfection, by overleaping our experimental footholds in reality and in current personal and political practice. It is obsessed with the delusion that because the pursuit of higher values on a larger scale *may* often advantageously replace attachment to some petty and limited aims, therefore the advance in valuational abstraction *means* a firmer grasp on the good, and a higher and wider horizon of values. Hence the appearance of a 'generous' thirst for 'perfection', whereas behind the façade of this inane idol of a *concept* of 'perfection' (though some less abstract value-word such as 'happiness', 'unity', 'freedom', 'spontaneity' or 'community' may be preferred) we find impoverishment, atrophy and obfuscation of the normal human sense of values, standards and decencies. Longing for 'perfection' and the actual pursuit of it are in themselves invested with a convincing and incontrovertible evidence of value, which may easily confer upon utopianism a deceptive appeal even to the ordinary consciousness of men.[28] Hence the psychological paradox: many of us, not belonging to the utopian type of mind but not trained to criticize it either, tainted but not centrally possessed by utopianism, manifest at one and the same time a utopian and a non-utopian 'will'. Such people would recognize that a certain utopian creed which has caught their attention means, after all, the very best of things, namely goodness itself, while their intrinsic desires and value-emphases are quite different, normal and balanced. They would, then, expect Communism, for example, to mean, in fact, something like a liberal-democratic order of things, only with more justice, fairness and kindness, less hypocrisy and corruption, and – to crown it all – more freedom.

Since the utopian mind is averse to reality – declining to take the rough with the smooth – and intolerant of its basic constitution, it has no interest in values, goods and qualities *proper*. It is interested only in the *one* idol of 'absolute' value, 'goodness' unopposed by contrast, limitation and contingency, the exclusion of countervailing aspects and patched-up solutions or settlements by compromise. Robespierre's totalitarian outcry –

> If you do not *all* for liberty, you have not done a thing. There are no two ways of being free: either you are *entirely* free or you return to being a slave. The *slightest opening* left to despotism will soon reestablish its power,[29]

Babeuf's horror of '*perfecting the imperfect*' (which helps it to survive, and thus keeps out perfection), and Marx's faith in the subversive virtue of ever-increasing misery,[30] are so many expressions of the utopian transference of valuation from 'the good' – in its primary, concrete, manifold and finite sense – to the single idea of its absoluteness, unlimited presence and unqualified purity. This 'dialectical' pattern of thought originates in Rousseau's fundamental thesis – the clearest exhibition, perhaps, of utopian logic – that civilization (organized polity and its artificial features, as opposed to the 'state of nature') is all to the bad until it be pushed to the point of total artificiality and the unchecked mastery of a single collective will, which shall be 'all good'. It may not be useless to recall here a letter of Rousseau's, written in 1767 (quoted in Pierre Gaxotte's *Le siècle de Louis XV*), which shows significantly how such a type of mind, despairing of total democracy but still clinging to the single value of 'totality' and indifferent to everything else, may then turn to flirt with a sort of fascism, as a second choice:

> ... une forme de gouvernement qui mettra la loi au-dessus de l'homme. Si cette forme est trouvable, cherchons-la....Si malheureusement elle n'est pas trouvable, et j'avoue ingénument qu'elle ne l'est pas, mon avis est qu'il faut *passer à l'autre extrémité* et mettre tout d'un coup l'homme autant au-dessus des lois qu'il peut l'être; par conséquent *établir le despotisme arbitraire et le plus arbitraire qu'il est possible.* [emphasis added]

> [. . . a form of government which will put the law above men. If this form may be discovered, let us seek it out. . . . If, unfortunately, it is not to be found – and I honestly confess

that it is not – I think that we must *go to the opposite extreme* and, at one fell swoop, put man as far above the laws as he possibly can be; and accordingly *establish an arbitrary tyranny – the most arbitrary there can be.*]

For even though 'despotism' implies one line of massive division – between the master and his subjects – as contrasted with the 'indivisible' unity of the *volonté générale* [general will], it still at least bears a signature of identity, totality and absoluteness, in sharp contraposition to a regime of constitutional limitations and diversified random privileges.

The divorce of utopian from common-sense human valuation is also behind the paradox of utopian exclusiveness and singularity as the reverse side of utopian abstraction and universalism. My pretension to supply mankind with a universal plan and a self-contained harmony of life is the exact opposite of my seeking communion and understanding with the universe of human thoughts, predilections and endeavours; and the concept of a 'perfect world' entails the uttermost isolation from the world and its treasury of relative 'perfections'. The 'self-evident' mediocrity of utopian desiderata – the 'philistine' aspect of the utopian worlds – is not an expression of the soul of mankind in its concrete, actual and living universality, which cannot be approached except in a mode of dialogue, composition and mutual recognition of diversity; rather, it is a fruit of immoderate abstraction, intended to fit a schematic anthropoid construct *in place of man*: not man in his actual, including his rational and spiritual as well as his vital and sensual, reality. The divorce is more directly brought about by the other aspect of Utopias – that of arbitrary eccentricity, hinting at a sharp transcendence of the 'ordinary' world of mankind and throwing into stark relief the fantastic preposterousness of the utopian venture: the pretension that another and perfect mankind of the future shall be conditioned and created according to plan – not (properly speaking) by an inferior preparatory mankind taken as a whole, however paradoxical even that may sound, but from the particular conception of *one* individual or sectarian mind which happens to emerge at one particular point in the history of imperfect mankind.

The point of this criticism may, it is true, be blunted by

considering the common features of the many particular Utopias, largely independent of the motley personal whims of their authors; and by taking account of the eagerness of the Marxists (and some of their rivals) to gear the Utopia to an 'objective' reading of 'historical necessity', and to disclaim any idea of determining, here and now, the actual complexion of the 'State of the future'. But the essential character of the utopian conception does not hinge on the choice of otiose arbitrary details. The class-less and state-less collective of tomorrow, decreed by a particular messianistic dogmatism born of a certain set of conditions in the landscape of nineteenth-century industrialism, expresses a classic utopian pretension amplified rather than contradicted by its pseudo-scientific trappings. If we refuse to fill in the details, that does not mean that we cease to determine 'the society of the future' (note the monistic and definite character of that imaginary concept), leaving it to be determined by itself or by contingencies; it means that we determine it to be so perfect as to determine itself forthwith, blandly certain of its further perfection, no matter what things it may prefer or what institutional details it may establish. It shall be essentially the product of *our* single-track emotive vision and plausible conceptual construction, whose *theme* it is, precisely, a perfect human collective which we need not and must not burden with the dead weight of our *more concrete* habits of thought, tastes and traditions – including even such traditions as are linked to earlier phases in the struggle for Progress, and evoke democratic associations.

In strict antithesis to utopian nihilism in respect of actual and present reality, and to the utopian claim of acting as the demiurge of a perfect future, Kipling's poem *The Palace* expresses the normal and reasonable attitude of an open-minded conservatism, proper to civilized man: man living by rights, and building for eternity, in his own perspective, yet aware of its limits and of its being only one perspective among others of equal status; living in touch with the mind of mankind but never identifying his own mind therewith; anxious to understand the values of old and to hand down his own to his heirs, hoping perhaps for a greater perfection in their work, to which his unfinished enterprise is meant to contribute, but knowing that it must be theirs as his own is not that of his forebears, and that he can neither foretell nor foreordain its perfection:

'And thy palace shall stand as that other's – the spoil of a king who shall build.'

I called my men from my trenches, my quarries, my wharves and my shears.
All I had wrought I abandoned to the faith of the faithless years.
Only I cut on the timber, only I carved on the stone:
After me cometh a Builder. Tell him, I too have known!

2
The Utopian Idol of Perfection and the Non-utopian Pursuit of the Good

1 BURCKHARDT'S CRITICISM OF THE MIRAGE OF SOCIAL PERFECTION

The Swiss historian of civilization Jacob Burckhardt, probably the greatest of anti-utopian social thinkers, emphasizes the *inherent contradiction* of utopian perfectionism rather than the mere excessiveness of its aims – the familiar aspect of its being 'too beautiful to be achievable'. The edge of his criticism is predominantly *logical*. This is in complete accord with Knittermeyer's remark,[1] that Burckhardt expects a salutary new direction to issue neither from man as a religious nor from man as a political but from man as an 'intellectual' or 'philosophical' being [*vom geistigen Menschen*], and it is entirely on the same lines that I am trying to develop my own train of thought.

Democracy, based on postulates of universal liberty, tends to bring into existence the Welfare State, and thereby necessarily the utter crushing of the liberties to which it continues to cling. Caesarism is certain to come, for 'the social demand imposes on the State an inconceivable load of tasks, which cannot be solved except by means of an equally unheard-of plenitude of power'. This fundamental idea of Burckhardt's – borne out amply enough, though of course not in a uniform fashion nor, so far, in all places and all contexts, by the events and trends of our post-1914 epoch – recurs again and again, with minor variations; but there are at least two passages in Burckhardt where I find an even closer, deeper and more synoptic approach to the theme of the utopian contradiction.

'Keeping everything persistently subject to discussion and change,' writes Burckhardt, 'democracy will end up with a host of irreconcilable contradictions.' These are set out more explicitly elsewhere:

The utmost freedom of the individual, along with a State all-powerful and providing for all ... domestic freedom, along with acts of violence (glorious ones, preferably) against foreign peoples; rights without end, along with a very dim awareness of duties, and a complete misconception of what is possible.[2]

A few words of interpretation may be called for. Glorious foreign wars do not exactly tally with the pacifist emphasis of more recent leftist utopianism; the idea still savours of the Jacobin and Bonapartist military romanticism of the earlier middle nineteenth century. But the French revolutionary pre-Marxist slogan *Guerre aux palais, paix aux chaumières* [Make war on the palace, leave the cottage in peace], with its very flexible range of application, will never cease aptly to express one inalienable facet of utopian thought: that *all* compulsion is evil, and that *no* violence is evil on the part of those who are possessed of this moral insight. As regards rights and duties, let us observe that what Burckhardt has in mind is not so much the current rightist admonition that men ought to be conscious of their duties rather than of their rights as the logical correspondence between rights and duties, claims and debts. This correspondence carries with it, of course, the hidden implication of 'duties without end' – that is, of the surreptitious imposition of charges, regulations and servitudes with no limits set to them, or in other words still, the self-stultifying bent of the pursuit of universal and effective freedom, the inescapable self-contradiction of Social Utopia. The added 'misconception of what is possible' seems to introduce a more vague and trivial emphasis on the exorbitance and unrealism of utopian endeavour as distinct from the inherent self-contradiction of the utopian conception. But, without wishing to labour the point at this stage, I should say that Burckhardt was far from wrong in assuming a close connection between the two: the logical standards of our thought-practice are inseparable from our awareness of the constitutive features of empirical reality. He who denies or disregards the fundamental economic law of scarcity, or the finiteness and defectiveness of human capacities, is not thereby committing a mistake in formal reasoning; but his thinking is not merely vitiated by errors of fact.

Here is a similar résumé of the utopian vision, conceived in a different and higher perspective, embracing an all-round perfection of human life:

> 'Glanzbild der Zukunft' ('A resplendent image of the future',
> but I might equally well translate 'The mirage of a future')
> in which the spiritual shall be reconciled with the material;
> religion, thought and life shall be one; between Duty and the
> Will there shall be no split; concord shall be established between
> pleasure-seeking and morality.[3]

It would be difficult to coin a better, a more essential, more
expressive, more terse and concise formula of the utopian attitude.
It is, by the way, extremely interesting to note how self-evidently
Burckhardt includes in the context of futurist utopianism proper
the philosophical schema of moral hedonism. The seductive glam-
our of Perfection will not inspire licentious dreams of subversion
alone, but illusory interpretations of the data of consciousness and
the basic features of the world as well. But despite appeal to the
authority of Burckhardt (and many others), I am perhaps on the
point of becoming too repetitive in proffering these polemical
generalities and displaying my own anti-utopian temper. Some
obvious pro-utopian objections have forthwith to be dealt with;
nor can we dispense with a closer analysis of the concept of
'perfection' and an attempt to make out what 'perfectionism'
exactly means.

2 IN DEFENCE OF UTOPIANISM

(i) Utopia proper and the pursuit of perfection

The objector may embark on a defence of 'utopianism' or 'the
utopian mind' taken in the sense of 'perfectionism', as distinct
from 'Utopia' proper, taken in the sense of 'placelessness'. He may
defend what I have been describing as an arbitrary vision of some
otherworldly state of things out of touch with historical reality and
the constants of human experience: 'There is certainly no reason
why we should slavishly dedicate ourselves to one particular vision
or personal conception of the Perfect, or commit ourselves to what
are only the opinions, desires and preferences of a solitary crank or
a small band of eccentrics. But neither is there any reason why we
should forbear from the bold, generous and persistent affirmation

and pursuit of what most of us evidently know to be, or can (if shown) with evidence discern to be, true perfection. What is wrong with Perfection, anyhow? And what is perfectionism but the pursuit of the perfect? Certainly perfection cannot as a rule be had for the asking. But we shall not devise the means to attain it unless we first ask for it. To say that the search for perfection is not worth the price is at best an utterly doubtful contention, if not – in general – a downright paradox. For what *else* can be worth any price at all? Every purpose, action or enterprise beyond the strict routine of everyday life can only spring from the pursuit of perfection; yet even the routine conduct of everyday activities would break down if we were to exclude *a priori* all hopes and plans to improve it, and all higher aspirations which provide it with a meaning.'

My hypothetical opponent begs the question in assuming that Utopianism exists only in its explicit, manifestly absurd, playful and irresponsible or baseless and insane form; and in assuming that perfectionism is identical with, or no more than a more emphatic expression of, the normal human striving to improve our lot and our character. It is precisely my contention that this is not so: that there is such a thing as a utopian attitude of mind, an ever-present human possibility. This is *not* identical with human purposefulness, planning and reformatory endeavour as such. While it is most characteristically expressed in 'properly utopian' speculations and writing-desk myths, it is more powerfully at work in social revolutionary beliefs and actions (and even in various aberrations of men's practical thought which are in no way directly connected with politics). Nor is it true that even the more wilful and fantastic among the explicit Utopias are merely a private affair of isolated cranks or clowns. They are constructed in terms of 'perfection' continuous with, or referable to, normal human categories of value, and are generally meant to elicit a wide intellectual and emotive response. And perfectionism is, I maintain, distinguishable from the mere pursuit of the good – moral, delectable, and other – by virtue of the more particular meaning we are wont to ascribe to the words 'perfect' and 'perfection'. This is primarily a *favourable* meaning, to be sure, despite the predominantly bad connotation of 'perfectionism'.

My opponent begs the question, but he certainly has the merit of *raising* questions. What *is* Perfection if not simply high value, or that which is very good? Is perfectionism merely, perhaps a purblind or incompetent pursuit of *some* good? How, and how far, can utopian be demarcated from non-utopian thought or endeavour? And may not our rejection of the utopian attitude commit us to a hidebound or flaccid, cynical or fatalistic, resigned and defeatist conservatism? The gist of my rebuttal, then, is not 'What you say is sheer nonsense', but only 'You have not shown that my criticism is pointless, or my enquiry unwarranted.'

(ii) Utopia as a mainspring of aspiration
'Utopias are precious, *if only* because they are never attained', I was told once by a glib and versatile leftist-liberal politician. The great German poet Hölderlin put it more subjectively: 'Him do I love who for the impossible yearns.' Another great poet, Oscar Wilde – hardly a typical utopian, and much less of a Romantic than Hölderlin – says more prosaically: 'A map of the world that does not include Utopia is not even worth glancing at, for it leaves out the one country at which humanity is always landing. And when humanity lands there, it looks out, and seeing a better country, sets sail. Progress is the realization of Utopia.' Similarly, Anatole France: 'Without the Utopias of other times, men would still live in caves, miserable and naked. It was Utopians who traced the lines of the first city. ... Out of generous dreams come beneficial realities. Utopia is the principle of all progress.'

Is it, after all, an unarguable matter of taste? Macaulay's lapidary remark 'An acre of Middlesex is better than a principality in Utopia' may jar upon our ears as a harsh outcry of defiant philistinism. But we can hardly say this of Wordsworth's lines:

Not in Utopia – subterranean fields –
Or in some secret island, Heaven knows where!
But in this very world, which is the world
Of all of us – the place where, in the end,
We find our happiness, or not at all!

Nor have all philosophers been convinced that a non-utopian and non-perfectionist attitude involves dullness and sluggishness, or moral indifference. Here are some representative voices: 'What you should mind in the first place is your present business'

(Pittakos, an early Greek sage); 'Do not apply your will to an aim that is not in your power' (Geulincx); 'No outer state of things should be willed unconditionally. ... Every endeavour may fall a prey to disproportion' (Herbart); 'Choose the best among things attainable' (Brentano); 'The situations of earthly life should not be looked upon as a random heap of occasions, each inviting us to realize some moral ideal, regardless of what is likely to result from these incessant moral responses as a whole' (Lotze); 'Contrition, not Utopia, is the greatest revolutionary force in the moral world' (Scheler); 'Le réel se constate et ne se construit pas' [Reality is not constructed but acknowledged] (le Roy); 'The question "What is the best state of things which we could *possibly* bring about?" is quite distinct from the question "What would be the best state of things conceivable?"' (Moore).[4]

I will concede to the objector the point that a bold and vigorous experimental spirit is as necessary for human practice as are traditions, continuity, and enduring standards. Clearly it is not such a spirit, *per se*, which I would call utopian or perfectionist; nor do I so consider the act of raising the question where, for instance, some morally objectionable state of affairs which has hitherto been deemed unalterable, or alterable only at the cost of disastrous harm which it would be very wrong of us to incur, is not perhaps susceptible to being mended in a way that does not exact so heavy a toll, and therefore a worthy object of reformatory action. It is in some such fashion that the 'utopian' spirit seems to be interpreted in the above quotations from Wilde and Anatole France. The real point of the objection is, then, that anti-utopian doctrinaires and people with vested interests are likely to obstruct useful innovations and rule out moral criticisms of the more profound kind by tagging on to them the vituperative label 'utopian'. This has indeed happened, and will happen; the admission is trivial enough. I would even add that the traditionalist mind may in fact be more utopian than the reforms it insists on rejecting, in that it may be prone to idealize the given state of things as a kind of sacrosanct quasi-perfection already attained.[5]

But all in all, this apologia of utopianism reposes on very shaky foundations. It apparently assumes that historical change is predominantly a change for the better – that is, 'progress'; but the palatable contrast between the 'caveman' and, say, our own civilized selves provides insufficient evidence for so general and dogmatic an assumption. (This is easier to understand today than it was some sixty or seventy years ago: and this growing doubt about progress *is* progress.) Indeed, the criteria and the very meaning of progress are highly problematic in a perspective of mentally discontinuous epochs or societies. Utopian imaginations and schemes of action sometimes precede, and initially inspire, wise and moderate piecemeal reforms which most of us are disposed to approve or welcome; but it is hard to say, and impossible to test, whether an *ab ovo* non-utopian conception of the same or similar reforms would not have brought about even happier results, perhaps more speedily and certainly at less appalling costs. Magical preoccupations did play a part in stimulating scientific research; but (taking it for granted that modern science itself is free from magic, and is an unmixed good) this consideration falls short of justifying magic; and the men who urged the cause of modest, sober empirical and experimental methods as opposed to irresponsible speculations and magical pretensions were most certainly promoters and liberators rather than destroyers or stiflers of science. No pursuit can be justified on the ground that it *may* contribute to the realization of ends which are quite *different* from its own, and happen to be good.

What is worst, however, in this patronizing admiration for 'generous' utopian dreams is the contempt for human reason and the frivolous view of human practice it betrays. Is it really a pastime worthy of men – something that brings out their nobility – to run after what they, or the wise sceptics among them, know to be fictitious goals; to set sail continually for the land which, by definition, changes its position whenever the sailors arrive within landing distance? Can we not use our time and energies more profitably, and above all more intelligently? It is, of course, imaginable that a scientist who devoted himself to the aim of finding a method by which to enable man to do without food and drink, or of producing a unisexual human breed, would fail at his task yet by accident discover, while engaged in its pursuit, an infallible cure for cancer; but there is no particular reason why this should happen, nor do we need, in order to get rid of cancer, any aim more 'inspiring' than that of getting rid of cancer. Error, like all evils, may work out favourably by accident, and is even a necessary means to knowledge or invention *in so far* as it constitutes the counterpart of 'trial ' in our proceeding 'by trial and error' (which implies an eminently un-utopian, critical and tentative attitude). But error, in itself, is bad, and the deliberate encouragement of error, including misconceived aims and unwarranted expectations, is not only bad but morally wicked and contemptible.

(iii) 'Yesterday's Utopias, today's realities'

As has been admitted above, many an aim that many or most people would dismiss as 'utopian' has come to be accomplished at some later period, which may mean a long succession of centuries, or only a few decades, or even less. But – prescinding from the cheap journalistic use of the word – an object which, in the perspective of some specified moment, appears impossible or all but impossible of realization is not therefore 'utopian'. I know not (and care less) whether television will ever convey smells as well as sights and sounds, but this is hardly my idea of Utopia. What would be utopian is the belief that such an achievement would prevent war, clear away the 'remnants' of tyranny or be both an expression and a mainstay of human perfection and untarnished happiness. Utopianism attaches to certain valuational conceptions of life rather than to definite projects, however ambitious or unattainable these may seem to those who first think of achieving them. To hope for a society cleansed from the conflict of rival powers is very much more utopian than to hope for the healing of the historic antagonism between France and Germany, or between Turks and Greeks; but, in its turn, to believe in the possibility of such a state of society is far less utopian than to believe it to be highly conducive to human virtue and human happiness. Again, some concrete and definite aspirations of the past, perhaps in the field of alchemy or of medicine, appear to our eyes in a utopian light not because they have proved pointless or impossible of fulfilment, but because they appear to bear the utopian sign of more global conceptions of existence in whose context they had their place.

Indeed, the question might be raised whether the actual *content* of any aspiration could be described as utopian at all; whether utopianism could be anything other than the *state of mind* in which an aim was conceived, or an enterprise conducted. There is nothing essentially utopian in a bold and risky venture; William the

Silent's words '*Nul n'est besoin d'espérer pour entreprendre, ni de réussir pour persévérer*' [You may act without hope, and keep going without success], if not exactly 'realistic', have by no means a utopian ring. Rather, what strikes us as utopian is overconfidence as regards both the agent's prospects of success in the direct and definite sense of achieving his purpose and – even more, perhaps – the felicific consequences and long-term effects his success is expected to produce. It is certain that 'the same action' – definable, that is, in clear-cut descriptive terms as 'the same' – may be undertaken in both a utopian and a non-utopian spirit. It may be done in an experimental and critical spirit (as a 'trial', in awareness of a possible 'error' and failure), or again in a spirit of enthusiastic certitude and purblind overvaluation. So far, it is true that whatever has – however justly – been decried as utopian may yet be attempted with an accent of realism, and become a reality more or less corresponding to its author's design; and that, therefore, care should be exercised in condemning a project as 'utopian' merely in view of its material content. Nevertheless, somewhat analogously with the fact that the rightness or wrongness of an action does not depend on the agent's good or bad 'intention' alone, a utopian conception is not simply a conception entertained with a subjectively utopian state of mind, independently of its intrinsic features.

The point need not be laboured here; suffice it to remark that the disjunction between 'what' I do and the 'spirit' in which I do things is anything but absolute. In particular, I cannot proceed by 'trial and error' unless I feel sure that the experimental change I have in mind is reversible, that the expenditure it requires is not disproportionately great, and that the risks (not to speak of the certain drawbacks) do not outweigh the possible advantages. Accordingly a non-utopian-minded administrator, critic, statesman or social reformer will tend to prefer, if only for this reason, the method of 'piecemeal' reforms, limited to well-circumscribed themes – 'points', as it were – seen against a background of stability and quasi-invariability; and to frown on sweeping change except in the case of urgent and evident necessity. He will shun all-embracing, missionary and redemptive concepts of reformatory 'activism'.

Utopia is not, then, simply a synonym for 'endeavour guided by illusions in the agent's mind'. Rather, it expresses general and objectivized types of delusion. Some kinds of assumption and purpose may bear on their face the stigma of utopianism, no matter how cunning, sophisticated and capable of realistic assessment their framers or sponsors may be. The 'utopian mind' is not primarily a matter of individual psychology. In other words, certain models of action and conceptions of the desirable embody, evoke and transmit certain states of mind. That one man's way of thinking may be personally more or less utopian than another's does not mean that no endeavour can be intrinsically utopian, or that there is no such thing as '*the* Utopian Mind'.

(iv) Perfection justified as a bargaining trick

Whether it is a question of claiming 'goods', 'possessions' and 'happiness' or of making moral demands valid, the objector may suggest: 'You have to ask for the maximum (or 'everything') in order to obtain a substantial amount (or 'a fairly satisfactory result', or 'anything at all').'

Even as a purely tactical principle, this holds only within certain limits, and is more applicable to some kinds of situation than to others. An exorbitant price may frighten the customer away rather than convince him of the great value of the commodity; arbitrarily raised and sharpened moral demands may provoke mistrust or despair, and a relaxation rather than a heightening of moral effort. Generally speaking, the success of the tactics proposed depends on the presence, in the subject's mind, of special motives for eagerness. Thus, many zealous priests treat sinners and prospective converts with the utmost indulgence and consideration, but are inclined to raise the standards of piety, orthodoxy and moral purity in proportion as the believer actually approaches the standards set for him. Moreover, the principle is applicable chiefly within the areas of, so to speak, an infinite continuum of values differing in degree rather than in kind. It is quite conceivable that a man, persuaded that he ought to be generous and selfless, will in fact become more disposed to be at least polite and thoughtful. But the overemphasizing of high virtues may also lead to the neglect of more ordinary and more stringent duties. Is it true that – as is sometimes alleged – monastic institutions, by deepening men's experience of the value and importance of chastity in general, have greatly contributed to enhancing the standards of matrimonial morality in Christian society? This does indeed seem very probable to me; yet there is also evidence of cases and periods of monastic depravity, owing, of course, partly to the inaccessibility of marital relations; and, on the other hand, of worldly Christians leading a loose life who allay their scruples with the argument that purity, an admirable thing, is, after all, the special business of monks and nuns. Any justification of the monastic 'counsels of perfection' must refer to the intrinsic value of the mode of life they recommend, not to its indirect usefulness for the 'lower perfection' of married life; and Christian matrimony is primarily established by our affirming it on its own merits, not as a toned-down emanation from the loftier substance of monastic chastity.

Except for its role as a vague accessory of the general moral training of men, the 'bargain' tactics of perfectionism breaks down in the context of strict obligations which can – and ought to – be neatly fulfilled, allowing little or no place for anything less than 'perfection'. If I owe a man £1,000 it is pointless to urge me to pay him £2,600 in the hope of thus prevailing upon me to pay him at least £400; crimes against life and property are prosecuted in order to suppress them as completely as possible, not to keep their frequency at an optimum level: yet they must be defined and prosecuted as such, not just expected to disappear under the effect of a sustained and fervent propaganda for neighbour-love and austerity.

In many other respects also – notably in contexts where 'demands' proper, with corresponding 'obligations', do not enter – we shall find the principle of 'aiming at the highest in order to get what is needful' inapplicable, or applicable only in a very general, indeterminate and peripheral sense. It is a meaningful purpose to abolish infant mortality altogether, and this may actually be within reach, but it can only be approximated step by step, and it will always involve medical attentions devoted to single cases, which may or may not prove successful; the formula 'Try to save 100 per cent of existing infant lives, and you will thus save the 85 per cent we really need' is empty of meaning. Again, artists have always been, and will go on being, inspired by great models; but we could see nothing more than a frigid joke, at best, in the idea of a music master urging his gifted pupil to 'aspire to be another Beethoven' and slily muttering under his breath: 'Perhaps he'll make another Puccini.'

Whatever the incidental successes of perfectionist 'bargaining' methods may be, their very principle lies open to the charge of untruthfulness; virtually, at least, they entail a falsification of outlook, misdirection of value-sensibilities, and distortion of emphasis. Excess in one line of endeavour is likely to breed defect in others; an imperative force attributed to aspirations and ideals will impel the agent to take genuine moral imperatives too lightly; and even within one dimension of values pursued, biting off more than one can chew increases the risk of failure – *Grasp all, lose all.* I have not thereby disposed of the problem of whether inspired and aspiring human endeavour is possible without an admixture of utopian perfectionism; my present purpose has been the more defensive one of warding off a cheap and abortive justification of it, and to bring to light its uneasy relation (to say the least) with intellectual probity.

(v) 'True' and 'sham' perfection

Again, an objector might remind us that the fact of idolatry may not disprove the existence of God, nor confute worship as such. To quote Blake's oft-quoted lines once more:

> The vision of Christ that thou dost see
> Is my vision's greatest enemy.

Not all 'vision[s] of Christ' need therefore be erroneous and misleading; to decide *which* vision to embrace may be more to the point than to impugn all visions because they are visions. Even in the realm of 'secular religions', perhaps not all perfectionism has totalitarian implications, and certainly there have been several totalitarianisms at loggerheads with one another. Many Christians and Liberals, loathing both Communism and Nazism, argued that the two were 'essentially the same': a wholly gratuitous and unreasonable opinion, born of the spoilt child's subjectivism which would define all things the child dislikes in terms of that dislike alone. Perhaps there is no such attitude as 'perfectionism' at all, but only conflicting ideas of perfection, some of them right and others wrong; perhaps all charges levelled at 'perfectionism' hit the target only in so far as the critic has mistaken and specious concepts of perfection in mind.

This objection is incontrovertible up to a point. It is obvious enough that not all 'perfections' envisioned by men are of a kind; and that there are (prevalently) good and (prevalently) bad causes, a good and a bad cause being equally capable of commanding fervent devotion and single-minded service: it is not the zeal of its devotees that makes it either good or bad. Nor are Utopias mere variants, differing by insignificant shades only, of one well-defined Utopia. But this does not preclude the existence of perfectionism and utopianism, or of the erroneous presuppositions and moral and practical dangers attaching to them. It is hard to imagine that any operative concept of perfection were *nothing but* spurious, and it is quite conceivable that an excessive craving for perfection as such, an uncontrolled fascination with the idea of perfection, may chiefly underlie the idea of 'sham perfections'.

3 PERFECTION AS DISTINCT FROM VALUE

(i) 'Correctness'

It is essential for my purpose to distinguish a special concept of perfection from Value, Good, and similar terms of appreciation, approbation and commendation; but ordinary usage is not rigidly consistent and directly or unequivocally informative, and I cannot rest my case on an arbitrary 'stipulative' definition of my own. The words 'perfect' and 'perfection' are used in various senses, and often in the rather loose sense of a mere synonym for 'very good', or 'right', or 'a good quality'; whereas 'good', 'fine', or other emotive terms may be used by a speaker who has something more like the special concept of Perfection in mind. Yet if such a special concept exists and has any currency at all, it cannot owe its life to a linguistic decree or choice of mine. I can but try to explicate that special concept *from some characteristic connotations* of the words 'perfect' and 'perfection' as actually used. Moreover, these words are emphatically *pro* words (except for the marginal cases where 'perfect' is colloquially used as a mere equivalent of 'complete' or 'utter', e.g. 'That was a perfectly beastly thing to say'), and it would be a futile and nonsensical attempt on my part to invest them with a *con* signature. If 'perfection' is anything, it is not a form of badness or evil but a special form of goodness or value (taken in a wide and indeterminate sense); it is merely with a view to laying bare the 'specialness' which constitutes it that I speak here of 'Perfection as *distinct from* Value' – that is, value *not* experienced or envisaged as perfection. The secondary, as it were silent, pejorative note inherent in 'perfection' – hinting at a peculiar possibility of perversion – will come to the fore in 'perfectionism', a word seldom used by good speakers at all but hardly ever used except with a mildly derogatory, ironical intent.

As has been said above, 'perfect' in broad usage may be taken simply to denote a high degree of value. More characteristically, it has a superlative or *limiting* connotation. What is properly 'perfect' is insuperable. Therefore, it is unidiomatic to call a man 'perfectly rich'; for though somebody may be the richest man in the United States, drawing an annual income x million dollars larger than anybody else's, it is easy to imagine an income of $x + 500$ or $2x$ million dollars, and quite possibly somebody else will earn as much tomorrow. Similarly, no athlete's muscular force is 'perfect', for some other athletes may be stronger, or one who is stronger may arise at any moment. But we do speak of an athlete's being 'in perfect condition', or a person's being 'in perfect health' or even 'perfectly sane'. Similarly, though mostly allowing for some amount of conventional exaggeration, we credit a person who has mastered a foreign language with a 'perfect command' of that language. For nobody can be in better health than a person who suffers from no discoverable ailment, however benign; saner than one who exhibits no sign of mental derangement; or more 'in command' of a language than one who wields it with correctness, ease and fluency. In short, that would seem to deserve the epithet 'perfect' which is best, or equal to the best, and indeed the best conceivable, of its kind.

This assignment of a superlative position, with the corresponding use of the word 'perfect', may, as shown by the foregoing examples, be soberly factual and descriptive, and entirely free – 'perfectly' free – from any mood or resonance of enthusiasm, infatuation or high-flown vision at war with reality. Perfection here approximates towards 'integrity' or 'wholeness' – 'haleness', as it were – in a *minimum* sense akin to *correctness*. What is thus perfect is no more than 'flawless', it being understood that perfection in this sense is not only possible but is the expected and unconspicuous thing, whereas the flaw or defect is that which evokes critical awareness of its presence. We might call this the 'regularian', perhaps even the 'trivial', concept of perfection. Its rationale lies in the fact that wherever conformity to a rule is all that matters, and is unequivocally possible, correctness or rightness *is* indeed perfection: it marks a minimum, seeing that nothing less would do; but it also marks a maximum, in so far as within the limits of the given theme or context, nothing more could conceivably be wished for. In respect of my obligation to pay X a certain sum within a certain time limit, I act with perfection in paying him that sum on or before that date; countless other men may be incomparably better than I am, even as regards honesty and trustworthiness, but none of them could discharge an analogous obligation more completely and punctiliously than I have done in the supposed case: I have here touched the limit of perfection.

But though it is still closely linked to categories like 'correctness' and 'the minimum', and fully embedded in experienced reality, the concept of perfection will rise above this level of triviality to display its higher and more proper but more problematical meaning if we turn from the domain of *rules* in the strict sense of the term to that of *standards* or *canons*. From the correct answer to one definite question or the correct behaviour in one definite situation, subject to unequivocally expressible and valid rules, it is a far cry to such concepts as an 'irreproachable character', a 'perfect condition of health', a 'faultless style', 'flawless beauty', or again, a 'perfect dachshund' or the 'perfect woman'. Although, in various ways and to various degrees, decision about the presence or absence of such perfections in the object under consideration may depend on straightforward arguments and tests of measurement, it nearly always requires intuitive appraisal, is rarely free from incertitude, and cannot in general be disconnected from more or less arbitrary, traditional, historically given, or fashionable canons of taste. Neat verification has partly been superseded by evaluation, and something of a 'gratuitous' element has entered into the complexion of 'the perfect'. Yet the suggestive force of the concept implies, precisely, a presumption of absolute and indubitable 'correctness'. This is not to say, however, that the phenomenon 'perfection of being' does not exist in any tangible sense, or that any application of the term is necessarily a misuse of language. My point here is merely that the delusional aspect of perfectionism appears somehow to be rooted in the very concept of perfection, although that concept is not as such chimerical or illegitimate.

(ii) 'Complete being', referred to a kind of thing

I have just allowed the phrase 'perfection of being' to slip from my pen. I did not mean to express anything ambitiously and nebulously metaphysical; I intended only to emphasize thereby the meaning of 'perfect' as applied to objects or entities, up to standard or conformable to certain canons, as opposed to answers, solutions or acts which are in accordance with a rule or fit a definite purpose.

A perfect work of art, a perfect specimen of some animal breed or some vintage wine, a perfect representative of a certain category of man, and so forth, embody primarily a kind of being, albeit secondarily standardized by the experts and striven for, fashioned or improved by human agency; whereas an answer or a solution has no significance except by reference to the proposed question or problem, and a regular or right action (as such) has none except by reference to the rule, statute, order, law, command or precept in point. So much for perfection, taken in a closer and higher sense, as contrasted with that elementary, if relevant, aspect of perfection by virtue of which it verges on correctness, precision, and conformity to law. But 'perfection of being', as interpreted above, may also help us towards working out the distinction between the concept of perfection and that of value or 'the good'.

Both some characteristic uses of the word 'perfect' (a perfect specimen of ... , the perfect ...) and its etymology reveal a significant difference from the eminently axiological general terms, such as 'good', 'value', 'pleasing', 'desirable', or 'preferable'. In a sense these terms, however open and indeterminate, point to qualities inherent in an object which are of a nature to invite appreciation, approbation, admiration, commendation, an appetitive or a reverential response, and in general a *pro* attitude, on the subject's or knower's part. I will not enter here into the classic problems and obvious sub-distinctions attaching to this fundamental topic, but merely observe that I am keenly aware of the difference between 'good' in 'good for somebody' or 'the good of the agent' and 'good' in 'a good man' or 'the goodness of the agent' (i.e. his morality: which in some important sense is also a good *for* the 'spectator', for the agent's fellows, and even for himself), and on the other hand of the technical use of 'good' in which it is interchangeable with 'perfect' ('a good dachshund', 'good eyesight'). Let it also be noted that 'good' – in all languages I am acquainted with – is an unanalysable primal word, while words like 'preferable' analytically and explicitly state the reference to an appraising subject I have been stressing; again, the origins of 'value' evoke a reference to power, capability and effect.

From this sphere of meanings, 'perfect' is sharply set apart by the note of self-contained being which its literal meaning suggests. As contrasted to pleasing, useful, beneficent, worthy of respect or preference, and so on, 'perfect' implies a primary emphasis on 'complete', 'fully done', 'achieved' – that is, 'fullness of being' in the sense of a thing's being whole, mature, fully actualized or executed, 'finished' (*parachevé*), or again, entirely itself, representative of its species, provided with the features that properly belong to its nature, and wholly what it 'should' be *qua* that thing. It appears, as it were, to stand justified, not on the ground of its favourably affecting the world or of its distinctive qualities worthy of appreciation, but on the ground of its being wholly elaborated and accomplished as the thing it is – regardless of whether being *that* thing is better or worse than being some *other* thing in its place. People who are impressed with perfection according to this aspect of its concept may assent to the Nietzschean 'imperative' *Be what thou art*; share the predilection, expressed in Revelation, for 'the hot' and 'the cold' alike, as opposed to 'the lukewarm'; prefer, at least aesthetically, the arrant scoundrel to the undistinguished, average decent person, or totalitarian enemies of their own cause to humdrum liberals and to the politically indifferent; or again, with more justification, place a good craftsman above a poor sort of artist. In some way, a hearty, lusty sinner may appear more 'perfect' than a thin-lipped, anaemic person who is afraid to transgress the law, or even the decent fellow who occasionally yields to temptation with an uneasy conscience, and is thus a more 'fractured', less 'of-a-piece' kind of being.

(iii) The artificial

With a modified emphasis, the same kind of 'perfection as distinct from value' clings to artificial products and mechanical contrivances as compared with more 'natural' goods. To be sure, I had to add 'with a modified emphasis'; for the perfection of machines or machine-like devices and arrangements is not primarily stripped of reference to the evaluating or appraising subject (as is the perfection of 'accomplished being' or 'being fully itself' *per se*) but, on the contrary, directly and unequivocally dependent on the enjoyer's, consumer's or planner's need and purpose. Wild horses, however we may appreciate their beauty and grace and perhaps their potential usefulness, exist independently of human management; even horses bred and trained by man are first of all *horses* closely akin to the wild horse: their character as racehorses, cavalry horses, and so on, is merely superimposed. Whereas railway engines, motorcars and the like owe their existence wholly to human want and invention; their very being is constituted by the purpose for which we use them. But therein, precisely, lies a species of 'wholeness'-perfection, peculiar to artificial things. If a horse needs to be fed, looked after, and treated for sickness, a motorcar also needs petrol, care and repairs; yet at least motorcars do not have to be humoured, as horses sometimes do. Their being is defined in terms of one human purpose or one set of human purposes; the being of no natural object – including, of course, the raw materials of which machines are made – is so defined.

Artificiality, then, provides one basis of formal perfection. Neither it, nor the mechanical and calculable (as opposed to precious things sought for and discovered, or discovered by chance), is the constituent feature of 'the perfect' in general; nor, again, is 'the perfect' characterized by its indifference from an evaluative point of view. Whatever is very good, supremely good, in its kind we tend to call 'perfect'; and conversely, whatever is whole, complete and characteristic of its kind tends to evoke our appreciation on that score. The impression 'It couldn't be better' connotes something in the way of perfection, and whatever is 'pure' and 'finished' has an air of peculiar 'goodness' about it. Artificial, machine-like and machine-made things claim appreciation under this particular category of value, seeing their more complete subjection to the human purpose they are designed

to serve and their essential determination by the fact of their being
so designed.

(iv) Perfection-emphasis

Yet, even though the very concept of perfection may imply at least
some assumption of intrinsic value – and possibly a high degree of it
– it also reveals at least a virtual *displacement of emphasis* from good
qualities in the plain and immediate sense of the word towards the
second-order quality, the synthetic feature, as it were, of a formal,
self-contained, harmonized and quasi-invulnerable 'completeness'.
This 'perfection-emphasis' may itself take very different shapes:
it may refer to the pure and genuine 'thisness' of an object, to
its transparent intelligibility or made-to-order disposability, to its
geometrical symmetry or perhaps (as in theology and in historicist
philosophy) its 'necessary' existence or emergence. In each case, it
is linked to a sense of compelling logical evidence rather than to
a properly estimative response. Our admiration of, or surrender
to, 'the perfect' by no means excludes our primary and manifold
appreciations of goods and qualities, but is set in a certain contrast
to them as one peculiar and different kind of appreciation. It refers,
as such, always to the selfsame formal trait of 'completeness',
whatever the substratum or dimension of that completeness may
be, unlike our primary appreciations, which do *not* refer to the
selfsame aspect of 'goodness' or 'value' in things but to this or that
among countless value-modalities. It cannot be inferred therefrom
that the pursuit of 'the perfect' as such, in some specified form, is
the *opposite* of the pursuit of values – as if, in yielding to the magic
of perfection, we chose the bad in preference to the good. This
would indeed be rank nonsense: I might as well prefer a man who
now and then twists the truth so as to suit his interest, not only to
a habitual liar (which I certainly do) but to a man of exemplary
truthfulness, lest I should incur the suspicion of setting greater
store by punctilious perfection as such than by veracity as such.
Yet though we naturally tend to associate 'perfection' with the
plenitude rather than the devaluation of value, its concept *is* in
fact separable and *sui generis* enough to admit of the *possibility* of
our seeking 'the perfect' at the cost of the valuable. Some people's
preference for consistent tyranny as against a defective regime of
liberty may come under this head; likewise, the overrating, in

industrial society, of mechanical efficiency at the cost of the
exquisite and the durable, if not also in some ways of the obviously
useful. But it is only in a later section that I propose to deal with
the error of perfectionism.

4 ASPECTS OF 'PERFECTION'

(i) 'Perfection' and 'hierarchy'
There is a class of evaluative concepts not mentioned so far in
this discussion, and much less popular with modern than with
Greek and Scholastic philosophers: I mean the *hierarchical* value
concepts such as 'nobility', 'height', 'rank', 'level', 'degree of
being', often identified with 'perfection' in traditional thought.
A kindred category of valuation is also *implied*, overtly or tacitly,
in the modern emphasis on evolution, or progress, or both. We do
not like so much to dwell on nobler and baser sorts of men, or even
of contemporaneous human pursuits – all work is noble; perhaps all
work should be, and will one day be, 'creative' – but we do like
to compare man proper with his pre-human anthropoid forebears,
to contemplate the height reached by present-day civilization as
contrasted with its more primitive ancestors, and to hope for a
mankind more highly developed than ours. Nor do we at all
self-evidently and consistently interpret these distinctions of value
in terms of 'felicity', of optimum 'satisfaction' or 'pleasure-and-
pain-economy', alone. Hierarchical level – or 'height', as I may
briefly call it – is a concept aligned with that of perfection in so far
as it points primarily not to the aspect of 'benefit', 'appreciation' or
'response' but to the object's mode of being seen in a self-contained
perspective. 'Developed', indeed, comes very close to 'complete'.

But, in contraposition to 'the perfect', evolutionary or progress-
ional concepts do not connote the idea of supremeness or totality
or, shall we say, of consummation. Rather, they suppose an open
horizon: what is more developed than it was in its previous form
may develop further into an even 'higher' shape; evolution has
no particular reason to stop at a certain point; progress is in
principle unlimited or 'infinite', the 'relative perfection' of today
becoming 'obsolete' tomorrow. Again, in the context of a static
order, nobler or higher things stand to baser or lower ones, not

in a perfective but in a complementary relation. The prince is not the perfect labourer – rather we may dream, perhaps, of a happy correlation between perfect princes and perfect labourers – and in general, higher beings are not the perfect editions of lower beings. And the concept of 'the noble' suggests a distinctive value-quality compelling admiration, analogously to goodness, beauty, grace or generosity, rather than the full being of a thing *qua* that thing. I do not think I can, or need, try to elucidate this difficult matter further here; my purpose in bringing it up has been to delimit 'the perfect' more carefully from 'intrinsic value' proper, as also to sketch the background for a more ambitious and comprehensive connotation of it.

(ii) The universal reference of particular 'perfections'
So far we have identified the perfect as that which is supreme in its kind, complete in its kind, and fully characteristic of its kind (which is entirely 'what it is', as it were). But a virtual ambiguity attaches to it. The things of which the world is composed undeniably divide into *kinds*, yet not in an *unequivocal* fashion. Sometimes we experience the self-contained 'departmental' or specific meaning of 'perfect' as massive, fixed, technical, and definitively satisfying; sometimes we do not. In 'a perfect dachshund', the emphasis lies on purity of breed and the single features which attest it, but there is also a reference to the functional aptitudes which huntsmen and wood-rangers require in a dachshund, and to some fashionable, slightly arbitrary, conventional standards decreed by experts. But the dachshund is a species of dog; and some people may not regard some perfect dachshunds as perfect dogs, or again, may not look for the 'perfect dog' in the dachshund species at all. In 'a perfect dog' – a looser concept – it is not characteristic doggishness that is emphasized so much, but perhaps pure breeding as opposed to mongrelism, perhaps the presence of such typically canine virtues as hardiness, intelligence and loyalty. But might not a utopian dog-fancier form the concept of a dog that were at the same time a perfect watch-dog and a perfect gun-dog?

Even greater problems will beset us if we turn to the varieties of human perfection. The 'perfect woman', so far as I can make out, is supposed to be very feminine; but femininity alone, as opposed to masculinity or to being 'undersexed', presumably falls short of constituting it: some more exquisite qualities are needed – or, in other words, the 'perfect woman' is something like the feminine, and perforce fully feminine, modality of the 'perfect man' (or 'perfect human being', man in the sense of *homo*, not of *vir*). In fact, to the erotic male imagination which created the mirage of the perfect woman, this fetish probably meant the most perfect of beings, a sort of deity rather than merely the female form of the perfect human being. Again, most of us will associate with the concept of a 'perfect physician' the image of a man in possession not only of vast medical learning and supreme professional skill but of high human qualities. In spite of the perfectional aspect of formal completeness or a consistent and integrated behaviour, we would less readily and less seriously speak of a perfect knave or a perfect burglar than of a perfect physician, scholar or statesman, or of the perfection of a saint: that is to say, we are readier to allow for particularized or departmental 'perfection' in so far as it may be looked upon as *representative* of a concept of *universal* – with an innuendo of unique, absolute, and quasi-divine – perfection.

Perfect in its kind ... but we may not mean it independently of the height, dignity and universal relevance of the kind in question. We may well feel it more proper, also, to speak of a perfect work of art than of the 'perfect' solution to some trivial problem of elementary mathematics or everyday practice. In other words, a thing perfect of its kind may interest us chiefly as a symbol of the perfection of being as such: an allusion to, or a pledge of, a perfect *world*. Perfect of its kind . . . but a 'kind' implies limitation, and therefore imperfection. Would not the really and wholly perfect thing redeem that imperfection, and form a flawless unity with its equally perfect *foil?* This is anything but idle speculation. Rather, we are approaching here *the key point of social revolutionary thought*. What if there is *one* thing whose perfection guarantees, automatically as it were, the consonant perfection of all things that form part of its environment or thrive within its matrix? If so, that particular thing of universal relevance and efficacy can only be the schema of social order. For the present, I must confine myself to this dialectical hint, which may also be put in the logical form that the perfection of a thing, conceived in an absolute and far-flung manner so as to comprehend also its outer relations, its invulnerability and its aptitude to typify being as a whole, implies the corresponding perfection of its context and, inversely, of its constituent parts and aspects. Such a movement of conceptual extension does not necessarily pertain to the concept of perfection, but its possibility is rooted in the primary meaning of perfection.

(iii) The 'minimum' and 'maximum' concepts of perfection: 'normality'
I will now once more confront this highly strung 'maximum' concept of perfection with its lowly initial or 'minimum' concept, and enquire about what they have in common by contrast with 'the good', or with value-concepts proper. At the supreme pole of perfection, we have the 'god-like', the 'transfigured', the 'absolute', the plenitude of value with no counter-aspect of disvalue to it; the man or the world of the bright future; or again, so far as it is the perfect body we are looking for, Adonis. At its lower pole, perfection merges into 'normality', 'integrity', the absence of marring or conspicuous defects: whatever is thus faultless, sound in life and limb – in a word, better than 'substandard' – passes as 'perfect'. Is this merely a matter of usage? When a French waiter asks me whether a *vin ordinaire* will do for my meal, and I answer *Oui, c'est parfait*, I do not mean that I take this to be 'the perfect wine' (however I may define that), but simply that it answers my present requirement, and that he should not trouble to offer me anything better and dearer, or any particular brand of wine. I presume the French *vin ordinaire* to be at any rate what I accept as 'wine', different from vinegary or poisonous fermentations which may also go by that name; but in fact it might – in some parts of France, at least – be a remarkably good middling sort of wine, though far enough from a first-rate vintage Burgundy, and still be 'perfect' in the stipulated sense. But if anything that ranges between topmost excellence and sheer acceptability according to the given context or situation is 'perfect', there seems to be little point in dwelling on the concept of perfection and distinguishing it from 'value-concepts proper': the very best is nothing but the highest degree of 'the good', and the up-to-standard is that which is good enough. Surely the supreme and the normal are not equivalent but mark the opposite ends of an extensive scale of positive values – all experienced, defined and tested in terms of value.

No doubt that is true, yet perfection-emphasis differs from value-emphasis firstly in virtue of its reference to self-contained completeness of being, which is conceivable independently of appreciation, and secondly to the idea of being *coincident* with value – this last implying a decisive modification of our primary experience of value as inherent in but in no wise identical with being, inscribed in the texture of reality but neither an expression nor the constitutive principle of that texture. This becomes clearer if we consider the equivocal concept of 'normality'. In current usage, we mean by that word something very near to the statistical average. It is normal for man to have five toes on each foot; most people are so born: indeed, how should we otherwise come to form the conviction that men 'ought' to be five-toed, that this is their 'normal' or 'canonical' shape? In matters less constant and innate – less 'essential', as some would say – usage is more variable. Even supposing that most people develop dental caries from early youth, we hesitate to call a bad tooth 'normal'; on the other hand, we do say that it is 'more normal' for an old than for a young man to have a weak heart, and more normal for a child than for an adult to get chickenpox.

Values and disvalues are presupposed from the outset: seen from one side, what is good enough (or better) is 'normal'; yet the concept of normality is centred in the usual, constant and typical, not in the valuable. A six-toed human foot would be regarded as abnormal, whether it increased or diminished the subject's ability to walk; though an inflamed nasal lining is not a normal condition, to have a cold from time to time is looked upon as normal; a moderate degree of some kinds of immoral behaviour is again spoken of as normal. Words very close in meaning to 'normal' and its opposite, 'abnormal' – such as 'ordinary', 'common', 'usual', 'extraordinary', 'uncommon', 'exceptional', 'outstanding', 'regular', and so forth – carry, in a fixed or a variable fashion as the case may be, a *pro* or a *con*, or an axiologically neutral, sense.[6]

But if we decide, as it were, that only the best is good enough, or raise the meaning of 'satisfactory' to that of 'consummate', we are interpreting normality in that perfectional sense which is often reflected in the word 'integrity' and which, ever since the Greeks – notably the Eleatics, Plato above all, and his more sober and cautious disciple Aristotle – has attached to the 'normal' or 'regular' in traditional metaphysics and theology. Even current usage shows some traces of this attitude in such eulogistic expressions as 'he is a *man*', '*truly human*', or 'that's what I call *wine*'. At a higher level, the impression prevails that anything less than perfection, anything that is liable to criticism and might be better, nobler and more flourishing than it is, denotes an incomplete realization of the essence of a thing, or a distortion of human nature; that anything that is not what it ought to be, or might be 'at its best', is not quite what it *is*.

The frequently used language of 'integrity', 'accomplishment', 'defect' and 'fault', as distinct from the language of 'good', 'evil', 'merit' and 'sin', is perfection-emphasizing in a similar way. The theological notion that actual human nature, being 'wounded' by the impact of original sin, lacks the 'integrity' it possessed in the first men before their Fall; or, again, the fancy that 'the saint' is the really 'normal' man, belong to the same realm of thought; equally, the philosophaster's claim that 'Being proper' and 'Good' are coextensive, and that evil has only a 'phenomenal' existence. Correspondingly, in spite of essential differences which cannot now be discussed, the revolutionary Utopia will connote a restorative trait: namely, the pretension of restoring to man what is 'rightfully his', and raising him to his 'proper stature'.

(iv) The relation to being
Although they are meaningless except in the context of being and therefore in fundamental accord with the order of reality, 'good' or 'value' bring to the concept of being an irreducibly novel and peculiar feature, adding decisively to the description of reality but neither defining its structure nor definable in terms of its concept. 'Perfection', on the contrary, suggests being as the definiens and the test of value and, conversely, value as the generating and governing principle of being. Revolutionary Utopia attaches, of course, to the latter aspect. But this is a matter for further analysis.

The distinction between perfection and value does not, then, mean that the concept of perfection implies no reference to value; 'full', 'complete', 'finished', 'total' and similar concepts, though fundamental to that of perfection (compare the frequent perfectional force of words like 'finish', 'integrity' and 'consummate'), fall short of its meaning inasmuch as they – in general, at least – lack any evaluative connotation except in the primitive functional sense in which a greater quantity of whatever *may* be worth anything is worth more than a smaller quantity of it, or a half-completed product of any kind is less utilizable than the completed one. Rather, the differentia of 'perfection' consists in a displacement of emphasis from value, with the manifold and particular appreciative experiences it evokes, to the abstract appeal of completeness of being, including the *supreme* value it is supposed *eo ipso* to embody and to reveal. The perfect is distinct from the good by virtue of its *special* reference to being, its paramount reference to complete, self-contained and rounded-off being which, *as such*, is seen to imply and exhibit all values pertinent to the object in question, and virtually all values relevant to an extended sphere of objects or themes, or indeed to human character and existence as such. But perfection may also be regarded as one modality of value among many. Hence perfectionism – the tendency to substitute perfection for the immense multitude and wealth of more primordial value modalities, by dint of the conceptual artifice to which it lends itself with peculiar ease.

5 PERFECTIONISM

(i) The 'perfectionist' and the 'common-sense' outlook

The briefest way of describing our ordinary, everyday attitude is to say that it maintains as self-evident the distinction and tension between Value and Being, seeing value in the context of the real world and its tendencies, and existing things or situations as possible bearers of values. 'Distinction' means that a thing is not good simply because it exists, or in so far as it is complete, or fully unfolded; and that values are conceived or conceivable without therefore existing or determining the nature of things and situations to which they refer. 'Distinction' means, further, that values are essentially (although in very different ways and degrees) separable from the things that display or embody them: what is good in one sense or context may be bad or indifferent in another; the goodness of an entity may change even without that entity's disappearing, disintegrating or being transformed into something else; if value penetrates being, somehow it always hangs loosely upon it. 'Tension', on the other hand, means that Value and

Being do not form a duality of mutually unrelated 'realms' but the meaning of value implies some kind of 'claim' on reality, and to realization; this may be expressed, in our consciousness of it, by an experience of obligation, of demand, of approval, of desire, of pleasure, of admiration or only of satisfaction with the presence of that value as contrasted with its absence. To the ordinary mind, the inherence of value in being appears limited, fragmentary, and for the most part virtual (and again, under that term, in part an object for various endeavours or pursuits). 'Tension' also means, notably, the presence in the world of positive disvalues or evils, connoting a virtual urgency for the task of suppressing or tempering evils.

The flexible relation between Value and Being, under the common-sense outlook, is further manifested by the rich gradation of shades of meaning attaching to the concept of value-'demands'. In some cases – concerning high art, for example – the normative categories 'ought' and 'should', however broadly conceived, are well-nigh, if not wholly, inapplicable; the value-demand finds its expression in the voice of individual yearning, inspiration, vision and ambition alone: 'I will', 'I would', 'I'll try', 'Could I but …', and so forth. Apart from that, compare such widely divergent uses of 'ought' and 'should' as 'He ought to pay his debt' or 'He should tell the truth' (the strictly deontic moral sense); 'He ought to spend more on charities' (moral but not strictly deontic); '*Gipsy* should really be spelt *gypsy*' (strictly regulative but non-moral); 'He is where he ought to be' (the British Prime Minister referring, in 1941, to a captured Nazi politician: some moral and some regulative connotation); 'It should be ready by now' (an expectation based on the usual course of things, deprecating a culpable omission or other possible source of disorder); 'You should see this picture' or 'You should come with us' (a friendly recommendation or invitation). Accordingly, the common-sense emphasis on values and their realization is selective, leaving a good deal to arbitrary choice, taste and opportunity, while setting apart the urgent and unavoidable. It distinguishes – allowing, of course, for a vast scale of interrelations – between the theoretical or contemplative appreciation of values and the practical problems of their accomplishment, acquisition, development, protection and communication. It is set in a perspective, fastening on selected or ineludible value-themes as contrasted with a total and systematic vision of them, but aware of their background and aura, their connections and tensions with other value-concerns, as contrasted with an isolated and self-contained conception of particular values. The common-sense outlook on value and its penetration of being is established in a mundane framework; it is based on a primary acceptance of 'the world', not from either 'optimism' or 'resignation' – such moods may alternatively and alternatingly attach, but are quite irrelevant, to the position I am trying to outline – but as a logical, or perhaps I should rather say pre-logical, constitutive presupposition of meanings, appreciations, ponderations, pursuits and practice.

In keeping with this, the common-sense outlook implies what may be described as an open perspective of universality, or a basis of actual and virtual consensus. It is essentially 'intersubjective' or 'multi-subjective': not identified with the consciousness and horizon of one particular person; one determined social group, type, body or institution; or 'mankind' as a supposed spiritual unity or organized whole. It is referred to those conditions, perceptions, valuations and needs 'men' are known to have in common (hence Common Sense), and may further prove to have in common by virtue of clarification by discussion and argument, and of mutual limitations and adjustments. In other words, common sense is keenly aware of the irremovable mundane fact of intersubjective and intergroup *friction*, of the division of interests and also of valuations and preferential scalings against a background of common modes of perceptions, common feelings and traditions; and in a virtually worldwide vista of attainable 'understanding'. Here is another, supremely important, aspect of the tension, as well as of the contingent, variable and ineluctably problematic relation, between value and being. Your satisfaction is not my satisfaction, and the two can even be opposed: your 'good' can constitute a hostile and opaque 'being' for me, against which my 'value-demand' has to be directed; although it may profit both of us if we both exercise self-control, clear away misunderstandings, come to some kind of agreement, and perhaps work out what is in our common interest and, possibly, specifically common to our aspirations. But the fact of *division*, taken in all its dimensions, is precisely the most 'common' finding and most universal category of common sense. Imperfection, limitation, variation and defect are our daily bread, and the *lingua franca* of our universal intercourse.

The common-sense outlook pervades human life, thought and civilization, but it is far from governing the mental activities of men constantly and exclusively, or invariably in its most genuine and characteristic form. Nor 'ought' that to be the case. Common-sense pluralism and perspective are comparatively alien, for instance, to such important spheres of activity as formal reasoning and fact-research concerning definite and isolable topics, mystical experience and religious faith, or heroic endurance in serving a task to which one is irrevocably committed. Indeed, it is part of the imperfection-consciousness inherent in the common-sense outlook to be aware of *its own* insufficiency and need of being supplemented by kinds of cognition and valuation that are somehow different from its own style. It is worth noting that a straightforward and exact expression of the common-sense outlook is often found impractical under its own rules, and is replaced by more precise-sounding, more sharply pointed and more effective types of utterance, it being tacitly assumed that informal modes of speech are not meant quite literally, indicate the drift rather than render the exact content of their meaning, and are held exempt from confrontation with other and perhaps contradictory informal utterances of the same person, made at no great distance of time but in a different context. Sentences like 'There is only one sin: selfishness' and 'Self-interest is the basis of all morality', or 'Go hungry, but dress respectably' and 'Wholesome and plentiful, well-cooked food is the prime necessity of man', or 'There is only one England' and 'There is no country like Spain' may express the arbitrary biases or one-sided manias or deep-seated doctrinal errors of different persons, or the changing irresponsible moods of one and the same person. But again, they may express, in an emphatic, abbreviated and misunderstandable form, well-considered and not really inconsistent points of view entertained by a person with a quite sane and balanced mind. This ambiguity, fragility and unreliability of ordinary language – the dependence on context and situation of the meaning it may convey – reveal a technical need for apparently perfectionist attitudes, conceiving of the provisional as if it were definitive, of the limited and vague as if it were exhaustive and clear-cut, of the partial as if it were total, of the conditional as if it were absolute. But if the black-and-white formulae and ephemeral quasi-absolutes or *ad hoc* value-realities of a perfectionist style of thought are a help even to making the common-sense outlook more articulate in its contents and more incisive in its modes of expression, again the necessities of practice, of purposeful action, the shaping of *pro* and *con* positions, effort, sacrifice, and so forth, to some extent inevitably call for the use of perfectionist models of valuation and, beyond that, give rise to states of mind more deeply vulnerable to the temptations of a perfectionist outlook.

Whatever good, value, aim or concern matters a great deal to me I shall tend to overrate in some way. First, as regards my subjective emphasis; this, indeed, is an entirely natural propensity, rooted in the very existence of subjects, but for which no affective and practical attitudes would be possible at all. 'Overrating' in this sense means something between the bare fact of my having some concerns rather than others, of my concerns being not anybody's or everybody's but *my* concerns, and the fact of my being passionately devoted to some of them beyond the mere fact of entertaining them, 'as if they were' of greater objective importance than they usually are. No error or delusion may be involved in such a state of mind; rather, as I shall argue below, strong loves and distinctive tastes may well play the part of anti-utopian forces by virtue of the clinging to concrete reality and the awareness of contingent subjectivity they seem to embody. Nevertheless, subjective overemphasis is rarely free from an innuendo of distorted perspective, for no clear frontier can be drawn between a quasi-belief proper and an actual belief tentatively, implicitly and informally held. Thus, at second remove, we may find objective overvaluation: the kind of love that engenders a definitely false picture of its objects, with its virtues grossly magnified and its unfavourable traits ignored, explained away, or one-sidedly interpreted in terms of its virtues; the conviction that the pursuit one is engaged in is highly important from certain public points of view, when in fact it is of meagre significance – and so forth. Thirdly, overvaluation (not as such perfectionist) may take on a tinge of absolute identification between value and being of some kind, and the value-modality in question may come to be credited with a universal claim. A thing or pursuit within the world will thus assume a supra-mundane status: a standard of 'perfection' over and above the ordinary, pluralistic and contingent experience of realities and values. Such conceptions, or perfectionist fixations, fly in the face of the common-sense outlook, although of course the latter cannot be simply crowded out of minds that live in the world but can only be overlaid, distorted, crippled and obliterated in some of its dimensions by perfectionist dominants. A few random examples may suffice to illustrate what is meant here.

I may point to assumptions such as that the morality of conduct is determined by its being *like* a specified person's ways of behaviour, or in keeping with a particular human type's or group's character or schema of preferences; that what is likely to serve certain specified *interests* is the epitome of morality; that moral conduct is that which is conducive to practical success, or inversely, that genuine moral conduct is a guarantee of practical success; that evolution, or vital growth and increase of power, means moral progress, or more ensured and general happiness; that better men and better institutions must mutually correspond; that there is some key value from which the plenitude of values is deducible and whose realization brings about that of the rest; that some concrete scheme of action, connected with a plausible moral postulate, morally justifies whatever is done or demanded to further it; that there is a predictable historical future, and that to act in conformity with its trend is to act well; that there is an unequivocal and knowable common good which is everybody's supreme good; that there are rules by which the immanent (prudential) rightness of practice, with or without reference to morality, can be unequivocally judged in the light of results, or even in advance, and thus secured.

What is it that distinguishes these or similar perfection-models of practical thought from the concept of actual value-realities as such, or meaningful and attainable ends as such? For 'goods', embodied values, reasonable endeavours, solutions of practical problems, and legitimate experiences of 'perfection' certainly exist in the common-sense perspective also. Scepticism, nihilism and inertia, a cult of 'randomness' and a wholesale mood of despair, are neither a fitting response to the aspects of order and the wealth of values which the world presents nor the gist of practical wisdom. Hardy's beautiful anti-utopian outburst, supposing that we take its second half literally, definitely goes too far:

> We are getting to the end of visioning
> The impossible within this universe,
> Such as that better whiles may follow worse,
> And that our race may mend by reasoning.

Why should better whiles not follow worse just as worse whiles do follow better; and seeing that reasoning obviously does sometimes promote insight and make self-control and honest ways acceptable, why decree that it cannot contribute to advancements of civilization, or bring about some mending of our race? Indeed, the point of my attack upon perfectionism is meant to be not that it exaggerates value-emphases and overstimulates our pursuit of the good but, on the contrary, that is is apt to warp our genuine response to values, and to misdirect our practice. Once more, then, what *is* perfectionism if not a high-souled, intense and determined aspiration for values?

Perfectionism is not the overrating of *this* value at the cost of indifference to *that*, as such. Rather, it is an insistence on 'perfection-type' values to the detriment of others, and a delusive belief in the universal possibility of perfect solutions, in the directive importance of perfect beings and goods, and in the universal applicability of perfectional schemes. That is to say, a monomaniac attachment – not simply to *one* theme, but to *the* one theme of 'perfection' as opposed to the mundane manifoldness of limited, uncertain and foreshortened goods, values, aims and concerns. The perfectionist mind is less interested, for example, either in justice or in prosperity than in the idea of achieving prosperity through justice, or of securing the reign of justice by creating universal abundance. It is prone to an idealistic disregard for reality as well as a naturalistic devaluation of values. Tending to conceive of 'the good' only in terms of 'the best', it is liable to deny a straightforward response to value-qualities. Being impatient of the tension between value and being, it will misinterpret reality as perfect, or easily and securely perfectible – at the cost of cheapened standards and self-deceptive techniques. Or it will misinterpret reality as devoid of value-content, compared with what it conceivably might be, and then endure it with passive indifference or engage in subverting its order.

On the plane of practice in general, the perfectionist attitude, averse to risk and intolerant of contingence, and animated by a craving for infallible guarantees, gives rise to a characteristic inversion: that is, a displacement of the 'necessary' or objectively evident from the sphere of knowing to that of willing, and of arbitrariness from the volitive to the cognitive side. Given a set of plausible constructions, uncritically accepted on the strength of the pragmatic prospects they offer and under the persuasive spell of their streamlined elegance or their mirage of a deep and all-illuminating explanatory power, practice becomes a matter of scientific exactitude. The agent may nurse the happy illusion that once in possession of this special arcanum of wisdom he is 'sure' to do the wise, the right and the seasonable thing (which in every situation must exist, and must be *one*) without having to resort to burdensome and uncertain choices between different points of view, without the necessity of painful renunciations and an arbitrary rearrangement of his preferences.

What constitutes perfectionism is not the belief, which is true and is implied in the common-sense outlook, that perfection-models exist: that 'many-splendoured' goods (inviting love and, as it were, compelling a degree of legitimate overvaluation) occur in reality, that widely differing values may centre in one concrete entity, and that to some problems of practice a capital, unequivocal and altogether satisfactory solution can be found. The perfectionist attitude consists in expecting too much of perfection-modes, and relying upon them beyond their solvency, with the intent of thus evading the jar of Is and Ought (in the widest sense) which is the primary datum that underlies the common-sense outlook. What perfectionism does is to overcharge perfection-models with imaginary functions of a universal key or remedy, or to fabricate such models where they are lacking, or unfitting to the situation; in other words, to substitute for the world, which is a *locus* of values, a theatrical scenery conceived *in terms of* values; or again, an automaton devised so as to ensure the realization of a concept of value.

(ii) Polarities and variants of perfectionism

It should be noted here that just as awareness of 'perfection' does not amount to perfectionism, and 'the pursuit of the good' essentially contrasts with perfectionism, so also the 'perfectionism' sometimes referred to in ironic colloquial speech is very different from what I have been talking about. It refers to the 'correctness' aspect of perfection and, at the same time, to the praiseworthy, if occasionally disproportionate, ambition to 'do one's best'. Zeal, meticulous care, scrupulous observance of rules, a taste for punctilious, exact craftsmanship, a painstaking attention to detail, may thus come in for censure or grudging admiration as cases of 'perfectionism', it being implied that such an attitude connotes some degree of misplaced emphasis or misapplied effort, of priggishness, pedantry or self-importance. I hold – though it is not my business here to argue the point – that the 'perfectionist' in this sense is likely to be worth a great deal more than those who find fault with him; at worst, he may be a sub-perfectionist in my sense of the word – that is, a man vaguely inclined to attribute to his neat or brilliant performance a universal import which is no more than imaginary. Though he is possibly a nuisance to others and beset by the temptation of overscrupulousness, the fount of self-defeating exertions, this kind of man is not fundamentally at war with reality and is distinguished by a keen (if perhaps limited) sense of value rather than by a proneness to abandon values for the sake of chimeras.

The 'perfectionism' of excessive zeal or regularian pedantry means an attitude of overtension, which only just borders on our theme. By contrast, the perfectionist outlook examined in these pages, with an eye on its delusive and utopian aspects or potentialities, necessarily involves a *negation of tensions* that is normally recognized and accepted: a hankering after some tensionless union of value and being. This is not to say that perfectionist thinking is simply unaware of tension and, as it were, satisfied with anything and everything; nor that it is not apt also to overemphasize tension and, in particular, to generate tensions of a new and peculiar kind. If it did not, how could utopianism ever play a revolutionary part? But revolutionary utopianism is not an unflagging zeal for long-overdue reforms, tightening of rules or watchful insistence on the proper execution of public duties. Rather, its background and entelechy is the vision of an unworldly world without imperfection, friction and creaking joints. And the more limited, less highly strung forms of perfectionism, whether they bear a quietistic or an activistic tinge, postulate in their turn the idea of things that are good just because they are what they are, or things that are real or realizable simply by virtue of their goodness (or evils which, just because they are evils, 'cannot go on for long'). Whether it is indulging in or systematically fostering pleasant illusions, or enamoured of smoothly working and painless solutions, perfectionism at least partially and inconsistently implies the belief that the resistance of brute matter may be discounted and the cussedness of things be extruded from the operational field on which attention is focused.

Correctness is by no means a perfectionist concept: it is meaningful to describe certain propositions, forms or ways of procedure as 'correct' and necessary, commendable or useful – be it, *mutatis mutandis*, in reasoning, mathematics, language, morality, law, manners or the sphere of crafts and skills. But a narrow-minded, subaltern kind of perfectionism may attach, overstraining and misusing it, to the conception of the 'correct': thus, the postulate that there must *always* be *one* 'correct' way (with no drawback to it) of expressing a thought, of acting in a given situation, of doing a thing, of arguing, of taking sides in a conflict. It has already been shown that the pragmatic desire – itself not unconnected with the common-sense attitude – of basing a decision on sufficient and compelling reasons is apt to encourage an arbitrary belief in unwarranted theoretical constructions and imaginary certitudes. In very different ways, perfectionist thinking may centre in the difficult and many-coloured but obviously ineliminable and far from meaningless concept of *nature*.

There are several forms, explicitly philosophical, political, quasi-scientific and popular, of identifying 'nature' with holiness and wisdom and 'natural' with 'good'; the demand, couched perhaps in Physiocratic or Rousseauian terms, for freeing, cleansing and disentangling the 'natural' from the haphazard institutional growths which have come to soil and to choke it, and to deflect the workings of nature from its beneficial, self-regulating and self-evidently right course; the rationalist, humanist and revolutionary undertaking to 'create a new nature', fitted to our needs and value-aspirations, through the man-made devices of machinery, artificiality and planning: so many ways, contrasting but partly also mutually confluent, of subordinating the pursuit of the good to the service of a perfectional idol. That the good is that which exists *of necessity*, or that it should emerge from a pattern of necessity; that evil is contingent, transient or 'merely phenomenal'; that the march of evolution or history is identical with a progressive self-revelation of the good; that good is the solid core of being and evil a zone of fleeting appearances which surround and hide it; or that if this is not so it ought to be so and might be achieved – here is another set of perfectionist suppositions and postulates of identity, closely related to the former. But the perfectionist emphasis may also fasten on *freedom* (from rules, from the allegedly irremovable data of nature, from necessity), on *reason*, on *intuition* or *le cœur* [the heart], as opposed to 'ratiocinative' reason, on *religious* concepts especially with a pantheistic tinge, and of course on the conceptions and embodiments of political power and prestige.

Very roughly, allowance being made for the manifold overlaps and sub-variants, the perfectionist claim to an identity between value and being may, with respect to its amplitude, be differentiated into a *particularist* or 'monomaniac', a *dualist*, and a *monist*, 'universalist' or 'totalitarian' type. In the first form, the overvalued and overcharged perfection-model, notwithstanding the universal or at any rate fictitiously extended relevance attributed to it, is of an essentially limited scope: it may be a person or a local community unduly reverenced, as if exempt from normal criteria of judgement; or again, a point of view, a method, a traditional or a newly discovered truth or technique of any kind whose importance and usefulness have been established and which is credited by the subject with next-to-miraculous virtues and with a range of applicability quite out of proportion with its real force. Dualist perfectionism erects some principle, system or scheme, of a universal scope of reference but confined to one plane of human relationships and dimensions of life – for example, utility, the economic *ordre naturel* [natural order], or the division of powers, or consciousness of duty – into an absolute, 'the one thing that matters': other themes and values of life, while supposed to be best protected thereby, are relegated into the realm of adiaphora and left so far to the dubious ministrations of men's minds as informed by the common-sense outlook. Totalitarian perfectionism, on the contrary, claims determination, and incorporation into the unity of 'perfection', of all things of any importance to men (or perhaps beyond that), though not necessarily by direct regimentation or utopian revolutionary planning; it admits no realm of indifference and no overt world, that is, no seat of relevant imperfection.

The general bent of perfectionism is monistic as regards theory, explanation and interpretation, and accordingly unitarian as regards practical orientation; it is averse to the common-sense world of manifoldness, tensions, distinctions and loose, ambiguous, contingent relationships. Chesterton's remarkable expression of the common-sense style of value-response –

There is one thing is needful – Everything –
The rest is vanity of vanities

– might be converted into its perfectionist opposite in some such terms as 'There is but one thing that matters: that ultimate "rest" which is really *one*; whereas *things* with their limited significance, their proper weight and their particular and in many ways antithetic values are vanity of vanities.' But perfectionism, being of the world though a rebel to it, is subject to the law of differentiation; the negation of tensions and the overpapering of distinctions cannot but conjure up a host of ineluctable *polarities* of emphasis, alternative attitudes to which will colour the various forms of perfectionism. If, for example, welfare and morality are supposed to be one, it will make a difference whether I interpret morality as an expression and instrument of welfare or welfare as a reward or a by-product of morality; though admittedly, the choice may not be rigorously dual, and I may also hazily conceive of welfare and morality as mere facets of a thing deeper than either – say something like 'flourishing life'. Let us now survey the most fundamental of the polarities which thus modulate the perfectionist outlook – aware, of course, of the obvious probability of their being rooted in one ultimate divergence, although they cannot be wholly accounted for in terms thereof.

'Value is the fullness of being' and 'Being is the self-realization of value': these antithetic perfectionist positions may be described, respectively, as 'naturalism' and 'idealism' – without prejudice to the various other uses of these hackneyed and long-suffering philosophical terms. Not in strict logic but in the sense of a quasi-logical implication, the naturalist emphasis may be expected to support a quietist, static and, as it were, embellishing attitude; the idealist emphasis an activist, dynamic, missionary or prophetic, postulatory or 'planning' one. The former experiences perfection as a 'given'; the latter experiences perfection as a task. Clearly it is the second that is more relevant to the theme of Utopia. But hybrid forms and supplementary, background interconnections play an important role. Thus the naturalist belief in a strongest and most highly energetic – and therefore, perfect – race may involve the idealist belief that it is the 'destiny', willed by a transcendent purpose, of that race to subdue and re-create the world, and the duty of each of us to aid it to do so. Conversely, straightforward utopianism may build round its idealist core a layer of naturalist ideology relative to the concrete 'cause', 'movement', leaders and camp that have come to represent it in the arena of historical reality.

Perfectionist thinking tends to 'formalism' and extreme 'abstraction' on the one hand (which corresponds more or less to 'idealism'), and to the cult of a 'concrete' and 'unique' value-reality on the other (which aligns with 'naturalism'). For example, an 'ultimate' and apparently 'all-comprehensive' principle like 'maximizing the good' will interest the perfectionist mind very much more than will good things or definite value-qualities; yet it may also bow to the universal sovereignty of one given object, person or organized collective which claims (or is made to claim) to incarnate and irradiate perfection. Perfection may be sought in a key formula of utmost generality, irrefutable self-evidence and a validity independent of any tradition, prejudice and historical context; or again, in a 'living' reality which manifests perfection already 'achieved'. Common-sense deontological or 'code' morality may thus be replaced by a more abstract pseudo-rational principle such as utility, consistency, 'energy economy', or 'conformance to nature' (here abstractionism merges into naturalism, in the above sense) or inversely, by a concentration of emphasis on supposed or selected exemplars of 'virtue', inviting allegiance or imitation (for this kind of perfectionist conception of morality, the label 'perfectionalism' might perhaps be proposed). And if a type of perfectionist attitude combines an abstract and uniform concept of value with the arbitrary ascription of such value to a concrete individual entity, as in high-pitched hero-worship or sectarian 'orthodoxy', this linking of opposite poles will be a direct and short-circuited one, quite unlike the pluralist and perspective structure of the common-sense outlook, with its manifold value-experience embedded in scales of conceptual abstraction and armature of references to concrete exemplars. The putative deciphering of the world or of life, with its value-implications and practical problems, in terms of a general key principle and the irrationalist mystique of erecting an unanalysable 'thisness' into a sovereign principle of value, are alike alien to the common-sense and germane to the perfectionist outlook.

Another important polarity concerns the mutual position of subject and object according to the perfectionist outlook. In my normal or common-sense relationship with values there is a most manifold interpenetration of the antithetic aspect of 'above me' and 'below me': on the one hand, I am 'subjected' to the compelling, obligating, fascinating, attractive, directive and formative action of values; on the other, I am 'the subject' of choices, decisions, confrontations and co-ordinations in respect of them, the 'person' to be benefited, satisfied and enriched by them. The two aspects interlink, of course, in a great diversity of proportions and modes. Perfectionism reveals a predilection for the two extreme poles: it tends to conceive of values either as 'absolutes' by which the subject is or should be unequivocally 'determined', of which his being were a mere function, *or* as instrumental goods, 'perfectly' to fit his designs and satisfy his needs. Misdirected religious pietism, 'superman' concepts, idolatries of power, instantiate the first possibility; atheist, emancipationist, humanitarian and democratic ideologies, the machine as the symbol of man's 'creative sovereignty', and reliance on mechanical methods typify the second. In the central concept of Utopia, man wholly 'spontaneous' and wholly 'socialized', the individual regenerated in perfection as product and bearer of a perfect scheme of society, the two aspects coincide: the subject is master of everything and slave to an all-embracing construction of desirability.

Finally, by contrast with the common-sense emphasis on distinction, discrimination, gradation, and differential recording of things, qualities and possibilities, the perfectionist outlook is likely to bifurcate into optimism and pessimism – though the platitudinous nursery-book optimism characteristic of naturalist illusions of perfection and of degraded forms of conservatism is apt to be boring, prim and joyless; while the pessimistic rejection of this imperfect world usually enshrines a hidden strain of cold optimism even in its most negative (stoic or passively and spiteful 'idealistic') variants, or is dialectically linked to an aspect of florid otherworldly or futurist optimism. The latter in its full-fledged, activist and revolutionary form implies a general optimistic preconception, more candidly manifest in Rousseau but more consistently effective in the Marxian mentality. Man in his purely immanent and earthly capacity, on the basis of his own wants and by means of his own forces, including reason, is to liberate himself from a hideous historical reality and to build a world of perfection all *his*. He is, then, good and happy according to his fundamental being (although it is not Marxist etiquette to say so), and the more so if his enterprise is worldwide and its success is a matter of certitude as opposed to mere wistful hopes and small-scale experiments. Revolutionary utopianism, challenging and unmasking the philistine illusions of hidebound traditionalist, saturated owners and stolid petty-bourgeois, is out to construct, at the price of oceans of blood, infernos of torture, ruthless slave-driving and a surfeit of obscurantist sophistry, a paradise of total philistinism no longer exposed to any conceivable stirring of the critical attitude – the fulfilment of the true, or perfect, being of man in which the tension of Is and Ought has no place or meaning.

(iii) The perfectionist fallacy

So far as 'tastes' *are* pure straightforward tastes, they admit of no argument. Some distinctive tastes are 'reasonable' in the sense that they spring from the somatic constitution of the subject and very probably answer its particular biological needs; like most thin and 'asthenic' people, I dread the cold more than even humid heat, while fat and rubicund people mostly stand up better to the cold and fail to enjoy even dry heat, and nothing could be crazier than our trying to persuade each other of the 'rightness' of our respective tastes. Other distinctive tastes – the purest 'tastes' – appear neither biologically 'fitting' nor justifiable or challengeable at all: if Eugenio d'Ors is right in saying that almost all people either prefer apricots to peaches or, like himself, peaches to apricots, I, who prefer apricots, feel no inclination either to be ashamed of belonging to my class or to try to convert any of those marked by the opposite preference. In other cases again, personal taste may display a more complex logical structure, involving 'convictions' proper and such valuational aspects as are arguable in terms of some generally accepted standards of value. I well might at some time, for some reason, enjoy Newbolt's verse more than de la Mare's, but if a man said he was more impressed by Newbolt's than by de la Mare's poetry it would at the very least be meaningful to suggest that his taste must be poor, unawakened or uneducated. A person who prefers Greek art to Egyptian and I, who place Egyptian above Greek, would not, for that reason alone, think of each other in similarly unflattering terms, but we might find a good deal to argue about, though presumably to little purpose; I might perhaps contend, clarifying it to a degree, that there was a dimension of purity and tenderness of soul to which he was unresponsive, while his hints at my deficiency in artistic vision or cultural sensibility might supply me with some food for thought.

Be that as it may, contrasting *attitudes* are not in themselves necessarily right or wrong, wise or foolish, and correct or erroneous, but they may well be susceptible of moral evaluation, and imply, intertwine with, and even repose on true and false beliefs, including valid and fallacious arguments. Thus, *some* among the many French people who in these days vote Communist are on the whole freedom-loving and generous men with a keen sense of personal dignity who have never understood the inmost essence of Marxism–Leninism, and would find life unbearable under Communist tyranny[7]; their attitude is based partly on leftist traditions, reminiscences and resentments, but partly also on the erroneous belief that the French Communist Party is chiefly interested in the welfare and civic status of the working classes of France, and on the fallacious reasoning that if the social fact that strikes them most obviously and proximately is that (some) French capitalists are too rich and (many) French workers are too poor, it follows that the paramount concern to govern their political conduct must be the breaking of the power and confiscation of the property of French capitalists. Notwithstanding the part played in all distinctive practical attitudes by primary emotive preferences and temperamental or accidental 'tastes', they require an intellectual scaffolding for their consistency and active vigour. The intellectual task of exposing the errors of fact, ideological obscurities and intrinsically refutable fallacies which underlie and support (though they may not constitute or engender) mistaken and deleterious practical attitudes is, therefore, not merely theoretically meaningful but of great practical – and, as the case may be, moral or political – importance.

Perfection as such, as we have seen, is not a fictitious concept at all, though it is a problematical concept inherently fraught with dangerous temptations; and perfectionism itself cannot be defined in terms of a fallacy alone. I certainly cannot, without further ado, 'disprove' moods, attitudes, likes and dislikes, and choices or pursuits at variance with my own predilection for the finite and limited, for the fragmentary and the imperfect – loved with a critical reserve – and for pluralistic and balanced perspectives – in a word, for consciousness of tension. But certain typically perfectionist errors *can* be disproved by experience or, rather, by arguments involving empirical tests: thus, the errors that war always (and necessarily) destroys liberty and engenders tyranny; that pleasure as such breeds disease, and labour breeds health; that liberal as opposed to non-liberal institutions are always conducive to prosperity; that health, longevity and happiness centrally depend on certain dietary habits, and so forth. It is clear that, in our context, sheer straightforward errors of fact are of no importance at all; they may accidentally be connected with false attitudes (a man may eagerly embrace an erroneous belief because it happens to flatter his personal or national vanity), but they essentially repose on misinformation and can be corrected by providing the subject with more explicit, ample and authoritative true information. Not so the element of *fallacy*: that is to say, specious argument and plausible but false – explicit or implicit – presuppositions, intimately bound up with the subject's desires and infatuations, and underlying factual errors in the sense of making the subject inaccessible to corrective information, preventing him from taking cognizance of factual data well within his reach, or forcing him into sophistical misinterpretations and distorted valuations so as to 'save' his preconceived belief at all costs. It would be pointless to see perfectionism at work in all emotive fallacies, except in the weak general sense that they necessarily serve the purpose of an illusory embellishment of reality from the subject's point of view and, on the other hand, perfectionist attitudes make use of many kinds of fallacies; but – summarizing in a way the content of this section together with the two previous ones – I may perhaps tentatively suggest a formula for 'the' basic *perfectionist fallacy*, implicit in all the various forms of perfectionist thought and attitudes.

In our pursuit of values and goods – in the widest sense of the term – we come to be aware of, and normally follow, some evident axioms of preference, which ultimately reduce to the tautology that 'the preferable is to be preferred'. More satisfying goods command a preference over less satisfying; what is altogether good has precedence over what is only partly good; values with a wider range of relevance and orientating or informing force overshadow those with a more limited range. A thing of value, complete as a thing, is better than the same thing incomplete; a full compenetration of value and being, with its suggestion of a necessary, automatic and permanently guaranteed realization of that value, is preferable to accidental and transient advantages; such value-experiences as bear within them a tonality of the highest and most definitive satisfactions of the mind excel mere 'here-and-now' gratifications, gains, or despatchings of duties. Our enjoyment of the sight and scent of roses does not logically imply our fingers being pricked by thorns, and in itself is better without such a pain or danger attaching to it. Again, areas of untroubled harmony between my environment and myself are obviously more worthy of appreciation than my haphazard and precarious successes in subduing outer things or fitting them to my needs, or laborious adaptations of my conduct to circumstances I cannot alter and claims I must needs recognize.

The perfectionist *attitude* no doubt consists in the agent's tendency to allow his choices not only to be influenced by this kind of evident axioms of preference, but to be predominantly *determined* by such, in an imprudent and obsessive fashion, *at the expense of* primary needs and duties, value-concerns, and practical necessities which do not carry this same kind of quasi-tautological, 'analytic' evidence, but do embody the substantial and urgent motives for action, as well as the genuine, deep and specific value and disvalue experiences, of man in general. Many of these primary needs and concerns will also be called 'self-evident' in ordinary language, but this is 'evidence' in a looser sense of the term only: the kind of 'evidence' proper to well-established and widely or universally known empirical facts, to customary beliefs and permanent data of consciousness; an 'evidence' based on our *world-experience*. We all expect one another to know that Stockholm is the capital of Sweden, that roses are lovely, or that peaches and apricots are delicious. I even expect my wife to know that I am peculiarly fond of peaches but more so of apricots: in all these contexts, and in the appropriate company, we may use expressions like 'evidently', 'obviously', or 'of course'. Yet none of these things is really 'evident'. What is 'evident', rather, are the inferences that can be drawn from these facts, once established: if I want to pay a visit to the Swedish court, I must go to Stockholm, and the like. It is not even 'evident' that man needs food, that there is such a thing as better and worse food, that some kinds of action are good and some evil, or that Rembrandt was an unusually great painter; though these and many similar affirmations are hardly ever called in doubt. We do, however, approach the plane of analytic self-evidence in proceeding to suggest, for example, that to provide men in general with plenty of good food should be one of the paramount concerns of mankind; that good conduct ought to be acknowledged and rewarded, and misconduct discriminated against and checked in *some* way; or that it matters a great deal to preserve Rembrandt's works carefully and to make them in some way accessible to many people.

It is inherent in the spirit of perfectionism to *stretch* this line of self-evidence, in the context of value-postulates, to excessive lengths – at the cost of underemphasizing the presupposed value-experiences and sensibilities themselves, and at the risk of getting entrapped in the snare of irrelevant, imaginary, self-defeating or self-contradictory schemes of ideas. Why not a scientific method of infallibly determining the degree of the quality of food and the right composition of meals, and a worldwide administration or propaganda to ensure that all mankind should eat well? The nutritional perfectionist who thinks on these lines may be unable to cook an egg properly and, more important, will quite possibly be unable, barring extreme cases, to tell good food from bad. If moral good should be promoted and evil curbed, why not envision a state of man in which good motives alone are at work, and evil impulses (deprived of whatever fostering-ground may breed them) no longer occur at all? The utopian moralist satisfied as to the 'evidence' of such a goal will perhaps approve of the use of utterly evil means to secure, in the future and 'finally', so sweeping a regeneration of man; what is perhaps even more to the point, his insight into actual moral problems is likely to be poor and superficial, for so long as evil exists, a trifle more or less of it may not seem worthy of passionate attention and patient assessment. And the man who is eager about the dissemination of high art will be apt to skip aesthetic appreciation, contemplation and discussion, and may weigh less in the aesthetic balance of mankind than any humble local craftsman or, indeed, any odd petty-bourgeois who is suddenly *struck* by the sight of some dilapidated chapel or forgotten etching.

I would, then, put the Perfectionist Fallacy roughly in these terms: 'The *degree of evidence* that guides us in our apprehension and manipulation of values is the safest criterion and guarantee of the height and wealth of the good we attain, achieve or realize for ourselves and others.'

The plausibility this fallacy is built upon is of a kind with the plausibility attaching, for example, to such typical and historically established fallacious reasonings as those employed by many Pacifists: 'War breeds war' (or 'Violence breeds violence') 'and peace, peace'; by Racists and certain kinds of apologists for aristocracy: 'A higher species of man generates and vouchsafes a higher morality and a higher level of society'; by religious pietists and aestheticists with Platonist leanings: 'The height of thought and conduct depends on the height of the objects referred to in its concepts and motives', or 'Thinking of beautiful things is what makes you a beautiful personality'; or again, by materialist reformers: 'The more prosperity, the greater surplus energies and, therefore, the higher culture'; and by pseudo-scientific believers in 'scientism': 'The more a proposition or argument is expressible in a mathematical, numerical or statistical form, the more incontrovertible it must be', and 'The use of a "dry" concept-language in the style of experimental science precludes error, imposture or uncontrolled fancy'.

All these fallacies include an element of self-evidence, trivial to the point of tautology and thus far carrying conviction in a strictly rational manner – and therefore also connoting a reference to some measure of factual truth – fused, more elegantly or more clumsily, with an arbitrary selection of facts, with unwarranted postulates, mere trappings of a rational approach, and verbal conjuring tricks. What *is* self-evident is *eo ipso* true, of course – 'self-evidently' true – *so far as it goes*. What is not true – and, of course, is *not* self-evident, but may easily appear so owing to the suggestive power of mere *association* and by virtue of man's craving for rational certitudes – is the assumption that arguments are correct, and beliefs true and embodying relevant knowledge, *in so far as they appeal to* self-evidence and seem to be permeated with the style and semblance thereof. Whereas doing wicked things cleverly means properly a misuse of reason, and fallacy in general an unskilful and falsifying use of reason, the philosophical, doctrinal or 'rationalist' kind of fallacy, as instanced above, means in especial a misuse *of the authority of reason* comparable to the manifold misuses of religious, political, personal and other concrete, incarnate kinds of authority.

The perfectionist fallacy, as distinct from the perfectionist attitude but inseparably wedded to it, is one variant of philosophical fallacy as here defined – or perhaps I should rather say *is* philosophical fallacy considered from the point of view of its informing the perfectionist attitude; indeed, all particular philosophical fallacies, or at least all those with a valuational or volitional theme, bear a perfectionist tinge. But no deceptive conceptual appeal can be so plausible as that of the extended perfectional 'evidences' which promise attainment of 'the best' and of a full and 'necessary' union of value and reality. Over and above the fictitious, short-circuited possession of this or that specifically desired good or value-quality it offers, the perfectionist fallacy offers the peculiar emotional satisfaction of a pure and all-round rationality pervading the subject's management of his concerns, which again will mould and colour his particular preferences, desires and pursuits. The fallacy remains a fallacy – and his professing and following of it may indeed tangibly and grimly avenge itself on the subject – but *within* the ambit of the perfectionist *attitude*, which it subserves and in its turn fashions, it partly '*comes true*' by actually charming the subject away, to some extent, into the false universe of values which represents its misinterpretation of the true world. By the same token, Utopia, while it cannot become reality, not only exercises a tremendous subversive impact upon reality but actually offers its addicts and slaves – temporarily, and mixed with anxiety and bitterness – a taste of utopian beatitude.

It should be added that the fallacy of all-determining self-evidences has greater force of plausibility in the field of a general valuational outlook than in purely theoretical contexts, or even in more specified and delimited value-contexts inasmuch as that field is but very indirectly connected with the disillusioning experience of 'plain, hard facts'. A scientific hypothesis, or any assumption relative to facts, can be convincingly falsified by experiment, observation or testimony; value-problems of a concrete, circum-scribed and comparatively technical kind are largely dependent on factual connections subject to straightforward intellectual tests, and on standard valuations unlikely to be called in question and thus assuming in some way the status of 'facts'. But the general outlook on value is not as such confrontable with stubborn facts of experience or committed to established axioms of valuation, like the basic *Don'ts* of ordinary Morality. It is capable of endless formalization and evasive reinterpretation. Thus the perfectionist fallacy may soar above any detailed tests, and the perfectionist attitude may *thrive upon itself.* Common sense is not only essentially imperfect, but a fragile and repressible thing in man: flagellants, stylites and herb-eaters may avow themselves 'happy'; knaves, profligates and corruptionists of the reckless and ambitious kind may live with a consciousness of moral superiority, despising decent people as philistines, pharisees and cowards; Communists may enjoy a vicarious consciousness of the plenitude of 'freedom', the thing being false and perverse and the phrase ambiguous and fallacious, but not a *mere* misuse of language.

It is further important to note that the perfectionist fallacy consists *not* (primarily) in mistaking for self-evident what is not so, but in mistaking self-evidence for '*the*' source of truth and information, for a self-sufficient basis of valuational and practical guidance. The mistaking for 'self-evident' of what is in fact only conventional, customary, habitual, familiar, frequent, or pertaining to a given environment and period, is indeed a most widespread human tendency, but even in its rabidly illusive forms it has no more than a virtual and remote connection with perfectionism. The ridiculousness of the fashions of the past or of a foreign accent or, in general, foreign ways is a cheap source of fun, but to deride this popular kind of amusement is also a cheap and easy way of asserting one's intellectual superiority. The sense of quasi-evidence attaching to the constitutive, permanent or very slowly changing data of our everyday existence is inherent in the routine of life, and thus an entirely commonsensical requisite of practice; nor does it necessarily involve believing that our habits, customs or particular maxims of preference are objectively perfect, and contrasting ones are objectively preposterous. (It need hardly be said that some of 'our' particular dogmas, traditions and usages *may* be well considered and objectively true, right or superior, while some alien, obsolete or novel ideas or practices *may* rightly shock us as absurd or revolting.) I may still smile faintly at the sight of Scottish kilts, Indian robes and turbans or, for that matter, glossy tophats, but at the same time I smile faintly at my own smile, and am far from having any definite views on the intrinsic superiority of my own less conspicuous adornments. No doubt tribal idolatry, uncritical sectarian or national self-esteem, candid and unreserved reverence for specified persons in one's social environment, and stubborn prejudice and unimaginative narrow-mindedness in general do approach or actually display the perfectionist attitude, but only in so far as they ideologically postulate the universal validity and directive competence of perfectional models, implying an overdraft on the 'self-evident' as opposed to the empirical, experimental and perspective modes of thinking, not in so far as they merely overestimate what looms large in the vital field of the subject. It may be a sign not only of ignorance but of foolishness and mental sloth to believe that an infusion of certain herbs is particularly good for a certain disease because one's mother and grandmother thought so, but it would appear forced and pointless to bring such an illusion under the heading of perfectionism.

On the other hand, the perfectionist attitude sometimes manifests itself by some features of wilful and provoking eccentricity, which might seem to give the lie to my reading of the perfectionist fallacy as a misuse of 'analytic evidence'. But, as paranoiac 'logic' shows, eccentricity and even insanity are opposed to common sense, not necessarily to consistency and rigorous inference. The conscientious objectors were certainly more eccentric but less inconsistent – less reasonable but at the same time more 'rationalist', and displaying a more purely 'evidential' conduct – than the multitude of woolly-minded but 'ultimately' sound-hearted Englishmen who first brazenly declared that 'war was the worst of evils', that 'war meant slavery anyhow' and that 'war could solve no problem', and then suddenly blurted out that 'Hitler couldn't be allowed to have his way', acting – a bit unfairly towards Hitler – on the latter principle. Neither triviality as such nor eccentricity as such has anything to do with perfectionism. But it may be said of perfectionism that it overdoes the triviality of a linear valuational logic and of an 'evidential' derivation of practical maxims to the neglect of widely accepted and firmly established – in a manner of speaking, quasi-evident – concerns, disregard for which, pushed as it may easily be to the point of demonstrative defiance, calls into being an aspect of eccentricity: just as a man who was excessively interested in his bodily health and his financial security, and interested in nothing else, would rightly be called 'pedestrian' and 'odd' at the same time.

Moreover, perfectionism is not only a self-defeating form of the pursuit of the good but is at least virtually bound to debouch in self-contradiction, for although truths, and therefore 'evidently' true principles, cannot mutually conflict, the purblind and imaginary following-out of one evidential line of inference will tend to obscure the subject's awareness of other genuine 'evidences' and their corollaries. Thus, while it is normal to be concerned both about security and about freedom, the perfectional pursuit of either will impair the agent's general relation to values, including the other of the two values here named, thereby reacting adversely on his fruition of security or of freedom itself. The more strictly perfectionist pursuit of both, in their supposed harmony or unity, will produce the self-contradictory position of seeking freedom as a putative result of 'maximum' security while expressly scorning freedom; or inversely, of deceptively expecting security from contemptuously putting aside, in an anarchic assertion of freedom, the prudential restraints, care and solicitude which in fact do not infallibly lead to security. But I shall try later to go more accurately into the theme of the 'utopian contradiction' as compared with the inherent imperfection of common-sense practice. My point here is that the fallacious overemphasis on consistency is not incompatible with contradiction ensuing in a wider context, and that, rather, consistency thus overburdened with a function it cannot discharge except fictitiously will break down at some point in a particular and glaring fashion.

It may not be amiss to note, in fine, that in spite of the abstractive and conceptual emphasis of the perfectionist fallacy, it would be a mistake to interpret perfectionism as an expression of the doctrinaire's or the 'intellectual's' mental attitude as such. It is not the military caste but the human animal that is prone to aggression and in need of defence; it is not the businessman but man who has to be practical and productive, and not the proletarian but man who is doomed to work. Similarly, perfectionism is not a professional disease but a classic human temptation; its various – including highly ideological – forms are rampant among men in all walks of life and in the most diverse situations. If it needs technical elaboration by intellectuals acting on behalf of men, so does common-sense wisdom. This is not to deny the possibility and usefulness of research about what psychological factors, sociological conditions and historical situations may render men particularly vulnerable to the temptation.

6 THE UTOPIAN CONTRADICTION AND OUR SUBMISSION TO AN IMPERFECT WORLD

(i) Perfectionism and utopianism
These two terms are sometimes being used here as if they were synonymous; in fact, they may roughly be said to overlap, but certainly not simply to coincide. We should keep in mind the axiological emphasis on perfectionism in order to understand the (so to speak) geographical, historical and political emphasis of utopianism.[8] It is less necessary to be aware of utopian visions and endeavours in order to analyse perfectionism; but at least we might venture to suggest that, given the perfectionist attitude, the emergence of utopian imaginations, conceptions and movements is to be expected.

Perfectionism as such is virtually or latently utopian:[9] it is, then, not utopian as such without any further qualification. The predilection of many people for streamlined solutions, infallible authorities or this or that 'arcanum' of successful practice, within a limited context which interests them, is obviously 'perfectionist', but to call it 'utopian' might evoke censure as an unduly broad and tendentiously forced use of that term. Some such people

may not be attracted at all by utopian visions (literary or not) of
self-contained perfect societies, may be politically indifferent, or
indeed may hold strongly conservative and commonplace views
concerning government and the social order: it would sound odd
to ascribe to them a 'utopian' outlook. Some cases will have to
be classified as marginal or transitional. Systematized perfectionism
relative to a particular sphere of concerns which is believed to be of
great importance to man – kept in bounds, however, by a normal
and unbiased attitude to other matters whose importance is not
denied – may be called 'partial' or 'departmental' utopianism.

A conservative in the conventionalist and conformist sense,
illusively oversatisfied with the conditions and standards of the
society to which he belongs, proud of the fact that 'the barbarisms
of old' are only 'an evil memory' but cheerful and easy-going about
present defects, ready to pooh-pooh complaints and demands for
reform, is a perfectionist of one kind – though not of the most
typical kind – but hardly a utopian. The traditionalist who clings to
some past epoch, that of his fathers or grandfathers or more remote
(perhaps the High Middle Ages), chosen as a perfection-model
and accordingly misinterpreted and misdescribed, and who urges
a restoration of that mental and social model at least 'in its essential
features', is a perfectionist in a more marked sense, and displays the
mentality of 'reactionary utopia' – which, to be sure, falls short of
the subversive and constructive claims of full-fledged utopianism.
In his turn, the characteristic believer in 'Progress' who insists
on perfectibility and on 'growth' as a guarantee of increasing
perfection may be averse to breaches of continuity and violent
upheavals, and thus in a different way again represent a restricted
or damped variety of utopianism. Plato may be looked upon as
a most prominently perfectionist thinker; but however important
he is in the history of properly utopian thought and literature, in
view of his reactionary aspects and of the playful, experimental and
aestheticist traits in his utopian speculations, we might hesitate to
call him a Utopian in as full a sense as, for example, the radical
millenarians in the age of the Reformation. His disciple Aristotle
is much less of a perfectionist but retains a great deal more of the
perfectionism than of the utopianism of his master; his account
of happiness, virtue and wisdom is well imbued with Platonist
perfectionism, although this takes a more hidden, reserved and

diluted form; while his conception of Society, though adorned with perfectionist conceptual decorations, is predominantly and explicitly anti-utopian.

If utopianism is perfectionism with an emphasis on its tendency towards universality, and deployed as it were on the 'macroscopic' scale of society, politics and history, has it, nevertheless, some component unconnected with perfectionism? If a mind may be more perfectionist than utopian, is the reverse also possible? What Utopia literally means – 'placelessness' or 'nowhere country' – is itself, as we saw above, a symbol of freedom from the limitations and divisions inherent in ordinary mundane existence. This seems to imply perfectionism at its highest, without revealing any content independent of it. The utopian turn from reality and conversion of a schema of social value into an imaginary 'concrete' construction, before descending on reality with the view of 'creating' it anew, likewise seems to correspond entirely with the perfectionist cult of abstraction, ordained to the pursuit of a complete fusion of value and being. Still, what might perhaps be discerned as a utopian motif conceivable without a reference to perfectionism is discontinuity as an end in itself, complete change or novelty desired for its own sake. Although such a yearning is hardly conceivable without a background of the experience of imperfection attaching to real life as such, it is logically compatible with the absence of any vision of perfection, or indeed of any belief that the new or faraway thing should be intrinsically better than the old and 'local'. A romantic unrest, hatred of stability and, as it were, revulsion from identity of this kind could not alone engender any Utopias or constitute anything like the utopian turn of mind, but is akin to the utopian challenge to reality, and may be more emphatically present in some utopian attitudes than in others. In this sense, some types of *rerum novarum cupidi* [those desirous of novelty], nihilistic in general, violently hostile to the established order, yet at the same time fairly sceptical about the creed and promise of the revolutionary cause they support (like Kirilov in Dostoevsky's *The Possessed*), may be credited with a mind more markedly utopian than it is perfectionist.

(ii) The utopian contradiction

Utopia is not a straightforward affirmation and cannot, consequently, be 'disproved'; but neither is it simply a 'temper'
which can perhaps be curbed in its manifestations and modified by
attacking its supposed causes, but not shown to be 'false' by argument. Preferences as such are unarguable, but practical positions in
general can be criticized, in varying degrees, as 'false', 'mistaken'
or 'wrong' – not merely in view of the purely technical or factual
presuppositions on which they may depend, but in a more intrinsic
sense also inasmuch as they involve a disregard for certain more
or less established standards, valuations and preferences which the
agent is not prepared expressly and definitely to disown. Mutually
conflicting desires, disparate wishes and contrasting tastes in one
man do not, of course, amount to contradiction: my desire to take
a walk this afternoon and my desire to avoid being drenched by
the rain which seems to be impending need not at all imply my
professing the maxim 'Whenever I feel like taking a walk I do
so' and at the same time the maxim 'Whenever rain threatens I
forbear from taking a walk'. Yet true contradiction *may* arise from
men's propensity to justify and solidify their various and changeable
attitudes by erecting their motives into principles with a universal
and 'rational'-sounding appeal, especially in regard to important
and controversial matters. Nationalism provides a standard example. It is not in itself 'contradictory' for a nation Y to struggle to
escape from oppression by a stronger power X and, possibly at
the very same time, to maintain its own oppressive rule over a
weaker nationality Z; but in such situations the Y nationalists will
tend to resort to the mutually contradictory ideological weapons of
the *universal* principle of national freedom in the one context and
of some equally universal principle, such as that of upholding the
traditional order of things or the right of the strong and noble, in
the other.

Contradiction, sometimes thinly disguised or disingenuously
corrected by *ad hoc* modifications fitted to the tastes of different
audiences, may in such or similar ways come into being, never
strictly speaking as a necessity but as an expedient of practice –
laying that system of practice open, at the same time, to logical
criticism and therewith to moral criticism more evident and more
difficult to ward off than the moral criticism it may intrinsically

evoke, and so making the latter more ineludible and strengthening its corrosive effect. Typical contradictions closer to utopianism itself can be observed in the more extreme kinds of political attitudes; thus, in counter-revolutionary 'rightist' traditionalism, the contradiction between condemning 'subversion' as such and the endeavour to upset existing traditions of a liberal nature; or in 'leftist' progressivism, the simultaneous glorification of 'courageous' dissenters or 'pioneers', and of 'the common man' or 'the masses'. I agree that the line cannot always be drawn neatly between merely 'paradoxical' or 'whimsical' attitudes and attitudes bound up with fixed or emergent principles which explicitly contradict one another; my point is only that such an entanglement in contradiction proper *is possible* by virtue of the inherent (though by no means general or absolute) need of practice to be propped by universal principles with the status of theoretical 'truths'.

The difference between contradiction proper being present in or absent from an individual's express positions may be a trivial one, with hardly any bearing on our judgement of his character. There are people who will sometimes fancy beer, sometimes wine; the slightly more primitive and impulsive kind will perhaps say, when relishing beer: 'A good beer beats wine any day!', and the exact opposite when enjoying good wine; whereas a more intellectual sort of person, but of like tastes, will rather reflect on the strange fact that preferences vary with occasions, and thus escape contradiction. Nor do the frequent contradictions in the ideologies of one concrete political party constitute a very interesting problem; they are a matter of hypocrisy and unscrupulous tactics, and as a rule indicate that the contradictory points in question are not the real theme of that movement. The Nazis bade fair that they would save capitalist society from the peril of socialism, and in the same breath posed as champions of the poor against the tyranny of capitalism: what they really cared about was something quite different. Only such contradictions are of interest to us as seem to be *inherent* in the very content of a practical conception or ideological position, independently of the psychology or morals of those who represent it.

Conceptions thus coming near to the mark of inherent contradiction must be of the perfectionist type which postulates a union of 'opposite extremes', with a claim to embody the fully – 'totally', or 'integrally' – desirable and satisfying. A cat can be all black, all white, all grey tiger, and so forth, or black and white, or particoloured in various ways up to the bizarrerie of a tortoiseshell with white and striped ginger patches, but the selfsame cat cannot possess the peculiar loveliness of, say, an all-black *and* that of an all-white, an all-blue, an all-ginger and an all-tortoiseshell fur. It is easier to dream of a perfect state of man incorporating both complete determination and pure spontaneity. Even in personal projects of life, highly strung utopianism is quite possible. A man may jointly pursue several ambitious goals which are in fact incompatible with his circumstances, and also intrinsically inconsistent: thus, social grandeur with the corresponding display of high living, and sovereign spirituality along with high thinking. Whatever the outcome may be, it will be widely different from the proposed aim, which cannot consistently be thought out, let alone achieved. Spiritual and moral corruption, intellectual dishonesty and a tissue of false pretensions are more likely to develop here than in the case of a man who, from the outset, has had in view little more than worldly ambitions; or again, a *compromise* between more modest and limited demands of comfort and security on the other. Yet, Utopia being a negation of Reality but utopian endeavour itself a reality, the life of our overstrung man, while blighted with a peculiar sickness of pervasive falsehood and *inconscience*, may at the same time actually reflect something of the splendour for which he has craved: to wit, the fact of his unrealizable but powerful intention.

An attitude is not a proposition or a set of propositions; it cannot as such, and as a whole, be proved or disproved; it cannot be contradictory in the strict and definitively annulling sense in which a theory can; it may depend more or less centrally on a contradiction (or several contradictions), and accordingly admit of 'degrees of contradiction'. Notwithstanding the contradiction implicit in the perfectionist fallacy – the contradiction, that is, between the claim to the plenitude of value and the corresponding readiness to put up with a lowered form of actual value-experience – perfectionism as such, with its range of choice between particular variants and incompatible poles, is less markedly contradictory than utopianism, that is, perfectionism as underlying a comprehensive vision of Society. 'Do the right thing regardless of consequences', for example, savours of moralist perfectionism inasmuch as it holds out the promise of a short-circuited 'moral perfection' or 'complete goodness' infallibly attainable, independent of circumstances, and possible in any kind of world; and also bears upon it an aspect of contradiction, since conduct as such *implies* a weighing of consequences; but it is unsuited to the utopian idea of a perfect society, and falls short of the utopian contradiction between the spontaneous goodness of all and the planned adjustment of all wants and preferences. The basic formal concept of Utopia itself exhibits a supreme contradiction not necessarily present in perfectionist attitudes: on the one hand, Utopia is 'nowhere', 'out of place' – too good, as it were, to be spatially located, an imaginary island separated from the world; on the other it is meant to be the full realization of Man, mankind as a whole; indeed, a cosmic empire (the contradiction is well brought out in Bruno Goetz's book-title *Das Reich ohne Raum* ['The Non-Spatial Empire']).

The question may be raised how far a practical position is nullified – proved evil or deleterious – by its logical 'refutation' in the sense of an exposure of the contradictions which mar its conceptual structure. Clearly, a false consciousness is a bad thing in itself, and dangerous inasmuch as it tends to breed misguided efforts and blur the sense of proportions in matters of moral emphasis. But not every attitude linked with contradiction is essentially condemnable or harmful. Thus, to my mind St Augustine's maxim 'Hate the sin but love the sinner' involves contradiction unless we resort to very artificial interpretations, for sin is not to the sinner what illness or misfortune are to the patient or the unlucky man, but (if its concept is to have any meaning at all) an essential, though not total, expression of the sinner's character, and so far qualitatively *identical* with him; hence indeed some act upon this principle in the fashion of excessively hating sin (and treating the sinner too harshly) in one case, while illegitimately loving the sinner (and condoning his sin) in another, according to their convenience; yet a morally sound and enlightened person who is not very exacting when it comes to logical rigour may profess Augustine's principle and translate it into the right kind of conduct, never excusing or explaining away moral evil but also never forgetting the universal commandment of charity, and never seeing in a sinner the sinner *alone*. It is different with contradiction pervading a comprehensive outlook upon life, or lying at the core of an ideological system which claims a universal directive force. The acceptance of contradiction – which, on such a supposition, must be somehow, and may be keenly, present to the subject's mind – means here that the subject refuses to acknowledge the rational test of consistency and, so far as his dominant practical themes are concerned, is in principle beyond the reach of argument: he may pursue preposterous or unrealizable aims while strenuously believing in success, to his own and to other people's cost; he may perpetrate, promote or whitewash satanic crimes in the belief that he is serving the cause of Good against Evil (in contrast both with the frail sinner and with the depraved miscreant). The moral guilt of such an agent is beside the point: we are dealing only with the practical, including moral, danger of ideological conceptions which involve contradiction. The practical complement of accepted contradiction is the ineffectiveness of balancing counterpoises – the exclusion of countervailing points of view – in the face of a seductive and obsessive appeal with the charm of rational evidence, moral heroism or spiritual splendour about it.

Acceptance of contradiction is closely linked, in the practical order, to the negation of the principle of *primum non nocere* [not to injure has priority] and of urgency: that is to say, the negation of the primacy of refraining from harmful and evil actions, and attending to the most pressing and obviously present tasks of reform and relief as contrasted with perfectional visions, exalted aspirations and all-inclusive plans. The contradictions implicit in pursuing gratuitous aims of supreme and universal happiness while wilfully inflicting suffering and disregarding men's actual wishes, or being satisfied with nothing less than a radical elimination of moral Wrong while flouting the rules of ordinary morality, do not disturb the utopian mind; rather, it derives from the experience of excessive evil a confirmation of its being committed to the total Good as distinct from doubtful, 'impure' and fragmentary realizations of the good. Again, given a certain degree of utopian tension and range of ambition (as opposed to mere moral idealisms and neatly determined partial aims bearing the primary emphasis, though fortified with perfectionist fallacies such as 'the just cause is sure to win'), contradiction between moralistic and immoralistic principles is likely to work out in favour of the latter, owing to their more direct linkage with manifest and impressive effects. It is easier to destroy than to create, easier to oppress (in a way bound up with some specious experience of liberty) than to establish and to foster liberty, and easier to mistake reckless beastliness for angelic grandeur than to credit lofty and scrupulous virtue with the pervasive and spectacular effectiveness it sorely lacks. If I may put it in metaphysical language, it is not correct to say that Evil is stronger than Good, but the reason why this is not so lies in the quasi-natural inclination of men to condemn Evil and to support Good in opposition to it; once Evil is admitted on a level with Good as a counterpart and a reflection of it, an *a priori* legitimate 'means' to good 'ends', it is likely to prove stronger than Good. Yet the central contradiction of utopianism lies not between Good and Evil equally willed but in the perfectionist concept of Good which implies, at the same time, an abstractive negation of reality and a full identification of itself with reality.

Utopia is 'nowhere': it is outside reality; a wish-world, in discontinuity with the real world, whose attractive features (not so much necessarily 'attractive' as meant to be evidently and incontrovertibly admirable and impressive) are perfectional symbols of a harmonious cosmos strikingly and defiantly dissimilar not to any given set of social spaces and times but to that which is unchanging in the structure of human reality. It is transcendent to 'this world': a 'kingdom of heaven' over and above tension, split, conflict, anxiety, want and remorse. But it is also 'of' this world – nay, more of this world than any ordinary reality in that it is meant to represent a self-contained, self-sufficient and definitively 'valid', 'fulfilled', terrestrial human world envisioned by the human mind and embodying a race of men whose only mode of existence is to live out their humanity fully and uninhibitedly. Moreover, utopian endeavour aims at converting this world into a non-worldly world with a transcendent, an abruptly different basic constitution, and therefore unknowable and unjudgeable for us except in the abstract, empty and purely postulatory sense of being by definition 'wholly other': non-worldly, splitless and tensionless. We set, then, as Utopians, our hearts on something out of context with our actually experienced concerns, strivings and satisfactions. We are trying to predestine for happiness and perfection a future kind of sentient beings quite unlike ourselves. As a bizarre pastime, this would not appear to imply contradiction; but it is done in the spirit of thus fulfilling somehow the meaning of our own lives and procuring a vicarious supreme satisfaction to ourselves, which does imply a kind of willing what we do not want, or wanting what we do not need, or believing ourselves to want what we know we do not want.

An attitude or a preference, however – let us remind ourselves once more – cannot be defined in terms of beliefs alone, contradictory or not, nor, in strictness, be logically disproved. Suppose this is precisely what we find inspiring and worthwhile: an aim with so boldly contrasting aspects as to evoke a sense of contradiction – otherwise, why should we be engaged in the pursuit? After all, a man is not always of one mind, nor does he want only what he can quite obviously and unparadoxically want, in everyday life. One may massively and without any countervailing desire want a meal when one is hungry, no doubt; but all endeavours are not of this kind. What point is there in many a man's drudging all through his life to amass wealth that will give him security for a brief remainder of years but no longer a life of enjoyment, or very little of it; or work in order to provide for his children a life of higher level and richer content which he cannot himself share, dead or even while he is still alive?

But, for one thing, it is part of my position that utopianism, virtually and inchoately present in our outlook and will as such, is an aboriginal possibility of the human mind, a temptation and a vice besetting Practice as such; and, secondly, the paradoxical or even preposterous types of ordinary human volition, with the disproportion and the *risk* of self-stultifyingness they may exhibit, fall short of the radical discontinuity and surrender of identity which underlie the utopian contradiction. It is one thing, say, to stretch my loyalty towards my family or country to the point of risking (or sacrificing) my life for their sake; another to seek the fulfilment of my own life in the 'perfect' life of an unreal realm of the future, the perfect complexion of which depends, in its turn, on my conceptual stipulations. As Utopians, we do not love a country as patriots, or admirers of some foreign land; nor do we want things for ourselves, our friends or next of kin, even seen in the perspective of our children's or our country's surviving us.

We want to create the object we *might* love if it existed, and want something that is not a compound or derivative of the things we actually want for ourselves and our fellows, nor a thing or aggregate of things which a strange race wants us − urges or entreats us − to procure for it.

To be sure, the utopian will cannot be contradictory altogether and in the strictest sense of the term; for it would not then, whereas it does in fact, exist and operate in reality. I should like to buy this book, but should also like to keep the money it costs: a trivial everyday conflict of desires which clash but involve no contradiction; but I cannot properly *will* to do both. Nor do utopian fanatics decide never to eat or never to clothe their children any more; they go on living, because they are human beings as well, and also because they could not otherwise plan and labour for Utopia. But this specific and comprehensive aspect prevails − a will to bring into existence reality contrary to the constitution of reality, and to represent the supreme satisfaction of man out of correspondence with the wealth of things men want. So far as such a will takes effect, it cannot be other than falsifying, obscurantist, misdirecting and tyrannical. Yet there must be some logical bond between what can be thus powerfully willed while 'at bottom nobody wants it' and what men in general really *do* want.

It is psychologically difficult to answer the appeal of the concept of Perfection with a resolute *No*; yet, as we have seen, the perfectionist emphasis runs counter to the experience of Value. Transposed into terms of a more explicit and fixed utopian attitude, of utopian *action*, that appeal takes the form of envisioning a state of man in which he has absolutely everything he may want. Surely this abstractive step from 'wanting a determinate thing here and now' to 'wanting to be able to get what I want' is entirely rational, legitimate and realistic; to condemn it would amount to condemning the use of instrumental and, in particular, of storable, convertible and many-valued goods such as machines, money and, indeed, corporative statutes and social connections. But the painful hiatus between wanting and having − the presence of imperfection, or one most prominent and universal aspect of it − is inherent in the human condition and in the very logic of our relation with goods (in the widest sense): if we had no psychic, prudential and moral defects we should have no laws, rules and statutes; if there were no scarcity of goods and services, no meaning could attach to money; if the individual's position and its adjustment to the needs of others were not a problematical matter (the problem being largely insoluble *per se*), status, office and connections would likewise lose their meaning; the idea of infused wisdom without hard study and 'trial and error', or of genius without one-sidedness, as well as the idea of a general and unlimited availability of the manifold primary goods we know, evoke in us, if we try to think them out, a sense of dullness, emptiness, unreality and self-contradiction. The concept of a good we can turn to *many* uses is meaningful, and so is the concept of a state of man globally higher than others known in history, including our own – though the more global the perspective of appreciation, the more uncertain the basis of comparison must become. But the concept of *getting* what we may want is empty except by reference to the things we *do* want; and the concept of a state in which we were sure of having, by preordained harmony, what*ever* we may want appears to be cut loose altogether from reference to our manifold actual wants. It suggests the prospect of our having been reduced, ourselves, to ghostly and degraded beings with an utterly drab and jejune experience of values; and, posited as a sovereign aim, it conjures up the idea of a will representative at once of wanting every imaginable thing and of wanting nothing in particular: a will not absolutely and analytically but *somehow essentially self-contradictory*. This is what I mean by the Utopian Contradiction: a central vice of utopianism, yet not incompatible with its existence as a psychic temptation and an effective social reality.[10]

(iii) The incongruities of ordinary Practice
It is not only fair but suited to my purpose to remember, at this stage, that the 'Common-sense attitude' or 'ordinary Practice' – or, shall I say, the characteristically non-utopian mode of thinking and willing – also evokes some standard doubts about its logical consistency and rational defensibility. The practical outlook of the 'rational animal' as a whole – for man can roughly be described (though not, I think, 'defined') in these time-honoured terms – is shot through with irrationality, or at any rate with points of questionable rationality, not only in the trivial sense that many people are remarkably foolish and everybody may behave

foolishly on occasion, but in a constitutive and ineludible general sense. However distorted into a gospel of nihilist and immoralist demonolatry, the existentialist thesis about the 'absurdity' of human life and endeavour contains a grain of truth, long known both to deeper and more contemplative religious thinkers ('Vanity of vanities') and to disillusioned cynical wits, but often overlooked by unreflective 'practical people' and methodically concealed by the professionals of theological, educational, scientific, commercial and political pragmatism and complacency.

Ourselves and our goods, satisfactions, aims and efforts are finite, limited, transient, perishable, tiny and tenuous things, yet wedded to stubborn biological urges and the more self-assertive as we cannot help apprehending the world and formulating our claims and anxieties in terms of universal concepts. We cannot manage our elemental, much less our higher, concerns unless we set them – partly, at least – in a perspective of quasi-absolute importance and of eternity; we strive desperately for possessions which are anyhow bound to vanish some day, and must ponder many of our decisions with a care suggesting, as it were, the fictitious assumption that the fate of the world depends upon them. We are continually confronted with practical problems which we are far from able to resolve with unequivocal certitude but which ineluctably demand a one-way choice, as if the course chosen could be the definitely 'right' and the other the definitely 'wrong' one: thus a man may be faced with the choice of establishing himself either in Paris or in Munich, with much to say in favour and in disfavour of either; it does not by any means follow that he can choose Basle as a midway 'solution'. We must, then, somehow arbitrarily treat the insoluble as if it were soluble. Our actions may be cleverly calculated (and at the same time morally impeccable), yet backlashing or 'contraproductive' by virtue of their unforeseeable (or even dimly foreseeable) consequences. As moral men with a sensitive conscience, it is still problematic whether we can avoid moral *guilt* altogether, but it is quite certain that we cannot avoid exhibiting certain moral disvalues and doing some amount of harm; much less can we avoid a good deal of social symbiosis and involuntary (but not necessarily unconscious) co-operation with grave moral evil. Some of our goals recede or become meaningless in proportion as we approach them. A lover is naturally jealous, yet either there isn't any ground for his being jealous or, if there is, he no longer has any right to be jealous (Karl Kraus). Our affections are, as many would agree, our most precious treasures, but they make us subject to endless suffering and condemn us to many deaths while we are alive: 'Give not thy heart to a dog to tear' (Kipling).

These incongruities of human existence, with their marginal areas of absurdity or inconsistency which might sometimes be construed into contradictions, are essentially irremovable. Many more could be enumerated; some may be tempered by practical wisdom, moral virtue and institutional reforms. Religious faith and a spiritual life shaped by it *can*, as many of us think, supply wisdom and virtue with more ample foundations and more satisfying perspectives; but religion introduces new problems and paradoxes of its own, and unfolds its action – helpful and ennobling, but not unconditionally so – *within* the context of this scarred and pitted world of ours: this *status viae* in which we have to, want to, and by religion itself are told to, live out our earthly lives. The false heaven of Utopia must not be seen against the background of a true heaven in whose possession we were living but for the intervention of utopian folly. A utopian critique of Utopia is invalid. The utopian war against reality cannot be countered by a forced interpretation of reality as Utopia already accomplished.

Our ordinary 'workaday' attitudes, arising as they do in the context of our particular concerns in the framework of real life and meaningless in the context of a desire to exchange reality against another kind of reality, escape the snare of the utopian *coincidentia oppositorum*. The incongruities they involve are – to repeat an expression I have used above – 'marginal': they envelop our practice, as it were, and attach to various special aspects of it, but they do not constitute its very stuff and dominant motif. Thus, we are corporeal and spiritual beings, and this involves tension, incongruence and even a virtuality of contradiction. There is, for example, something 'absurd' about our being conspicuously subject to bodily needs, urges and ailments while 'dedicating' ourselves to spiritual concerns, and a man may *feel* rather deeply, almost at the same moment, that he *is* his body and that it is only the spiritual that *matters*. But it belongs to the utopian as opposed to the common-sense outlook to vision away the tension between the two poles, conceiving of man as a being of *uninhibited* corporeality and *unencumbered* spirituality. Again, it strikes us as slightly illogical, once we bring the two different contexts into one conspectus, that we should emphatically try to escape from danger of death whereas we know that eventually we have to die anyhow – and it makes little difference, in this respect, if we believe in the immortality of the soul, though we then also tell ourselves that our death does not mean, anyhow, the end of everything for us – but this state of consciousness is not really fraught with contradiction unless we commit ourselves to the dogma that nothing temporal can be worth anything.

The utopian tendency may be either to expect the creation of an immortal human race or to plan for a total oneness of the individual soul with that of Society, or again to slur over the 'occurrence' of death, thus maintaining the fiction of a human existence cleansed from its ineliminable tragic and catastrophic feature. Again, the incongruity of having to take unequivocal decisions in spite of the incertitude of practical judgements implies no contradiction except on the perfectionist view that practice should not only be reasonable but also be rationally deducible from the concept of what we need plus fact-knowledge, so that our acting upon an uncertain estimate would contradict our feeling 'I'd better do *this*' – an idea of practice utterly at variance with the constitutive features of human practice as we are able to imagine it. Yet again, there is something paradoxical about the fact that we are morally obliged to follow our conscience while our conscience may be erroneous – nay, in some fashion ungenuine or perverted – and the fact that we may, and at times do, disobey the command of our conscience, even though its utterance be incisive and unequivocal. But this state of things, far from amounting to a contradiction proper, is connected with the very nature of conscience, which is essentially neither identical with the agent's will nor, on the other hand, independent of his moral quality; thus it can be both disregarded and come to be distorted, and is always fallible though somehow representative of the moral claim as recognized by the agent. It is the utopian conception of morality *without* a cleavage in man – without 'the jar of right and wrong' – and thus of a morality without conscience which is properly self-contradictory. To be sure, that contradiction can be made to disappear by substituting for the only concept of 'morality' that is meaningful to us an utterly different concept of unchallenged and perfect 'goodness' in whose orbit the moral theme of right and wrong does not arise at all. In this way, the moral self-contradiction of utopianism reduces to the fundamental utopian contradiction implicit in the concept of an endeavour starting from and operating in the context of reality yet directed to aims devoid of meaning in that context except for their psychological association with the purely formal abstract idea of 'supreme desirability'.

To sum up. The manifold *scissure* (split-ness, as it were) of man in his mundane existence is apt to arouse in various ways a sense of contradiction or, more properly, a sense of imperfection, limitation, tenuity and incongruity, including, notably, the incongruity between the frailness, futility and dispersion of man on the one hand and his partial possessions of value, height, satisfaction, union, power and achieved progress on the other, which make him an essentially 'aspiring' being again and again exposed to disappointment and foundering on the hard cliffs of reality. Utopianism rejects the common-sense *submission* to the human condition and 'pursuit of the Good' *on its terms*, erecting in its place the idol of a perfect human condition which would not be a human condition and which demands the *self-surrender* of man to an alien, unreal and (as to its actual features) inconceivable construct of his abstractive mind. Linked therewith is a mirage of the all-comprehensive perfect Good, discontinuous and out of tune with man's actual pursuit of value-achievements in the framework of a reality which is not identical with the Good but logically inseparable from any meaning man may attribute to it.

(iv) The non-utopian pursuit of the Good

Obviously, everyday practice in the service of current 'need-fulfilment' has nothing utopian about it, even though it be the everyday practice of people with strongly utopian mental tendencies or people devoted to some fixed conception of subversive utopianism. The qualification is necessary, however, that the management of even very ordinary concerns may be strongly infiltrated by perfectionist schemata such as 'a just cause is sure to conquer', 'a calamity must be due to some mistake which could have been avoided', and the like.[11] In this concluding passage of the present chapter, I would point to *some characteristic*

aspects of Non-Utopian Practice in an ampler sense, including more
extensive, ambitious and specialized forms of the 'pursuit of the
Good' beyond the mere current business of life.

A non-utopian spirit of Practice will, in the first place, be
characterized by *awareness of imperfection*, not only as regards the
'goodness' (the worthiness, capacities, virtues, and so on) of the
agent himself but also as regards the 'goodness' of the intended
aims and the conceptions, projects and prospects they imply.
Awareness of incertitude, risks, drawbacks and the possibility of
relevant unforeseen consequences is part thereof. So is awareness
– it may be called 'meta-perspective' – of other concerns of
the agent, not belonging to the given thematic field of his
action, but perhaps of paramount importance to him or to his
associates or whatever other communities in whose interests he
may share. In other words yet, a non-utopian agent is conscious
of his practical subjectivity, howsoever buttressed by objective
justifications, universal directives and consensual appreciations and
concepts of value. He knows that his 'pursuit of the Good' must
involve *his decisions* - considered and arguable decisions, to be sure,
but still decisions proper, which might have fallen differently, and
which are not a clear and quasi-necessary self-realization of 'the
Good' through the instrumentality of his infallible wisdom or
unproblematic inspiration. This is by no means meant to convey an
appeal for inaction, or any discouragement from bold, zestful and
far-sighted initiatives, or from single-minded and heroic efforts.
The point is precisely that a man's worth – his vital level, his
power of decision, his practical reason, his strength of character
and stamina – shows itself, not least, in his ability to endure
incertitude and the ambiguity of values and hopes, to engage in
sustained and vigorous action in spite of countervailing aspects, to
reason out a situation or a broader conspectus of practice without
rationalist illusion, to stand by his preferences as such (legitimate
but incapable of 'proof') and, as it were, to give his wholehearted
devotion to limited aims, and pursue strenuously what he knows
to be finite, fragile, and in some way problematical goods.

It has not been my intention in the foregoing lines to draw a
portrait of the ideal 'non-utopian' man of my predilection, to
adumbrate a set of the axioms of practice or to propound a
table of recommendations;[12] least of all, to claim to possess the

secret of optimum success in life. What I emphasize is, rather, that a young hero nursing bold dreams of conquest, an ambitious man of talent in any walk of life, a reformer sworn to the cause of righting a definite system of wrongs or raising a dispossessed social group to a respectable level of life, the champion of one social group or nationality or type of culture as against its rival, a musing imaginative artist or a contemplative, disinterested thinker may *alike* be guided by (predominantly) non-utopian conceptions. Supposing that my formulations of the anti-utopian criteria of 'awareness of imperfection', 'consciousness of subjectivity' and 'acceptance of limitation and incertitude' were to exercise a practical effect on a certain number of people, this might in some cases be a paralysing effect, deterring the hearer from actions of a wider range and from highly consequential planning by confronting him more keenly with the necessity of relying on his decisions and diminishing his assurance; but in others it might equally be a stimulating and encouraging effect, accessible to the insight that it is worthwhile – and the only reasonable conception of practice – to act and to pursue high aims on *non*-perfectionist assumptions.

Again, the 'non-utopian pursuit of the Good' will bear a *pluralist* sign as contrasted to a monist and reductionist confusion of value-categories or the postulatory fiction that what is 'really' good from one point of view *must* also be good from another relevant point of view. (This is not to say that such happy solutions never exist and are not to be looked for; on the contrary, to find quasi-natural unions of values and combinations of utilities is what practical skill largely consists in.) One aspect of pluralism will manifest itself in the linking-up of long-term perspectives with short-term calculations, immediate experiences of value, the realization of urgent needs and the sense of intrinsic obligation apart from determinate advantages. It is repugnant to the non-utopian mind to think in terms of abstract and general values or aims projected into a distant future – out of time, as it were – without connecting them up manifoldly with direct intuitive valuations and needs or demands felt to be a present reality or, at any rate, an impending desirability continuous with the problems of the present situation.

So far as the 'pursuit of the Good' implies change in the sense of specific, abrupt, large-scale reforms, institutional or not – turning points or changes of direction, as it were – non-utopian thought will conceive and devise them within a framework of *constants* – of a given and accepted structure of realities, values and goods, that is – as opposed to total concepts of reversal and renovation. The antithesis is not a tactical but a logical one. The acceptance of a groundwork of invariables is not a stratagem applied in order to allow the desired change (or set of changes) to slip in more imperceptibly and comfortably, with less resistance to overcome; rather, it is what renders it possible for the change to be meaningful, for without a relative fixity of standards and a general permanence of their background and environment in reality, no change is susceptible of appraisal and no reform can lay claim to the character of an improvement. Anything so far established that comes to be questioned – owing to the rise of new value-experiences and sensibilities, or to dislocations in the texture of factual reality which call for a rearrangement of valuations and codes – can be questioned meaningfully, and with a view to arriving at a relevant judgement of it, only by reference to other established things which are not themselves questioned in the same breath. No doubt, un-utopian activities of reform will often have to extend their scale in the process of their execution, or even of their conception, perhaps far beyond the primary need for change or demand for redress or enhancement which has been their point of departure; while, on the other hand, utopian planning and subversion also make use, psychologically, of such presupposed and ambiguously maintained constants as a given society, a set of urgent or fashionable problems of practice, or again, value-categories capable of widely different and breezy or fuzzy interpretations like 'prosperity', 'justice' or 'culture'. But the utopian emphasis lies on the vision of a perfectional value-reality in contraposition to given realities, valuations and goods as such, including specified areas of change and limited themes of reform; whereas the non-utopian 'pursuit of the Good', concerned with the authenticity of the values it means to implant into reality as distinct from the concept of a consummate value-reality, is focused on singled-out 'variables', in the context of a given and accepted world, as the fit object of reformatory endeavour.

Respect for universal and intrinsic *moral laws*, especially as regards their basic prohibitive meaning and emphasis ('Thou shalt not …'), constitutes an obvious corollary to the anti-utopian principles of the incertitude of practice, of limitation, of pluralism, and of the recognition of constants and selection of reformable variants within their context. All negation of moral 'absolutes', standing out in sharp relief amidst the malleable stuff of practice and providing a schema of fixed boundaries within the flux of yearning, aiming and planning, savours of utopianism – thus, utilitarian or evolutionist ethics – although, of course, a rejection of intuitional and deontic morality does not, as such, amount to utopianism, and Utopia cannot be defined or exhaustively described in its terms.

Lastly, it is natural to the non-utopian 'pursuit of the Good' to be conceived in *adjustment* to the desires, preferences and valuations of persons *other than the agent*. This does not mean anything like the superstitious beliefs that the 'general will' or 'the people's verdict' are infallible, or that 'the majority' is always 'right'; neither does it imply that a Prince enacting a salutary measure over the opposition of an ill-advised public opinion must be of utopian will; and least of all, that in general my opinions are 'true' in so far as they conform to a fixed body of traditional views or are derived from the fashion of the moment, sensed directly or farcically computed by opinion-pollsters. What is meant is only the *anti-tyrannical*, but not, therefore, necessarily democratic or hedonistic, Aristotelian principle that men's apprehension and pursuit of the Good cannot be conceived, instituted and guided independently of their appetites. (Which again by no means commits us to the Aristotelian myth of an objectified universal 'Good' to which all appetites are 'ultimately' directed, and in whose terms Morality also can be accounted for.)– Sacrifices can be exacted legitimately, sensibilities awakened and tastes educated meaningfully, but men cannot be made to 'pursue *the Good*' by their subjection to a perfection-idol thought up by a visionary Mind not theirs – that is, to pursue the Good against their own wishes, preferences, experiences of value and consensual standards. In other words, whereas the utopian mind is essentially solipsistic, bent on identifying its conception with a virtually unitary conception of the mind of Man and consequently, by its active impact on reality, on achieving an identity of the thinking and willing of mankind with its own, the non-utopian attitude is characterized by an irrevocable and sentient *awareness of alterity*. The non-utopian agent may aspire to significant unity by consonance and convergence – including the element of conviction, and not excluding a marginal role of coercion – but will abhor the idea of unity in the sense of indivision, something to be secured through the sweeping away of the differences, scissions and partition walls inherent in the state of a multisubjective mankind. He is aware that the minds of men can be neither a reflection of his own nor *one* 'other mind' at variance with his, as 'wrong' opposed to 'right'. He may naturally, on many grounds distinguish between preferable and inferior or deplorable, better and worse, inclinations, habits, traditions and standards in his closer and wider social environment, but not without losing sight of the great pluralist truth so wisely and strikingly put by Tennyson:

> And God fulfils Himself in many ways,
> Lest one good custom should corrupt the world.

Unity in the utopian sense of collective solipsism is, indeed, not only a thing of impossibility but also a false and self-contradictory object for the 'pursuit of the Good', for 'one good custom', prevailing throughout to the exclusion of others, could not but dry up the founts of 'goodness' in men by stifling their apprehension of the variety of aspects and tones of value, and thus inevitably 'corrupt' instead of ennobling them. The non-utopian agent may well fight for the *predominance* of a conception of his choice as against its rival or rivals, but not without strictly disavowing the delusional claim to re-create mankind in his own image.

3
The Utopian 'Godhead of Man'

1 IMPERFECTION AND EVIL
> *Evil thrives never better than when it is presided over by an ideal.*
> *(Karl Kraus, 1915)*

To the utopian idol of 'Perfection' as distinct from 'the Good' corresponds an essential inclination to confuse 'Imperfection' with 'Evil'. Visionary optimism and the Manichaeist critique of existing reality form, as we have seen, inseparable counterparts within the selfsame attitude, though the degree to which either is conspicuously emphasized may vary. But to approach the matter, as I am proposing to do now, through the *negative* terms of 'imperfection' and 'evil' appears to me to be the most apt method of prying into the utopian conception of morality and of action – beyond valuation, wishing, thoughts and hopes. For action depends eminently on the spur of *urgency* – the sense of having to get rid of an evil – and, not unrelated to that, of course, moral incentives in their most characteristic, genuine and effective forms are centred in the experience of 'sin', 'transgression', 'wrong', 'pollution', 'disgrace', and the like. There is no question of denying the metaphysical prius of 'the affirmative': the 'positive' presuppositions of being, value, goods, life, satisfactions, accomplishments, personality, goodwill, virtues, and so forth: in a word, of that which is *impaired*, disturbed, hurt, mutilated, disfigured or soiled by defect and evil. Nor is there any question of denying the obvious empirical fact of 'desiring a good thing and getting it' without having resented its absence as a torturing pain, or the existence of properly 'prescriptive' besides 'prohibitive' moral norms: of 'duties of commission' and 'sins of omission' in contrast with moral 'taboos' and the kinds of misconduct they bear upon; or again, of the value of charity, generosity, and high-minded designs besides that of self-control, detached objectivity, and virtuous abstention. Yet a feeling of *want* – rather than the anticipation of joy – is what most imperiously

compels action; and at the centre of the sense of moral obligation
lies not so much the goodness of fulfilling as the evilness of breaking
the law. The absence of what we really want is hard to bear; and
if prohibitive conscience tells us 'Thou shalt not do A: it is evil',
prescriptive conscience may still tell us 'Thou shalt do B: to omit
or evade it is evil'. Accordingly, utopianism, in translating itself
into a motive for action, will start with *rebellion* against Reality
as beset with non-moral evils and *condemnation* of the moral evil
which pervades its structure.

We shall presently see how this very attitude involves a confusion between moral and non-moral ('practical' in a stricter sense,
or 'prudential', or 'utilitarian') points of view; for the moment,
I would set aside *this* distinction and keep my attention fixed
on the more general one, not unrelated to it but challenged
even more fundamentally by the utopian mind: the distinction
between Imperfection and Evil, applicable to both the moral and
the non-moral fields of values. What do we mean, or perhaps
what various kinds of things do we mean, when we speak of
imperfection and of evil as distinct from each other? What does
utopianism mean in disregarding or denying the distinction, and
what consequences does this negation entail? I shall first give a very
brief and broad answer to the first question, then go on to answer
the second, and, in dealing with possible objections, try to clear up
what has been left in the dark as concerns the distinction itself.

Imperfection and evil are clearly not two classes of objects
like plants and animals, or even two types of sensation like
tearing pain and constricting pain; but neither are they merely
objectivized expressions for two different degrees of our aversion,
such as 'unpleasant things' and 'intolerable things'. No doubt, the
distinction leaves ample room for relativity, fluidity and transitional
forms: the same thing may be an imperfection in one context,
and an evil in another, and the change of circumstances and
perspectives may shift the status of a disvalue from 'imperfection'
to 'evil', or inversely. Any imperfection may be looked upon as a
virtual evil: vulnerability means the comparatively high probability
of suffering a wound. And evils are to some extent interpretable
as imperfections: thus, a moderate incidence of colds pertains
to the 'normal' imperfection of a healthy person's health. But
in some significant sense the distinction between the absence

of a good which should *fitly* be present and the presence of a positive evil which should *strictly* be absent remains an absolute one. Ignorance, however massive, is primarily an imperfection; error, however slight, is primarily an evil. A weak and untrained body is primarily an imperfection, however great reason it may give for anxiety; ever so slight a pain is primarily an evil. Drab moral mediocrity and lack of distinctive virtues (not of moral sense or conscience) is an imperfection; sin or an immoralist attitude are evils. Some evils must be tolerated (for some time, or indefinitely); while there is no reason why all imperfections should always be tolerated. For imperfection in the stronger and relevant sense of the word – the sense according to which it is not an 'imperfection' in a horse that it is not human, whereas it is an imperfection in a writer to lack a keen awareness of syntactic exigences – merges into evil, and the acquisition of a formerly 'missing' perfection may amount to something like 'liberation from an evil'; and again, the indirect or remote pressure of an evil that is 'kept in bounds' comes close to a mere imperfection of our being. Nevertheless, to have to put up with an evil is a painful necessity, while to be able to remedy an imperfection is a happy possibility. The vanishing of an imperfection is a 'net gain', a progress, an ascension; the elimination of an evil is, rather, in the nature of a restitution or compensation. *De facto*, we endure many evils and surmount many imperfections. Essentially, however, we experience evils as (so to speak) deadly alien bodies in our flesh, and the elimination of each, as a *prima facie* absolute; imperfections, on the contrary, as something inherent in our constitution or that of any particular kind of being or individual entity, considering their possible cure *prima facie* in the perspective of other important concerns and the finiteness of our resources. In the face of an evil, we first take up an unconditionally negative position, 'costs' being a later consideration; in the face of an imperfection, the question whether concentrating on fighting it would be worthwhile, or how far it might be dangerous and perhaps suicidal or at any rate unwise, arises immediately.

Roughly speaking, it is *prudent*, in the general framework of practice comprising both vital and moral points of view, to treat imperfections gingerly, conservatively, not attacking them except in a cautiously selective fashion; whereas in regard to evils an attitude of resolute hostility appears to be dictated by either a vital or a moral *imperative* (or both). Our concrete application of the distinction depends, according to case, on an immensity of data and circumstances, and is within wide limits a matter of arbitrary decision; but all normal practice, in its countless departments and various styles, is permeated by this basic duality. Now the optimist world-view of 'classicism', 'perfectionalism', or 'belief in a cosmic harmony' pretends to assimilate evil to mere imperfection; and this may lead to quietist resignation and to more gravely immoral consequences as well: such as a diminished capacity for moral indignation, connivance at corrupt practices in the guise of 'sublime wisdom', callous indifference to the suffering of others, and the cult of sloth and selfishness in general. But the similar confusion with an inverse emphasis which is engendered by properly utopian Perfectionism will work incomparably more destructive effects – tending, as it does, to subvert reality (instead of merely degrading it by false justifications) and to uproot morality in principle, turning it upside down, as it were (instead of merely making it anodyne and inoperative). In contraposition to the optimistic interpretation of the world as 'harmonious' and the corresponding reduction of evil to a status of mere imperfection – often mistaken for 'realism' and, by virtue of the resignation it fosters, for pessimism – the utopian attitude is, of course, optimistic in a more highly strung sense; this aspect is often stressed unilaterally by its conservative critics. The difference may be schematically expressed by a conceptual model like the following, crudely simplified and overdrawn as it undoubtedly is. Suppose I am ill: men of the quietist illusion will say that I need not be treated but should patiently bear with the imperfection, which is 'ultimately' ordained to my good and even more patently subserves 'the greater good of the whole' (nor is all this *entirely* false); in his turn, the utopian subversionist will say that by my illness the world as it is stands condemned, that a *really* harmonious world cleansed from the possibility of such monstrous evils can and must be substituted for it, and that it doesn't matter what sacrifices in terms of imperfect human welfare and conventional morality the process may demand – I may perhaps be killed instead of being treated, but this would happen so as to bring about a state of affairs in which I could not again become ill. I, the patient, definitely prefer the mockery of the first kind to the perfervid interest taken in my health by the second kind of quack.

Evils misread for mere imperfections will be interfered with too little and will too complacently be left alone; but imperfections resented as evils will be interfered with too much, and this means that the comparative importance of existing genuine evils will be underrated, and, worse, that new and greater evils will recklessly be wrought.

Of course, even the most extreme fanatics of utopian activism and totalitarianism do not actually think that World Revolution is the cure for every ill of every kind here and now, or at any time in the future; or that the aim of preventing influenza in men would by itself justify the slaughter of any number of them. Thought-patterns of this kind, however, accord with their turn of mind. More than any other brand of human power, one inspired by a strong and sincere faith in humanism can be lavish with human lives. It is highly characteristic of Marxism that while on the pragmatic plane it describes the 'class enemy' in terms of moral indignation, as an incarnation of fiendish evil (robbers, brigands, war criminals, and so on), its deeper philosophical concern is not to liberate the innocent proletariat from its bloodthirsty oppressors but to liberate *man* from its *imperfect condition* called 'alienation', and to implement the law of historical progress which guarantees his rise to the status of an integrated unity of mind and will. The imperfection of a tedious, bewildered, chance-dependent, inadequately 'fulfilled', somehow *unsatisfactory* existence of men is crystallized – or shall we say projected – into the shape of concrete bearers of massive and malicious evil proper, the theme of their ruthless extermination commanding the impetus of passion needed by 'History' for the overcoming of the imperfections which have so far circumscribed, disfigured, paralysed and adulterated the lives of men as such. The fact that the concept of the 'class enemy' is extended to embrace petty bourgeois, peasant owners, 'Social Fascists', deviators and class traitors, including unintelligent Communists, is not a self-refutation but a confirmation of the *genuine*, deeply and essentially utopian, Marxist theory. Imperfection is evil, and ruthless evil inspired by the purpose of suppressing imperfection is good.

But for utopian-minded aestheticist intellectuals, most of whom had no class affinity at all with the proletariat and very many of whom have hesitated to espouse or come definitely to reject the

Communist cause, Communism would never have attained its present hegemonic position in the world – or, indeed, any position worth speaking of. I remember a text written by one such man in Hungary – a consistent *non-Marxian*, and later for many years known, especially in America, as an anti–Bolshevist – in the autumn of 1918, on the death of a 'revolutionary syndicalist' friend of his:

> He would surely not see eye to eye, on all points, with Lenin and Trotsky … but, as surely, his soul was incomparably more in accord with the vision, terrible but full of greatness, of bleeding Russia than with the land of sleepy compromises on the Danube.

Imperfections are despicable irritants; great evils, specifically opposed to *them* at any rate, are above all *great*. This is the spirit I mean, and though it is most naturally and fruitfully political in emphasis, as a fountainhead and a tool of subversive tyranny, it is by no means confined to political contexts.

We all know moods of this kind in our private lives, and such moods may indeed have their justification; there are several reminders to this effect in the Gospels. Imperfections have an aspect of *insidious* evils: the habit of acquiescing in them too readily may render us insensitive to more serious and avoidable ills, and abjectly slow to resist them. Man not aspiring to greatness, not in living contact with aspirations after greatness, is in danger of losing his dignity and falling below acceptable ordinary standards. But to bear this in mind is one thing; a fundamental perversion of proportions is another. It is better to suffer want a little worse than one would otherwise have to (want amounting at times to an 'evil') than to go always and uniformly without luxury (a grievous 'imperfection') but, given a scarcity of means, solid austerity is absolutely preferable to a system of pretentious shams; it is far better not to be always meticulously correct than never to be generous, but to commit crimes or base actions in order that one may keep one's family in opulence, or to shower gifts on one's friends, is absolutely condemnable. The 'profit motive' for doing productive work, as contrasted with intrinsic, altruistic and spiritual motives, may be put down as an imperfection – and to circumscribe its radius of efficacy and destroy the fiction of its universality is a meaningful and noble endeavour indeed – whereas revolutionary spoliation and terror devoted to the aim (even if it were not an impossible one) of suppressing men's selfishness and desire for gain are monstrous crimes wilfully increasing the misery and indignity of the human condition. The utopian perversion, in confusing imperfection and evil, will operate both ways: attack imperfection as an intolerable evil, and justify evil as a 'transitory' and 'inevitable' means to the realization of the ideal, that is, the suppression of imperfections.

To return to the distinction between imperfection and evil as such. That distinction, falling short of a massive dichotomy and undefinable in terms of a single criterion, appears to me to exhibit five aspects which have one feature in common. It is this – that imperfection brings out the *'merely human' stature* of man, and evil, the *threat of annihilation* against which that human stature itself, with its implications of a relative permanence and of intrinsic worth, stands in need of being guarded.

(a) Obviously the distinction is *also* a matter of degree. Blindness or deafness, formally *prima facie* an imperfection, may well be called an evil by virtue of the greatness of the privation it constitutes. A slight pain, in spite of the 'positive' *novum* [new thing] it means, may well be felt as an imperfection attaching to a phase of one's existence, and even a severe acute illness I have suffered may remain in my experience as testifying to the imperfection rather than the 'badness' of my life. In a sense, small evils rather than great remind us of the insurmountable imperfection, the 'merely-humanness' of our condition. Mediocrity or 'moral failures' may irritate the perfectionist consciousness more than glaring sins or immoralist principles.

(b) Obviously again, *negative* defects bear a tinge of imperfection, and *positive* ones are more properly described as evils. The metaphysical interpretation of evil as 'the absence of good' may be beside the point: the Platonist, Augustinian or Thomist who clings to this formula of consolatory decency will still, when he goes down with smallpox, notice in his condition something more and worse than a diminution of this former appetite and vigour, and will similarly in practice appreciate the difference between a weak-willed man and a man of wicked will. But it is true that the line between what is 'negative' and what is 'positive' cannot always be drawn with self-evident ease. Are the nagging pains of hunger, the paralysing effects of cold (caused by want of food or, respectively, of fuel and appropriate clothing), something purely negative? How far is a 'weak heart' a purely negative, how far a lethally positive defect? Cannot faulty reasoning arise from sheer lack of brains or of intellectual training; incapacity to see the truth be underlain by a biased and perverse will? Habituation may induce us to experience an inveterate evil as a mere imperfection; the loss of a 'superfluous' good hitherto possessed impresses us as a positive infliction. Yet the distinction stands: boredom is one thing and torture another; lack of wine one would like to drink is quite different from being offered, and having to drink, a repulsive brew; an indolent and selfish ruling set, however afflicted with and conducive to positive evils, has an essentially more negative and imperfectional meaning than an insane or diabolical tyranny, though the latter in its turn may not be unconnected with primitivity, ignorance, and a sense of weakness. Again, the practical priority of avoiding positive evils over remedying negative wants is by no means absolute; it may be quite sensible and advisable to endure *some* special sufferings in order to obtain *some* 'extra' advantages. But under common sense it is a more urgent necessity, within proportions, to guard against superadditive evils than to accumulate missing perfections. To the utopian mind, this axiom suggests the idea of a fundamental resignation. Submission to imperfection, incongruity and limitation ratifies the fact that man is not all-powerful, all-wise and all-one – in short, divine; and positive evil is counted good in so far as it reveals the bankruptcy of reality as given. The fact that we are deficient is evil supreme; submission to tangible and substantive evils *may* reveal our determination to flout and our power to overcome an order of reality not made to order – not our own creation. In Marxian language: violence must be pushed to its extreme so that coercive power in society may vanish altogether. In existentialist language: our freedom of choice avers itself in our choosing 'gratuitously'

– in other words, perversely – as opposed to the rule-ridden 'unfreedom' of choosing what hurts less and debases less.

But indeed, why not choose the 'greater good' rather than 'lesser evil'? Because, I should answer – and only in such a frame of reference does the axiom of the primacy of evil hold at all – the most obtrusive evil determines the most urgent task. Maiming and corrupting evil has the first claim to be dealt with; and the farther out of context it is, the wider the space granted to our free selection of perfective or corrective purposes. Translated into 'positive' idiom, this is equivalent to the principle that the pursuit of the good, though never a mere assent to reality (as pre-utopian 'perfectionalist' thought would imply), has a meaning only *within*, not *regardless of*, reality. For it is under the pressure of positive evil that the protection of the value-assets established in reality become a paramount concern of practice. The taunt of imperfection elicits our aspiration after improvement; but the challenge of evil compels our basic affirmation of the good: the presupposition that conditions the meaning of reforms, ambitions and advancements within the bounds of actual and irrecusable reality.

(c)   We tend to describe defects as 'imperfections' rather than 'evils' in proportion as they appear to be *inherent in the constitution* of a real entity, for example, a person or a nation or culture. Thus it is with my morally unfavourable dispositions as distinct from my sins, or the incongruities and irrationalities in a pattern of social relationships, as distinct from the actual malpractices and abuses that may thrive on their soil. Again the distinction is anything but fictitious, and is nevertheless highly relative and often inapplicable except in an arbitrary and circumstantial manner: perhaps more so in regard to collectives than in regard to individuals, seeing that in the latter case it is easier to delimit 'natural' constants from voluntary acts and impositions from outside. Certainly the moral evil inherent in slavery could not be conjured out of existence or reduced to a mere imperfection by calling the slave system a 'peculiar institution'; yet one may well deplore, as many thoughtful observers have done, the violent crushing of the Confederacy and the type of civilization (with its likewise 'peculiar' noble and lovable traits) it represented.

The argument may cut both ways: if I ardently wish that the Bolshevist regimes of Totalitarian Terror be wiped off the earth, I do not know that I desire as unequivocally the extirpation of the collectivist systems of production and modes of life they have implanted in the unfortunate societies subject to their control, for I may respect an established style of existence which I find unsuited to my taste and believe to be objectively inferior in value. In general, the possibility (in principle, at least) of its elimination *not* implying the destruction of the organic inferiority of type or character to which it attaches appears to be one of the tests of 'evil' proper in contrast with 'imperfection'. In the medical context, I would sooner attack a 'disease' proper than the 'diathesis' which may give rise to it; in the political context, I incline to distinguish between a disgraceful rule and an objectionable social order; I would reserve energetic combative action for tasks in the nature of 'warding off a menace' and prefer advisory, adjuvant and adaptive methods in dealing with inadequacies and promoting wholesome change. No doubt, evils are real, and in fighting them we are fighting bits of reality, not merely trying to alter the bad features of a thing of reality we axiomatically want to maintain in its identity. Yet 'evil' is not primarily what constitutes the particular shape of a 'thing', the identity of 'individuals' (including social, cultural and institutional types) which make up the manifold texture of the world; it is, rather, a 'disturbing' attendant quality, a configuration of attitudes and intentions, a habit or relation more or less isolable from the 'individual' taken as an identical constant, an action detachable from the agent howsoever 'his own' and engaging his responsibility; an extraordinary or morbid condition, or again, an outer 'enemy' threatening the survival, integrity or welfare of the particular entity which lies in the focus of our practical perspective (of the given thematic situation) and commands our service or loyalty, or at any rate our attention. As bearers of a non-utopian will, then, we shall fight evils but not fight evil indiscriminately; fight evils with selective concentration, in response to the urgency of their presence in 'our' fields of action and their interference with what is or may somehow reasonably and naturally be made a province of 'our' concerns; not, however, wage war upon the existence of evils in the world, which pertains to the imperfection of reality, and is to all intents and purposes inseparable form the fact of its manifoldness, dividedness and richness in tensions. Fight evils, to put it differently, without – as the fallacy of radicalism would postulate it – transferring the same stress of hostility to their undergrowth and surrounding tangle of imperfections; and again oppose imperfections in a different key, as it were, in a way limited and modulated by their conceptual distinction from evil proper, attuned to the measure of their inseparability from given beings and their particular nature.

It may be rephrased thus: in the concept of Imperfection, the emphasis lies on the *bearer* or the *area* of defects, on a being whose constitution is not defined in terms of disvalues but is relatively inseparable from certain kinds thereof; whereas in the concept of Evil we experience disvalue, disorder, aggression, vice or error as *constituting*, seen in some significant perspective, a force in reality. For example, while no person as such may be regarded primarily and properly as 'a black-guard' analogously to his being a man of racial complexion X, nationality Y, and professional training Z, 'the criminal' or 'the villain of the piece' are, within limits, legitimate concepts of practice; and while tendencies such as unruliness, a taste for violence, disrespect for alien property, and aversion to orderly work are not themselves ghosts of evil stalking along the streets or across the countryside but are grafted on natural dispositions potentially good as well as evil (perhaps love of adventure and independence) peculiar to certain types of personality, an organized gang of ruffians defacing and tormenting some corner of the human world may well be described as a neatly identifiable, 'subsistent' force of evil. Over and above trying to disrupt and put out of harm's way now this, now that criminal gang – treating them as beads on a string, as it were – it may certainly also be a meaningful project to fight criminality on more general and preventive lines, wherever some conditions appear specially to favour it; now, the utopian mind will attach greater weight to this more problematic and optional task, and greater still to the more remote conditions underlying the first-named conditions, to alight on the 'faulty' social order – the intolerable imperfect condition *of man* – which is responsible for the occurrence of such imperfections as banditry.

(d)   Another point of distinction, though closely related to the above three, is that which concerns *limited* and *stationary* (let alone evanescent) evils on the one hand, *rising*, *expanding* and *aggressive* ones on the other. The former, in common-sense experience, approach the category of 'imperfections': they are more symbolic of mundane and human imperfection in general, with which we have to live; to attack them demands a more arbitrary decision than does resistance to new and advancing evil; the problem whether it is worthwhile, and not perhaps likely to do greater harm than good, is more in point. The distinction is self-explanatory, and may be interpreted as a variation on the theme of *urgency*. Perhaps it will be found, even by minds not deeply bitten with utopianism, that I am insisting too much on leaving the initiative to 'the enemy'. But why should I be war-minded in an aggressive sense, intent on planning for a world empire, rather than in a defensive sense, my attention focused on such enemies as really arise and offer a threat? Our field of discourse here is the subversive Manichaeism of the utopian mind (with its complement of perfective optimism), intolerant of the imperfection of reality with a corresponding loss of sensitivity to specific evils: it is not the problem of activity or practice in general. Fighting an enemy, in whatever sense, is not the only mode or aspect of our pursuits. Freely chosen high aims may be achieved, good deeds done, useful innovations carried out, beautiful things made, many kinds of values created or encouraged without being bitter about imperfections as if they reflected the presence of a salient and monstrous evil.

(e)   Finally, the distinction between imperfection and evil is significantly related, although by no means equivalent, to the distinction between '*the non-moral*' and '*the moral*'. That grave evils utterly remote from mere imperfection may be of a purely non-moral nature (whether preventable or not, whether in some way involving human causation or not) is a truism, and so is the existence of moral imperfections proper, for example some forms of levity, carelessness, vanity, or any kind of morally undesirable weakness that falls short of malice, corruption or unprincipled conduct, that is, wilful misdirection. Nevertheless, moral evil is 'positive' evil in a pre-eminent and distinctive sense of the word, in that it connotes an intentional *affirmation* of evil as such (be it even not 'for its own sake', which is the less frequent and less typical case, though not so rare as commonly thought), while non-moral evils, it might well be argued, are more of an inevitable concomitant of the imperfection, limitation and dividedness of reality. In an inaccurate and abridged phrasing, but not irrelevantly, it might be said that non-moral evil, including our own bodily and mental deficiencies, is only an evil we *suffer* from, while moral evil is that which we *do*; or that non-moral evil attaches to *condition*, moral evil to *action*. That much non-moral evil is *wrought* by immoral conduct (thus, the death or sufferings of criminals' and tyrants' victims) and that, on the other hand, we cannot help causing a good deal of non-moral evil knowingly *without* any moral misdirection or defect on our part (thus, by legitimately thwarting somebody's will or disappointing somebody's expectations, and so forth) cannot alter the fact that in one fundamental sense man is merely *subject to* non-moral evil, along with imperfection, but is the *author* of moral evil. No doubt, many non-moral evils, underlain by no moral guilt, could be avoided by greater insight and skill, apart from strength; and again, some morally undesirable states of fact cannot be avoided or mended at all, or certainly not by any degree of goodwill alone; still, in its essence or principally, non-moral evil is involuntary, and cannot be the object of blame except improperly or indirectly, whereas for moral evil the opposite holds. Perfectionist optimism tends to explain moral evil away: crime is a 'necessary' consequence of poverty; aggressive malice, of an inequalitarian and competitive social system; unchastity of overcrowded tenements or, in the rich, of socially compulsory idleness. But in the subversive bent of utopianism, the same confusion operates with an inverse emphasis. Imperfections and evils in general are 'blamed on' – with the full force of *blame* – morally faulty institutions and arrangements which are tainted with guilt and deserving of wrath. Or, at any rate, they are regarded with scornful impatience which, even if it is explicitly distinguished from the moral condemnation reserved for single criminal actions (or perhaps ruled out altogether as 'un-scientific'), has the colour and style of moral indignation. The imperfection of ordinary reality, of the non-utopian world, is equated to evil taken in its most proper and central sense. And – in conformity with the idealist mood which disregards the category of the permissible and ignores the thematic primacy of evil proper – perfection, including 'happiness', takes on – to recall a singularly unhappy phrase of R.L. Stevenson's – a specious and pretentious appearance of 'duty'.

2 THE MISUSE OF MORAL EMPHASIS

Moral experience in its primary, central and most evident form is 'negative' and non-comprehensive. His conscience accuses the agent of the evil he has done, and warns him against the evil he is tempted to do; it does not provide for him a personal plan of life. Moral laws and standards, more conspicuously prohibitive than prescriptive and prohibitive in their emphasis even where they are prescriptive (the moral emphasis of *pacta sunt servanda* [agreements must be kept] is focused on treachery rather than on a sanctification of contract-making, for instance; and the moral emphasis of patriotism is focused on treason rather than on one's normal attachment to one's country), brand certain kinds of conduct with the stigma of 'evil'. They do not impose on man a scheme of ends, pursuits, attitudes and institutions. There is, to be sure, an intimate compenetration between moral points of view and the immensely manifold human pursuit of values as a whole; but the latter – including its highest levels, such as religious assent, aesthetic experience, disinterested thought, or the shaping of personality – cannot be brought under the concept of moral imperatives, nor can these be made dependent on a conspectus of human aims and desirabilities as grasped by the private agent's or the political planner's mind. The moral law does not command me to create 'a moral world', and my interest in the moral tone of 'the world' does not license me to infringe the moral law in my actual conduct. My awareness of and attention to the morality of 'others' is certainly an indispensable and important part of my own morality and of my social practice, but it is secondary, variable and, beyond certain limits, optional rather than implicit in my duties (though it may still be commendable, and deeply experienced). No vision of an ultimate good or goodness or perfection of mankind can be justified in blurring the standards of good and evil as applicable to the intrinsic quality of my actions. For this I am responsible in a primary, direct and absolute sense (with the proviso that the measure in which my actions may be morally 'admirable', or 'well advised', or 'fertile', is not a matter of my free will). For the moral level of 'the world' I am, generally speaking, not responsible – or, to put it more exactly, am responsible only in an indirect, perspectivally limited, problematic and attenuated sense. Thus formulated, the principle is true in regard to everyone, including the man of civic and educative preoccupations, the philosopher and the political thinker, the ruler and the reformer.

'Idealist' presumption tends to see things in a different light: a sublime breed of men in place of straightforward normative morality; a 'moralized' world answering the 'moral claim' *of* man in place of the 'abstract' principle that man, any man in any context, shall recognize and honour the moral claim *on* man by pursuing legitimate ends in abstention from wrongdoing. But while religious or philosophical 'idealism' may content itself with diluting moral emphasis proper in a luxuriance of edifying and all-embracing speculations, and with relying on 'supra-moral' motives in the minds of the secure and the refined, the 'pious' or the 'enlightened'; while perfectionism may renounce moral emphasis, complacently superseding it with illusory conceptual constructions, the utopian *will*, with its insistence on a decisive rupture of continuity and an active subversion of reality, cannot so dispense with moral emphasis, which is one of the most potent and elemental incentives of human aspiration, a most deadly paralysing venom when used against any opponent thereof.

Utopian subversion, not itself moral in its deep primal motivations is strictly compelled, – and, indeed, not unnaturally inclines – to wield the combative, destructive weapon of moral appeal: rather than despise and 'soar above' moral emphasis, it will distort it into Manichaeist hatred of imperfect reality and the concrete supports of imperfection; rather than circumvent or uproot moral emphasis, it will misuse it by levelling it against the inadequate target of imperfection as opposed to its proper concentration upon genuine moral evil.

In other words, revolutionary disregard for moral norms requires a *moral* justification. Whether the language officially employed is that of '*vertu*', of 'social justice', of 'the liberation of mankind', of 'the fulfilment of the meaning of history'; whether opponents are abused as 'tyrants', 'exploiters', 'brigands' or 'traitors', Utopia presents the conflict between it and unregenerate, unredeemed, crude, contingent, mundane reality – between what is and what is not of itself – as an issue; or rather, *the* issue, joined between Good and Evil. Certainly the innermost theme is not morality; it is not the righting of definite wrongs, the punishment or stopping or prevention of crimes, the dispossession of scandalously immoral rulers: such motives may intervene in revolutions accidentally, or may even be the essential ones, but then rebellions and insurrections – or, indeed, 'revolutions' – may not be utopian at all, and should not as such be confused with 'the Revolution'. Nor is it a moral theme in the sense of moral education, reform, refinement, 'uplift' or 'humanization': that would inspire various kinds of social initiatives, propagandas and attempts at organization, but is unlikely to command the hatred needed as a leverage of social subversion. Rather, the utopian theme is a fundamentally 'other', perfect mode of man's being, which has an oblique and ambiguous relation with morality: it connotes a concept of moral perfection tied to the concept of overcoming the tension between Right and Wrong, of the elimination of sin-consciousness and of the moral imperative which entrenches upon man's spontaneous and self-contained pursuit of his vital concerns. Nor does utopianism in general pretend to be based on a properly and predominantly moral theme, such as enforcing respect for the Ten Commandments or the Golden Rule or *Honeste vivere* [A life with honour]; it often prefers non-moral to moral language, especially at a higher level of its self-expression: straightforward moral appeal, as also a crude appeal to the appetites, belong, rather, to the secondary terminology of popular agitation; and such direct terms of moral condemnation as 'tyrant', 'oppressor', 'thief' or even 'exploiter' are less peculiarly characteristic of its vocabulary than are words like 'aristocrats', 'bourgeois', 'surplus-value', 'anarchy of production' or 'private property' used with a vituperative intent. Utopian subversionism links up with the moral criticism applied to rulers, authorities and established institutions by what may be described as the leftist opposition; but the grand antithesis assimilated to Good and Evil is not, for the utopian mind, that between regard for others and (individual or group) selfishness, high-minded responsibility and cynical pleasure-seeking, justice and injustice, equity and heartless legalism, or even equality and inequality of rights: it is the antithesis between Itself and what is not Itself, 'my vision and my vision's enemy', Utopia and the world as Reality outside Utopia.

Because moral intuitions are essentially and irreducibly plural, and capable of mutual tension, any moral overemphasis entails the danger not only of practical unsoundness and unwisdom but of moral underemphasis and defaulting in other respects: harsh and loveless justice, and excessive benevolence to the detriment of justice and truthfulness are standard examples. This has nothing in itself to do with utopianism, except that blind and unconditional insistence on *one* dimension or aspect of morality may procure a false sense of 'unbroken' completeness, 'maximal' correctness or 'all-goodness', and thus correspond to a perfectionist illusion. However, social utopianism – that is, the goal of a perfect human *universe* beyond the presence of Wrong – embodies a mirage of 'the Good' incomparably more prodigious and bemusing than a mere one-sided moral concern, whose area of reference is no wider than the quality of the agent's own conduct and its effects upon his immediate environment. Such a goal, neither unconnected with ordinary moral concerns (such as justice, benevolence, self-dedication, and perhaps a formal concept of 'purity') nor in any way definable in their terms, towers so high above 'conventional' moral standards and conscientious scruples as to leave them without any autonomous validity and to make any moral restraint that may stand in the way of its pursuit appear part and parcel of the '*evil*' world it claims to supersede: the tangle of petty interests, prejudices and powers of inertia whose place it is called, and bound, to take. Moral emphasis is thus not only arbitrarily narrowed and sharpened into one particular direction but transferred to a principally non-moral – shall we way, a para-religious, 'anthropological', or 'metaphysico-historical' – aspiration, while retained with its specific sharp note so as to be misused for the *discrediting* as 'evil' of the non-utopian given reality. For it is a vital exigence of the utopian will that to surmount that reality shall impress its servants and the undecided or indifferent as being not only desirable, and not only perhaps a 'scientifically' demonstrable necessity, but a *duty*. In the perspective of its utopian counterpart, once erected into a goal of striving which can actually be willed, the imperfect world of men, of human nature operating in a medium of contingency, takes on the character of *evil*: the dark background which supplies Utopia with its moral credentials.

3 UTOPIAN HUBRIS AND THE CONFUSION BETWEEN MORALITY AND PRACTICE

If, on the one hand, the aim of establishing man as a sovereign Lord of his infallible and harmoniously happy Practice constitutes a paramount moral demand, nay, the epitome of Morality – non-utopian 'brute' reality being a mass of evil and a mess of impenetrable disorder, in whose midst particular and single pursuits of value are sterile and ineffectual – on the other hand, the right Practice, once attained, automatically implies and ensures moral perfection, thus making away with the necessity of taboos, obligations and self-critical conscience. While the philosophical confusion between Morality and Practice, between the theme of 'the goodness of man' and the theme of 'the good of man', is not necessarily utopian in inspiration – or not so except in a broad, virtual and inchoate sense – and is on the whole, perhaps, conservative rather than subversive in spirit, there may be few features more characteristic of utopian thought than the tendency to take the identification between the moral and the practical perspective of human action utterly seriously. The reason lies in the peculiarly thematic manifestation, by Morality as distinct from Practice, of the *split within Man* – and of Man's *submission* to that condition of splitness. This constitutes pre-eminently what is intolerable to the utopian consciousness, attached to the mirage of the godlike indivision of Man and all the more specifically opposed to man's acceptance of the scission as the right and sober mode of tempering its painfulness and controlling its possible disruptive effects: in other words, to his recognition of the Moral Laws.

To be sure, Practice itself reveals even more immediately and self-evidently the inner division and fragmentation of man, and also the necessity of his constantly dealing with that basic fact without any thought of its global elimination. The multifarious divergence of his desires and valuations, the ever-present tension between his aims – including that between his short-range and long-range values, or again that between his thematic perspectives – forces him constantly to choose and to renounce, to take risks and face incertitude, to endure delay, to accept compromise, to economize his resources, to limit his strivings, and to submit to limitations of all kinds. This precisely is called 'Practice' in the stricter sense of the word, as distinct from the tranquil enjoyment of a good already secured and completely satisfying here and now, in its own place, or from the unfettered flight of thought; or again, from the technical execution of a 'single action' complete in itself and, at the point of being carried out, dependent on no further choice. Now, without doubt, moral demands on the agent made valid from outside are assimilable to the category of outer pressures and impositions in general, and moral demands recognized as binding by the agent himself are correctly described as part of his own concerns, interests or preoccupations. Yet moral demands, even though they belong themselves to the *materia* of practice, at the same time 'trench' or 'impinge' upon the open texture of practice in a unique fashion, manifesting a new and entirely peculiar dimension of that dividedness and subjectness of man which utopianism is committed to suppress.

For moral demands are experienced as *unbarterable* 'absolutes'; not as a pursuit – albeit a noble one – within the agent's practice, but as imperative conditions of his practice's being justified, his pursuits' being valid, his status's being defensible at all. In the moral perspective, the agent has not the same latitude of choice as in the practical. Undoubtedly he has to make moral decisions in view of the frequent incompatibility between different *prima facie* moral demands relative to the same situation (say, between justice in a not wholly strict sense and the good of his friend, or next of kin); undoubtedly, on the other hand, even in practice outside the moral imperatives he is not restricted to the consideration of agreement and utility proper but is also confronted with the hierarchy of values, with high values which claim his reverence and dedication. Moral performance unfolds, and therefore moral intention itself operates, in the framework of practice; and practical, as distinct from purely technical, themes will seldom fail to connote at least a hidden, virtual or subtle moral point. Yet the fundamental contrast remains that flexibility is the normal and prevalent mode of practice, the agent being 'sovereign'; not, indeed, in regard to facts or to the world, but in regard to any of his particular concerns – sacrificing A to B or favouring A above B 'as he chooses', though as a rule he may be well advised to stick to such practical maxims as he happens to adopt, so far as they apply to the matter in hand – whereas the normal and prevalent language of morality is the imperative, the agent being not sovereign but subject, and responsible in regard to any moral law that has a bearing on his particular situation or theme of conduct, even though it may be objectively impossible for him to comply with it. Either he *bona fide* submits to the moral demand as best he can, or he is '*at fault*', whatever kind of 'penalty' that may entail and in whatever way and degree it affects him psychologically. The scission between *my will* and *my conscience* is capable of being healed from case to case, and even in a relatively permanent and stable fashion, by my outfit of 'good dispositions' and 'solid virtues'. But since I always remain *subject* to the moral imperatives, though I may for long periods comply with most or all of them 'gladly', spontaneously and without any notable inner opposition, the scission is never eliminable in any essential, final and total sense, and is of a quite different character from the scission implied in the multiplicity of my divergent concerns. Between these, I 'arbitrate' with a 'sovereignty' much like an owner's in the management of his estate; whereas in the moral perspective of my will under trial in the court of my conscience, I am *accountable* for my governance of my affairs in a way reminiscent of the position of a responsible agent, official or servant acting on instructions and disposing of goods which are not really 'his' but which he only holds in trust.

He may misuse his power – perhaps with impunity, or apparently so – but is powerless to oust the rightful owner and take his place himself; he may acquit himself well of his task, but even so he does not change his status and enchant himself into identity with the true Owner.

It should be added that moral experience presents us God as a *Deus absconditus* [hidden God], not as a Person Who addresses us in supernatural Revelation, much less as an object of our metaphysical construction; its deep background emphasis lies not on the perfection, power and goodness of the Lord but on *our not being*, ultimately, lords over our own lives, or mankind the Lord of the world. In Practice we are not, of course, actually independent of God; in Morality as such, outside religious faith, we are not formally and explicitly servants or children of God. But if the two were one – practice all suffused and sanctified with morality, or morality a mere function, epitome or abridgement of an immanently well-ordered practice – Man would look a great deal more like God; and for an incarnation of such a Wisdom-Goodness utopianism would reclaim him. The harmonious, concerted and infallible Practice of man – *another world* which *is* 'a kingdom of this world' – is installed as the cynosure of morality. Diversified moral rules, 'universal' and 'absolute', not linked to *this* projected or nascent world of perfection, are contemned as paralysing fetishes and philistine inhibitions. Just as all reductionist ethical theories attempt to 'prove' at least part of the consensual moral intuitions of mankind (the so-called 'conventions') as a consequence of something else, such as utility or conformity to nature or whatever other arbitrary axiom, the fabrications of utopian fantasy and subversive *hubris* always flaunt some morally pleasing aspects according to our 'conventional' conceptions of Good and Ill. But this is an accidental token and by-product, not an intrinsic test of the unique excellence they embody. Utopia is perfect not because it satisfies such and such traditional criteria but because it stands for perfection, and expresses the oneness in Man and his world of Being and Value. The city of Man, conceived as a structure without rents and fissures, is incompatible with those intractable grim reminders of man's imperfection, proneness to evil, incertitude and inward division: the moral rules. Human practice cannot attain to the stature of self-contained perfection so long as it has to rely on the crutch-like props and respect the hard barriers of autonomous morality which cannot be accounted for simply in terms of its own exigencies. The claim of morality proper must be denied; conscience must not be allowed to stand in the way of the planner's construction.

Some classic corollaries of the confusion between Morality and Practice which keep within the context of the appraisal of persons and of general value and disvalue qualities are irrelevant to utopianism: thus, the tendency (allied to Thomism, though not necessarily inherent in it) to mistake strength of will with a right direction of the will, prudence for virtue, and unruly sensual passion for *the* principle of moral evil; or again, the pious and gratuitous postulate that a man must be 'happy' in proportion as he is moral. Although a totalitarian flavour, in the wider sense of the word, is discernible in these and similar fallacies, they do not transgress the open perspective of 'abstract' universal principles of judgement applied to the actions and life of 'any' individual, and so far they remain in tune with ordinary standards of both morality and practical wisdom. On the contrary, what characterizes the utopian turn is the *en bloc* identification of morality with the practice of one specified – imagined, projected, or already emergent – world of perfection. It is not that Jones must be moral because he is clever and self-possessed, or that Jones, exhibiting features of great virtue, must be regarded as happy, but that Jones (the dreamer, warrior, engineer, ruler, or citizen, of the Higher as opposed to the Ordinary world, of the City of Man as opposed to the mundane medium of men) incarnates the Good because he represents that *different order of things* in which being and goodness, Is and Ought, Does and Does Right are *a priori* designed to *be identical*. The secret key is presumed to have been found to the realm in which, and by reference to which, practice is automatically sanctified.

EDITOR'S NOTE TO CHAPTER III

Indications as to how this chapter might have been finished are provided by the not wholly perspicuous 'Running notes', which I have mentioned in my introduction, and also by a list of section headings, which reads as follows:

1 Imperfection and Evil
2 The misuse of Moral Emphasis
3 The confusion between Morality and Practice
4 The Utopian negation of Conscience
5 Sin and Utopia
6 Ethical Relativism and Utopia
7 The misconception of Practice
8 Omniscience and Omnipotence
9 The non-transcendent Divinity
10 The mirage of the Future

This chapter was in fact projected as the fourth, and was to have been preceded by a modified version of The Moral Theme in Political Division, which constituted Chapter III. The other three chapters were entitled 'The Utopian Concept of Society', 'The Utopian Mind in Politics and Civilization' and 'The Anti-Utopian Consciousness'. It is, however, worth repeating here that many other projected versions of the book exist.

OTHER PAPERS

The Moral Theme in Political Division

1 MORALS, POLITICS AND CONTROVERSY

In this paper, I try to show that antithetic political positions appear to imply different moral attitudes not only accidentally but essentially, yet in a peculiar, limited and ambiguous fashion; and that political relativism or pluralism is far from implying moral relativism or pluralism in a corresponding and coextensive sense. In other words, the gist of my contention is that men may be agreed about the basic universal laws of morality and none the less (or, indeed, all the more significantly) differ in their response to various moral requirements and points of view as emerging in specified contexts of human practice. Political positions are not as such derived from moral demands, nor consequent upon moral errors; nor do they, as such, determine the moral convictions of those who hold them; but they tend to be associated with distinct kinds of dominant moral emphases rather than simply to respect or to disregard morality.

Although political life is partly made up of discussion and by no means of stark fighting and clear-cut clashes of interests alone, and while moral attitudes also involve discussion and dissension as contrasted with a straightforward application of indubitable universal rules, the domain of political positions is *controversial* in a primordial sense in which the domain of moral demands and appraisals is not. Political partisanship is not, logically, on an equal footing with moral belief and direction of conduct. This is, of course, most conspicuous in the medium of the multi-party constitutional state, in which political opinions are presumed to be optional, whereas morality is characterized by our considering some kinds of conduct as intrinsically illicit and some as intrinsically obligatory. We do not see in the parties for and against which we vote embodiments of Good and Evil. We may be, or usually are, influenced by moral motives in our political choice, and may, for example, welcome a Socialist victory at the polls as a happy event full of bright promise or lament it as a national disaster. But even so, we do not regard our political position as universally valid and binding, and a different position as a disgraceful anomaly. Controversy and a solution by compromise, as expressed and codified in the party system, are the very stuff of political life; whereas in moral appeal and argument a quasi-'innate' consensus about standard taboos and obligations is presupposed.

The distinction roughly sketched in the foregoing passage does not depend on the concept or practice of the liberal-democratic type of regime. It is less manifest in the pre-liberal forms of state, with their absolutist, theocratic and oligarchical aspects, and is deliberately blurred in the modern totalitarian one-party state. But it always is and remains valid and known. Men might, on moral grounds also, prefer Athens to Sparta or support Sparta against Athens, but that this was one thing while virtue and vice or justice and injustice were quite another was clear to them. When (as recorded in Dickens's *A Tale of Two Cities*) George III was styled in an English court of law 'our most gracious and sovereign Lord', while the head of an enemy state was drily referred to as 'the said French Lewis', this did not delude anybody into thinking that George and Lewis were the meaning of Right and Wrong, or stood for opposite moral laws. Although parties, cliques, sects or sponsors of this or that policy might identify their respective cause with 'good' and that of their opponents with 'evil', men did not cease to be aware of the difference between the conflict of rival powers and the tug of temptation and conscience. Again, those who, with Hegel, place 'concrete' *Sittlichkeit* (the moral mission, majesty and performance of the state, especially the state one belongs to) above 'abstract' morality, still know that the two are not the same thing; and a modern totalitarian who believes that, say, to be an imperialist brigand or a class traitor is infinitely worse than to be a knave in the ordinary sense of the term, still leans on men's 'abstract' moral repugnance to brigandage and treachery.[1] The existence of political division, often called 'party' long before our legalized institutional parties were even dreamt of, is inseparable from political existence – that is, from social order implying some kind of government, and thus virtually from human life.

In a sense, conflict of groups and the controversial character of politics are not so much obscured as overemphasized in the totalitarian systems. It is true that Ourselves and the Enemy are equated to White and Black; that, accordingly, a ruthless suppression of the Enemy is made the principle of policy, and – in the pre-eminent Communist type of totalitarianism at least – his eventual disappearance is foreseen. Compromise, therefore, is apparently accorded no place here as an essential complement of division but only as a purely pragmatic and temporary expedient. Still, it can safely be said that the philosophy of the state as an instrument of class struggle conforms to an agonistic and partisan conception of politics. The Fascist variants of totalitarianism held to this in a more moderate but at the same time more unequivocal fashion, rejecting as they did class struggle but affirming compulsion and violence as eternal principles. It was Carl Schmitt, perhaps the ablest political philosopher connected with National Socialism, who described 'Friend and Foe' as the central category of politics. There are, of course, ideological tendencies (particularly in some forms of religious conservatism) which minimize the role of controversy and interpret politics in terms of a universal 'good'. There are others which challenge the validity of 'abstract' moral standards (as in manifold types of naturalism, nihilism, scientism, activism and totalitarianism). Nevertheless, I venture to abide by the assertion that division, conflict and compromise are connatural to politics, whereas disagreement is looked upon as a puzzling and anomalous peripheral element in morality, and infringement of accepted moral standards primarily as a 'wrong' rather than as the expression of a different kind of 'right'.

2 POLITICAL PRACTICE AND ITS RELATIONS WITH MORALITY

Politics thus constitute an area of controversy, first, because they represent a field of human *practice*. Although moral rules are supposed to circumscribe and regulate my practice, as also to enter into its contents, they cannot create the tissue of my life. This is made up by the vast multitude of my desires, needs, interests and purposes – primarily non-moral, though many of them connote a moral theme. And, seeing the manifold conflict and competition between my various concerns, my practice – the administration of my concerns – requires continual acts of choice between mutually exclusive courses of action, with their antithetic advantages and drawbacks: 'deliberation' means controversy, argument and division within myself. Even on this level, within the practice of a single subject, controversy is present in a very real sense, in no way reducible to mere reflection, clarification and calculation. The agent cannot, in general, decide validly and with certitude what is 'the best thing' for him to do, but has to settle, in part, the order of his preferences *in actu* [in the act], and side in a more or less arbitrary manner with one of his concerns or sets of concerns as against the rival 'party'. Such practical maxims as he may have adopted can help him in making his choices, but cannot imperatively direct his conduct or be the test of its prudential 'rightness'. They represent not (like moral laws) sovereign demands on him, but subordinate tools of his skill in shaping his life, however unwise it may often be for him to disregard them. In the first place, then, politics are necessarily controversial simply by virtue of their forming a part of human practice – that is, the choice between goods mutually incompatible or difficult to harmonize, the ordering of preferences and reluctances, and the pursuit of 'interests' and 'ideals' as distinct from the respect or contempt for laws, the fulfilment or evasion of obligations.[2]

But, in the second place, the controversial nature of politics is amplified and made more salient by the fact that they refer, not to the practice of men in general, taken as individuals, but to *social* practice in its *concerted* form – that is to say, the practice of a collective body taken as a unitary quasi-agent which in some significant way stands for the concerns of a multitude of individuals. Division has a far greater scope here than within one agent's practice as such, or even within a field of private lives with their more enduring or more transitory mutual relations. For on the one hand it includes the divergency of interests, the mutual indifference and possible hostility, of distinct persons and more or less fixed groups of persons; and on the other hand it is evoked and sharpened by the requirements of collective unity: the world, or even a town, may be large enough for A and B, who disagree with each other, to keep out of each other's way; but one state cannot be smoothly run by several governments at loggerheads with one another, nor a given field of commonwealths submit, without conflict or tension, to rival claims to hegemony.

Though political exhortation, discussion or deliberation rarely fails to involve moral arguments, and may indeed sometimes centre in a moral emphasis, political and moral argument are essentially different things. 'Should the armaments policy (or the Balkans policy, or the labour policy) of our present Ministry be changed, and if so, what kind of policy should take its place?' is a properly political problem, though obviously dependent on moral considerations also. In 'Should we succour a friendly country threatened by an aggressor Power' the political and the moral problem interpenetrate. 'Can I, in conscience, maintain my allegiance to the leader of my Party, now that in one important matter he has pronounced in a sense strongly opposed to my own conviction?' is a properly moral rather than a political problem, though it refers to political, not to private, life. Political (like ordinary practical, or pedagogical) argument is not, primarily and necessarily, about a moral obligation valid for anyone in a *kind* of situation. It is about the good of a determinate community of persons in a determinate set of circumstances, interpreted from certain standard (including, probably, moral) points of view. A fixed and irremovable opposition of interests is often implied in the context, taken for granted, or harped upon as a central theme. Demosthenes' *Philippics*, meant to rouse the Greeks into resisting the Macedonian menace, are not addressed to Philip. Party propaganda is intended to fan the zeal of adherents and to win the floating and wavering elements of the electorate rather than to convince decided opponents. Some parties appeal to some social classes only, stressing the antagonism between them and other classes; and some parties express and encourage a national particularism in a state of several nationalities.

Political positions are not an application or translation of so many moral positions. Their connections with morality may be wholly trivial or accidental. Thus, parties engaged in a bitter struggle will accuse each other of deceitful slogans, attempts to intimidate, and electoral fraud. The political enemies of a Parnell will easily discover that adultery, of which perhaps they would formerly have taken a more lenient view, is the most heinous of crimes. Some people may join a political camp out of moral indignation at the particularly unfair methods used by its opponents. Certain moral points of view, such as equal justice or reward due to merit, are self-evidently invoked by the votaries of certain political doctrines. Again, some co-ordinations between political bias and moral emphasis seem to change with historical circumstances or the more specific elaborations of doctrine. Traditionalist positions may naturally seem to be linked with stricter, subversive movements with laxer standards of sexual morality, but Cavaliers and Puritans, as well as several other political antagonisms, do not fit into this scheme. 'Advanced' parties are charged by their critics both with a cult of unbridled individualism and with a worship of the masses portending a total disregard of personality, while 'reactionaries' are rebuked for their reliance on 'mere charity' and on legal formalism alike. Pedestrian utilitarianism and materialism, doctrinaire indifference to realities and highly strung unpractical idealism – these opposite charges are frequently levelled at one and the same political school or party, seen from different aspects and attacked in different contexts.

But the glib irresponsibility and ideological trickery of party propaganda may not account for the content of these one-sided polemical (or, in turn, self-advertising) descriptions. Nor is the problem disposed of by obvious considerations of the kind that parties imbued with ideological fanaticism are likelier to make light of moral restraints in general, or that power groups with little doctrinal emphasis will very possibly tend to think up ethical justifications of a moderate degree of swindle and corruption. Granted that political positions *are not* equivalents, reflections or applications of moral positions, and that very different types of moral character are compatible with very different kinds of political attitudes, it still appears natural that political divisions of a comparatively general, deep-reaching and permanent import – standard ideological attitudes, in a word – should *imply* relevant divergencies of moral emphasis, and thus be *interpretable* to some extent, though by no means *definable*, in moral terms. Thus, the socialist plea for economic equality (within certain quantitative and structural limits) and the 'individualist' defence of ownership (with a conservative accent on the right of 'prescription', or a liberal accent on the freedom of acquiring property) do not issue from contrary moral commandments.[3] Apart from their non-moral aspects, they both refer to basic evident concepts of justice. But it appears as if we had, on the one side, a moral protest against an unjust social order or pattern of human relations; and, on the other, a moral protest against a proposed or actual performance of unjust actions, meaning overt or veiled expropriations and the imposition of arbitrary constraints. It might be suggested that, in the two antithetic positions, the way in which morality is geared to practice – that is, to men's pursuit of their primary concerns – is conceived of in a different fashion. Stress is laid, by socialists, on fitting human activities and levels of life into a plan apparently devised, in terms of the prevalent concerns of all, by a just mind; while the defenders of property rights insist that men and governments, in the pursuit of their various ends, should be mindful of the direct commandments of justice. These two points of view are by no means identical.

It is to a closer scrutiny of a fundamental contrast of this kind that I now propose to turn, trying to interpret – chiefly in a moral context – what are called the political 'Right and Left'.

3 RIGHT AND LEFT AS ASPECTS OF POLITICAL DIVISION

Right and Left, rightism and leftism, are terms of a frivolously accidental origin which have acquired a fairly definitive technical status. Their meaning, though far from being well defined or rigorously constant, seems to refer to an important aspect of political attitudes discernible in very different historical situations, and to deserve philosophical attention in spite of the carpings and mockeries of over-nice purists and ardent specialists.

It is true enough, however, that Right–Left is far from being the only significant axis of political division. Thus, unionism or centralism and particularism or regionalism, extremism and moderation, the pragmatic pursuit and the moral appraisal or use of power, and of course the domain of foreign politics – of international contest of power and co-operation – do not, as such, express the polarity of Right and Left. Again, the thematic predominance of the Right–Left division varies with time and space. In the context of many a great political issue, it is less characteristically present than in the historical ambit of the French Revolution or, perhaps, of the struggle of Athenian democracy against oligarchy and dictatorship. Furthermore, the position on the Right–Left scale of certain standard political concepts may shift to some extent with historical change. Within the wider purview of the present generation, 'liberalism', 'democracy' and even 'socialism' have lost somewhat of their Left, 'conservatism' and 'monarchy' of their Right connotation. The Left or Right ideological sign of nationalism has been subject to sharp swings. Nor can any political complexion, whether of a party, a statesman, a doctrine, or a regime, be described in terms of rightism and leftism alone. Finally, in every leftist (or rightist) structure a residual deadweight, a balancing safety-valve or a dialectical counterpoint of rightism (or leftism) can be found.

As regards the salient *prima facie* aspects of the Right–Left division, we may conveniently refer to such current formulae as (i) Authority versus Liberty, or Order versus Anarchy, or Dogma versus Criticism; (ii) Tradition versus Progress, or Stability versus Change, or the acceptance of natural and historical facts as opposed to rational planning; and (iii) Hierarchy versus Equality, or 'Classes' versus 'Masses', or 'Privilege' versus the 'Common Man'. Between these three main groups of motifs, there is nothing like a strict logical co-ordination; in fact, for example, rightists chiefly attached to tradition and rightists chiefly attached to monarchical absolutism have often been at variance with each other,[4] and so have leftists more concerned with civic equality and others more concerned with rational innovation. Nevertheless, seen in the context of typical social situations and recurrent tendencies in a diversity of social media, the different aspects of the Right–Left division reveal a certain consonance of meaning which underlies, and to some extent warrants, the use of the 'Right–Left' terminology. If every political attitude connotes features other than that of being rightist or leftist, many political attitudes, on the other hand, are emphatically rightist or emphatically leftist above all else, and there are many more which display an unmistakable rightist or leftist tinge.

4 THE MORAL EMPHASES OF RIGHT AND LEFT

To live by a set of established traditions and to undergo change, which both evokes and is effected by a reformatory criticism of that tradition and its various aspects in the light of moral and rational postulates or 'self-evident principles', is normal to a civilized society. Criticism, reform, and a rational revision of some prerogatives and inequalities will essentially be linked up with the direct interests and wants of the social groups excluded from important privileges –

the *tiers ordre* [third order], the 'common people', the 'disinherited', the 'underprivileged, as the case or the denomination in vogue may be – though leftism is not, of course, a revolt of the utterly wretched and despoiled, and indeed could not exist at all as a social force if it were not based on certain positions of power,[5] some elements of wealth, and a measure of intellectual equipment. Again, the primordial framework of traditions and beliefs is embodied in a hierarchy of privileges, formal or informal, and entrenched in a vast and manifold system of loyalties, prejudices and vested interests, ramifying into the humblest layers of society. These forces of the Right will try to withstand the pressure of leftist demands, or to ease it by limited concessions; will dispute the criticisms proffered and the projects of reforms proposed from leftist quarters; and also, in their turn, will contribute to change by alternative reforms destined to render invulnerable the more essential stock of traditional positions at the price of sacrificing more expendable ones.

In both these orders of political endeavour, moral and immoral conduct – in recognized universal terms – is possible and occurs, though the partisan mind will tend to identify its own cause with standard implications of morality as such, and to impute reprehensible motives to apparently fair and beneficial actions of opponents. The supposition of rightist and leftist 'antithetic moralities' is disproved by the largely identical moral appeal of the two sides in their reciprocal polemics. They each stress, according to the situation and to their more special or local doctrines, justice, sincerity and loyalty in general, religious, utilitarian and common-sense standards, and again and again accuse the adversary of falling short of his own principles. So far, Right and Left do not seem to present any ethical interest, though the sociologist might still embark on an empirical examination of the average moral conduct of confirmed rightists as opposed to leftists.[6]

But if, instead of searching for contradictory moralities in the strict sense, we turn to the indirect moral implications or presuppositions of rightist and leftist thought, we may well discern a significant asymmetry. Like all possible findings of philosophical enquiry, it has been hinted at in many different ways, some of the current formulae being these – that the Left displays an 'abstract', the Right a 'concrete' approach to morality; that whereas the Left would 'realize the ideal'; the Right 'idealizes reality',[7] that the Right may be all too prone to content itself with order instead of using it to ensure justice, but the Left, prone to forget that without order justice is plainly impossible;[8] that the Right will easily lapse into hypocrisy, the Left into attitudes of moral nihilism; or again, that the Right thinks it needful for man to look up to something better than himself, while the Left believes in human perfectibility.

It is clear that whatever an established tradition with its hierarchical guardianship or embodiment and its cluster of privileges means, it does not mean the moral imperative and its urgency in the conscience of men. It is, I submit, equally clear that the leftist demand, whatever its moral credentials may be and howsoever it is couched in a moral language, is fundamentally distinct from the moral demand: it stands, primarily, not for a demand on men, addressed to their conscience, on behalf of right as opposed to wrong, but a demand of men, or on their behalf, for 'rights' as opposed to a sense of 'being wronged'. The central experience of moral obligations, including those of justice, benevolence and loyalty, does not in itself bear either a rightist or a leftist tinge. What, then, are the respective moral points of application of Right and Left? The answer to this question seems to me to be, briefly, that the rightist moral emphasis harks back from moral conduct to its social basis, conditions, inspirations and guarantees; while the leftist moral emphasis swings past it towards what might be described as its results and expressions in the pattern of social relationships. The rightist political mind is interested in 'virtue' – that is, human quality as connoting morality; the leftist, in a morally approvable 'state of things' in which morality has been given effect and produced its full effects. The leftist desire for a morally unobjectionable scheme of social institutions, appreciations and habits, joined to the faith in perfectibility, reflects the moral attitude that has sometimes been designated by the ungainly word 'perfectionism'. If I may be excused in proposing an even uglier technical term, I would contrast therewith the rightist tendency to derive the moral tone of society from the predominance and exemplary function of 'perfect' or 'noble' human types as a form of *perfectionalism*.

How this connects up with the rightist attachment to tradition, lineage, hierarchy, particularized sets of dogmas and standards – 'prescription and prejudice' – on the one hand, and with the leftist aspects of abstraction, social criticism, reform, progress, planning and a non-distinctive affirmation of human rights and interests (i.e. egalitarianism) on the other, may not perhaps require, here, a detailed discussion. But before I go on to what I am most concerned with, the rightist and the leftist conception of the relation between the moral and the non-moral, I would mention two points of obvious interest.

(a)   It would seem to accord with the foregoing description that 'men' versus 'measures' – that is, a comparative indifference to the intrinsic justice and apparent usefulness of institutions and an all but exclusive attention to statesmanlike and civic qualities – is the distinctive mark of the rightist as opposed to the leftist attitude. This, I think, is half true: it may undoubtedly be surmised that Pope wrote

> For forms of government let fools contest;
> What'er is best administered is best

in a rightist rather than a leftist mood; at any rate, it betrays a keener yearning for a wise, benevolent and powerful (if enlightened) king or prime minister than for the most perfect device for popular representation. Yet though Pope's religious position may also be labelled as rightist, the subsequent lines

> For modes of faith let graceless zealots fight;
> He can't be wrong whose life is in the right

savour of orthodox liberalism and 'abstract' moralism rather than clerical particularism and authoritarianism. Certainly the rightist attitude cannot be defined in terms of institutional and doctrinal neutrality, nor is the Left necessarily devoid of a discriminating appraisal of concrete policies and personalities. There exist, moreover, such things as Right doctrinairism and Left opportunism. Nevertheless, the rightist mind has more natural affinity to political indifference and to an emphasis on statecraft (including high standards for the administrative personnel), and is less keen on doctrine. Non-political and 'middle-of-the-road' attitudes are sometimes a disguise for rightism, or at any rate a propitious soil for rightist persuasion.

(b)   This asymmetry is connected with the essential fact that whereas a historical priority is proper to the Right, in an exquisitely political sense the Left constitutes a primary and the Right a secondary, 'reactive' (resistant or counter-attacking) force. The traditional – as it is sometimes over-stated, 'grown' not 'made' – order of society may so far be called pre-political; it is with the rise of the Left that the classic division begins.[9] Expediency and the 'art' of government are more consonant to the rightist mind; 'system', though not strictly alien to it, sits on it more lightly. Accordingly, the Left alone unfolds into a classic spectrum of 'isms' (suffice it to mention the basic triad of liberalism, socialism and anarchism); the manifold 'isms' of the Right, apart from the obvious polarity of moderate conservatism and counter-revolutionary speculative utopias and fanaticisms,[10] are of a very much more contingent, *ad hoc* and historically 'unique' character.

5 MORALIZING SOCIETY VERSUS MORALITY IN SOCIETY

In the rightist vision, the moral theme is inseparably intertwined with non-moral values, dependences, directions and standards. This is reflected in such expressions as 'aristoi', 'optimates', 'our betters', and in the moral use of such words as 'high' and 'noble'. Distinctive human value, an established social position and the refinements that go with it, a well-begotten, well-shaped and well-bred type of human being, are looked upon as a seat of moral virtue and a source, a guarantee and a *prima facie* yardstick of moral conduct; and a moral life is seen as implicit in the wider concept of a 'good life'. But although, in a more extreme modern rightism of Nietzschean inspiration, there have been suggestions of superseding *Gut und Böse* (Good and Evil, Right and Wrong) altogether by *Gut und Schlecht* (Good and Bad, Noble and Vile), and the concept of moral conduct by that of *Formniveau* (level of being; cf. 'good form'), the relation between a heightened form of being and morality is in general meant in the sense of a correspondence rather than a one-way reduction. The specific character of the moral theme and the validity of the moral law are not denied. Indeed, the superior education of the 'noble' or 'ruler' is presumed to include moral education proper; or again, the man of 'independent' position is credited with a higher capacity for just, disinterested and impartial judgement, and the man who has 'a stake in the country' with a reasonable degree of public-spiritedness. That the rulers are not above the moral law or arbitrary creators of it, but subject to it, is recognized and sometimes symbolically stressed under the Christian dispensation, and probably in most kinds of religious traditions.[11] But it is inherent in the rightist attitude to conceive of morality as incorporated in a whole of qualitative, social and metaphysical hierarchies, and – partly, at least – as a function of a mode of life ordered on such principles; and to believe that, on the whole, morality will fare better if rulers are not meticulously called to account under the moral code but loosely presumed to embody superior virtue in a comprehensive sense. Though it is perhaps not specifically linked to rightist politics in the Greek city-states, the ideal of *kalokagathia* is fairly expressive of the relation between moral and non-moral values as visualized in a rightist style. Morality is seen in a kind of unity with, and partly of subordination to, vital and other non-moral excellence; but its distinct meaning is hinted at by the very composition of *kalos* and *agathos*, joined together by a 'k' which stands for *kai* (and). The rightist contention is not that goodness is a mere synonym for or a mere – and necessary – manifestation of power (i.e. power of high quality and breeding, connoting the aspects of vital force, beauty, 'form' and 'nobility'), but that it is the goodness exhibited and made valid by power,[12] and the kind of goodness more in keeping with the exercise and appreciation of power, which counts in the world and impresses a stamp of goodness on reality.

In contrast with such a conception of morality as embedded in the manifold of social reality, leftism aims at adjusting social reality to the moral demand. It regards social order not as a dispenser of moral values, but as a – so far, inadequate – projection of the moral order and the state, as an apparatus for the securing of moral claims. Thus, approaching social order critically 'from outside' and judging it by the test of 'abstract' postulates independent of the authorities and powers actually prevailing in it, the leftist mind apparently steers clear of ethical naturalism and starts from a neat distinction between moral and non-moral modalities of value, and from stressing the antithetic as well as the consonant aspect of their mutual relation. This is expressed in the demand for strict commutative justice, equal rights and freedom from all discriminations on the one hand, and in the demand for compensatory provisions for 'the weak' and in revolutionary polemics against 'distinctions' (in the widest sense) on the other. While utterances like 'Handsome is as handsome does' or 'When Adam delved and Eve span, who was then the gentleman?' are straightforwardly moral or common-sense protests against the rightist mumbo-jumbo of the substantive superiority of some breeds or strains of men, the Left thinks up an opposite mystique, not necessarily of the moral purity of 'the people' (or 'the common man') or the historic mission of the proletariat – though such a tendency is inherent in its position – but of non-discrimination, neutrality in respect of distinctive quality, and the extension of the sphere of 'equal justice', as a leverage for the moralization of life. Just as, in rightism, emphasis is displaced from moral conduct proper towards the moral connotation and moral usefulness of the social pre-eminence of a complex of qualities, vantage points and disciplines, in leftism emphasis is so displaced towards a morally pleasing groundwork of Society: an objective state of things representing, as it were, morality in operation, which to a large extent would ensure the fitting and salutary behaviour of men automatically, without engaging personal conscience.

Clearly, *this* kind of thematic withdrawal from the sphere of conscientious morality is more consonant than is the rightist kind with an emphatic experience of morality in separation from other concerns, valuations and reverences. If I am set to devise, on a clean slate, a moral order of public relations for men as such, without knowing their various personal and collective accomplishments and without any pre-established biases and appreciations on my part, I shall be inclined to put in equality before the law, universal equal suffrage and an equal distribution of property (except, perhaps, for a sector of state-owned capital and public services) rather than specified persons or families born to rulership or to whatever kind of privileges or enjoyments, millionaires, clerical castes, superior races, and the like; and to add provisions for amendment, correction of abuses and the widening of intellectual scope rather than a fictitious landscape of traditions.

Leftist thought, especially as regards its critical phase and its initial impulses, is thus inclined to dwell on the direct enforcement of moral exigencies rather than on indirect supports and probable strongholds of morality; and, in reference to any given state of affairs, to be aware of the cleavage between what is and what ought to be, displaying a *prima facie* neutral and formal approach to different human realities and their possible contents of value unconnected with the clear moral postulate in question. Yet this very concentration of moral emphasis and its challenge to reality implies, virtually, the counterpart of a radical identification of moral with non-moral concerns, and of a naturalistic submersion of the moral theme under the absolute of human need-fulfilment and sovereignty of will.

The leftist insistence on justice, with its inherent tendency to extend the range of that concept, is subject to an ambiguity between the idea of 'righting wrongs' and the idea of espousing the interests of those (presumably) wronged as identical with what is morally right.[13] Hence the classic confusion between interests – or wishes – and rights, between claims raised and claims morally sanctioned, and between rights in the weak sense (e.g. man's right to prosperity, which entails a strict right to no more than not being forcibly prevented from his lawful pursuit of wealth) and rights in the strong sense (e.g. a man's strict right to repayment of a loan he has made).[14] Again, the pretension to correct whatever *can* be meaningfully brought under the concept of 'injustice' and in a debatable way resented as such – for example, incongruities or stark contrasts of social positions, perhaps in an arguable continuity with grossly unjust acts of the past – quasi-logically develops into a pretension to rearrange the pattern of social relations altogether. Further, the 'realization of morality' on the social scale, as a comprehensive goal, opens up the vista of a 'moralized state of man' in which the pursuit of human concerns, no longer falsified and diverted to destructive channels by invasive powers, arbitrary authorities and perverse or outworn institutions, cannot but run along morally satisfactory lines. Hence, a morally self-contained and *a priori* secure functioning of society would make the intervention of conscientious morality pointless and superfluous, and the moral theme, in its distinction from directly vital and practical themes, irrelevant.

The myth of a 'primitive', *pre-civic* 'state of nature', whose lost 'integrity' we may hope to recover by a thoroughgoing conscious rearrangement of society, raising man to an *altogether civic* status of existence, is meant to provide the leftist conception of the straight coincidence of morality and natural fact with a kind of metaphysical or meta-historical sounding-board. That the will of man, unless it be thwarted, divided, enchained and thrown into disharmony, *is* goodness constitutes – not, indeed, a principle underlying all patterns of thought or practical projects of the Left, but the presupposition of its irrepressible belief in a boundless perfectibility of man, and in mankind's task of ridding itself of moral imperfections and blots through a machinery of rights, an organization of its will and an adequate supply of resources and of information. Accordingly, although it leans on an experience of some strictly and unequivocally moral postulates, the Left at the same time is prone to an integral *subsumption* of morality under the concept of 'the Cause': that is to say, progress, revolution, emancipation, the production and diffusion of wealth, technological and scientific advancement. It thus transfers moral emphasis, with its psychological weight and acuteness, to morally irrelevant or peripheral themes and, owing to this predominance of one morally hallowed pursuit over moral restraints, perhaps even to positively immoral directives of conduct which are then revered on the same footing with evident and urgent moral demands. The starting point, as it were, may be purely and distinctively moral reflection, reminder, or protest, but the ideological flower in its full unfolding may be a neat supersession of intrinsic morality by a pragmatic vision exclusive of all autonomy of the moral theme. The rightist counterpart of this aspect lies in a propensity to modify, grade, colour, subdue or inflate moral emphasis so as to keep it closely in tune with pliancy towards authority, docility towards the powers that be, conformity to traditions, and the particular atmosphere of a given community or some of its ruling sets.

6 DUTIES VERSUS RIGHTS

The well-worn rightist adage 'What matters is the duties rather than the rights of men' is literally an absurdity, for rights and duties rigorously correspond to each other:[15] the creditor's claim and the debtor's debt are one and the same relation, just as 'A is B's husband' and 'B is A's wife' mean the selfsame relation of marriage.

But on a freer interpretation, the maxim ceases to be nonsensical and becomes defensible, as well as open to criticism. It appears to suggest three orders of consideration, in close connection with one another.

(a) It is quite meaningful to say that men should be invited to mind their duties rather than encouraged to nurse their rights, seeing that a man's attention to *his* duties and his attention to *his* rights are very different and indeed, in some sense, contrary, though by no means contradictory, states of mind. Whether or no a society is better served by duty-consciousness or by consciousness of rights prevailing in its members, the two can plainly be distinguished. And a prevailing duty-consciousness may be expected to be more conducive to peace and co-operation, as also to a higher level of morality, *in* society. On the other hand, so far as the structural characteristics of society, its legal, administrative and economic regime, *can* be an object of moral appraisal, leftists might argue that the morality *of* society was likelier to benefit from men's being keenly aware of, and unwilling to brook the infringement of their rights.

(b) The word 'duty' is also used in a wider moral sense, as a synonym of what the agent ought to do so as to acquit himself as 'good' or morally 'worthy'; and duties in this sense comprise, besides duties to others which imply corresponding rights on the part of these 'recipients', other kinds of duties which may be called 'duties to God' and 'duties to self', or again 'duties *per se*'. There is nothing absurd in maintaining that I have duties of self-improvement, and though it may not be easy to say precisely what these are, it would be very much more difficult to say, except for possible accidental details, to what other person or persons I owe them – that is, who may claim my strenuous pursuit of self-improvement as his or their 'right'. The rightist may, then, express a deeper, more complete and more properly conscientious view of morality, tied to a greater emphasis on human quality, as compared with the leftist concern about a social order fitting the postulates of justice. Again, it might be retorted that the single-minded and active service of a stringent moral task –

that is, the securing of disregarded human rights – is a more important test of morality than is the scope and refinement of moral experience.

(c)   Finally, the meaning of 'duties versus rights' resides in the non-moral aspects of these moral concepts. A case may be made out for discipline, submission and loyalty as opposed to self-interest, covetousness, ambition and envy, which are linked with the leftist ideology of 'rights'. But neither is the first set of attitudes purely moral: it connotes force of habit and inertia, mental sloth, superstition, tribal self-admiration, and the like. Moreover, the vices of greed, lust for power, and the rest are not more conspicuously alien to the rulers than to the ruled. Ideologists of the Right may counter this objection by pointing out that the vices they censure are more dangerous to the permanence of society than the drawbacks clinging to the virtues they preach, and more corrosive of social order in the multitude of ordinary men than in the ruling circles, where they are offset by special virtues and attainments. It is better, they may argue, to screen and tolerate wickedness in high places than to encourage and breed it in people at large under a moral pretext. The leftist answer may be that moral resignation cannot but stultify morality, and that the moral claim on reality must be pressed even at the cost of temporarily adding fuel to the fire of some kinds of selfish or evil passions, for otherwise morality will have proved to be illusory.

7 LEFTIST MONISM AND RIGHTIST HOLISM

Among the doctrinal expedients used by the Right, the 'organism' theory of society has perhaps pride of place. The duty of subordination is made intellectually more palatable by its being interpreted as a subordination of the members (or cells) to the body, and thus supported also by a reference to the logical truism that the part is subordinate to the whole. Those occupying higher positions in the social hierarchy are presumed to be 'better' in some significant sense, and entitled to reverent submission on the part of the 'lower orders' – not only on the strength of their possibly nobler substance and the merits which may have contributed to their rise, but inasmuch also as they more directly represent the good of society as a whole, a broad conspectus of its concerns, and its continuity, identity and survival.

By contrast with this 'holist' view, the leftist mind inclines to a 'monist' conception of society: more exactly, a conception of monist rationalism and voluntarism, as expressed by Rousseau's 'general will' or by the term 'pantisocracy', occurring in late-eighteenth-century English radicals' writings. The premiss may be described as individualist: it is a postulate of justice and an epitome of the 'rights of man' that a person must not be subject to any human will except to one that is really his own. Such an axiom conforms to the model of the state of nature and to the principle of the neutral starting point, falsified so far by the loaded dice of actual civilization. But how can man become his own and sole master? Not unless society is either abolished or perfected into a self-determining single subject of consciousness and will, in which the sovereign wills of its every member, informed by the same reason embodied in each, are united to the point of being identically one.[16] This may seem a construction of ideas even bolder and more out of touch with reality than the organism theory, which derives some plausibility from the fact of the functional interdependence of social groups. But facets or approximations of a conscious identity of minds and wills also exists in reality: it seems to be 'the same Reason' in us that apprehends analytic truths – for example, mathematical theorems; and in some situations all members of a more or less extensive social unit pursue the same object from the same motives with a clear and emphatic conception of it which seems to be identical in each individual mind. Identity of insights and of aims is an aspect of social reality, as is the individual's incorporation in an organized 'whole'. Holism and monism are both arbitrary, tendentious misconstructions of actually existing basic features of human existence.

While moderately rightist and moderately leftist attitudes may obviously come very near to each other, if not actually interblend, in their awareness (however different the primary emphases) of the joint or linked, as well as of the distinct and partly antagonistic, interests of men, holism and monism alike tend to inspire extremist political positions, disdainful of the non-political manifoldness of human concerns. Right and Left forms of totalitarianism or quasi-totalitarianism will thus again exhibit some very similar formal traits, and even borrow a great deal of each other's techniques of coercion and persuasion. But apart from the political contents and symbols on either side, the underlying logical patterns are different. Holism aims at imparting to the ordinary individual the belief that his 'true good' lies in his reverent surrender to the superior and transcendent good of the 'whole' to which he belongs, and in his vicarious sharing in the grandeurs, values and wisdom embodied by its elites and leading personalities; on the moral plane, this is linked to an emotive experience of 'duty'. Monism, on the contrary, endows the ordinary individual with 'sovereignty'; on this view, there are no realities or qualities over and above him, and his will is meant to be the ultimate standard of the good. Yet this rehabilitation of man's being implies that his will has been ascertained and purified to be his 'true' will, identical with the true wills of his fellows. Hence, the individual must be so conditioned as to fit the institutions devised to formulate and to make valid the true will of men.[17] The one and indivisible will of man, thus evoked and enthroned, can neither do nor suffer wrong, for there is no valid will besides it which it could oppress, nor any powerful will besides it by which it could be thwarted. Man, in the monist conception, is subject only to himself, and no one can violate his own rights. The sovereignty of the collective individual – of which electoral democracy presents only an inadequate rough draft – will at the same time mean that postulates and facts, rights and actual relationships, morality and reality, have become one.[18]

8 RIGHT, LEFT AND THE TENSION BETWEEN IS AND OUGHT

To sum up: Right and Left differ, from the moral point of view, not so much in their moral evaluations or even by their respective affinity to opposed systems of ethics as by the contrasting attitudes they take to the tension between 'Is' and 'Ought'.

The rightist attitude accepts that tension as ineliminable. In its properly conservative form it may do so with a measure of laxity – as it were, 'cynicism'. In general, it inclines to rely upon the concrete, given *points of junction* between Is and Ought: the virtues and relative perfections embodied in particular human entities and social traditions, and the habits of dutiful conduct as implied in social hierarchy and dependence. In its more extreme forms, rightism may further erect some present or past (arbitrarily interpreted and embellished) social order into a moral standard; and such circumstantial utopias of traditionalism or reactionary imagination may be bolstered up with holist theories of a more explicit and abstract kind which 'deduce' moral obligation from the *a priori* 'allegiance of the part to the whole'; and bestow upon the ordered 'Whole' as such the status of a moral absolute.

The leftist attitude, on the contrary, tends to *overemphasize the disjunction* of Is and Ought, experiencing their tension as intolerable and always in need of urgent redress. In its moderate forms, leftism is chiefly critical and reformatory, allied to analytic reason rather than bent on utopian construction.[19] The complementary vision of a *natural identity* between Is and Ought is allowed play merely as a schema of reference in the background of political thought. But the application of moral rules and tests, the righting of various social injustices, and the institutional curbs placed on power and ascendancy fall short of making away with the tension. By mitigating it, they broaden the basis of moderate conservatism; by giving rise to *new* incongruities between positions of power and intrinsic value, they are apt to provoke rightist reactions and to disappoint leftist expectations.

Left extremism, whose visionary and abortive early manifestations often precede the emergence of a cautious and temperate leftist outlook, may thus revive after a period of piecemeal reforms and progressive achievements, adopting perhaps a non-utopian scientific concept-language and a realistic technique of political action, as in the case of Marxism and Leninism. By contrast with the rightist sanctification of specified powers and facts, which even in its boldest totalitarian forms remains necessarily selective and therefore ultimately tolerant of the tension between Is and Ought, full-fledged leftism is committed to the aim of attaining an integral fusion of human reality and the humanly desirable, as expressed above all in terms of a social condition of man that is no longer open to criticism. The rightist attitude, be it ever so flexible and disposed to compromise with change, is self-perpetuating; it would for ever maintain moral awareness as a corrective ingredient of an irremediably imperfect world. By the same token, it is tempted

to restrict, to tone down and to blur moral awareness; to render
it ineffectual, not to say innocuous, in many directions: not,
however, to get rid of it. Whereas the leftist mind is haunted by
the dream of its dialectical self-elimination through the fulfilment
of its striving. In the state of perfection, the pre-eminent original
functions of the Left, vigilant criticism and the vindication of rights,
would have lost their object and been doomed to disappear, as if
the wheel had come full circle. Leftism is distinguished, at the same
time, by its keen response to the tension between Is and Ought as a
motor of moral endeavour, and by its impatience to see that tension
vanish as an unendurable thorn in the flesh of man.[20]

In so far as the Right tends unduly to interpret natural and
historical facts as signs and pledges of intrinsic superiority, positional
values as qualitative, and particular qualities of value as moral virtues
and standards, we may say that it is essentially liable to indulge in
illusions.[21] In so far as the Left is driven unduly to extend the scope
of evident moral postulates into a structural framework of society,
so that human situations in general shall be determined by man's
justice,[22] and man's justice become one with man's will, we may
look upon it as essentially vulnerable to a paramount *delusion*.

But the antithetic kinds of moral emphasis implicit in rightist and
leftist politics, though inevitably fraught with the danger of these
aberrations, are not in themselves corruptions of morality. Rather,
they form part of the practical applications of moral appraisals
and demands. The basic moral intuitions of mankind – which
Right and Left alike cannot but take for granted as a premiss
for their respective moral appeal – provide no solution, except
in a prohibitive and limiting sense, for the permanent or topical
problems of political organization and choice. But the practice of
men in Society, with their divided interests, divergent tastes, and
conflicting purposes in need of being aligned and concerted, calls
for moral guidance and inspiration. Political controversy involves
moral issues. Genuine moral experiences will thus come to be
evoked, actualized and deepened but, on the other hand, dragged
into the tussle of non-moral concerns and adapted to the exigencies
of ideological argument and of the self-assertion of rival camps.

The Utopian Mentality

1 UTOPIA AND UTOPISM

For all the diversity of literary utopias, and the great variety of other forms which more characteristically reveal it, there exists a *utopian cast of mind*. It consists in the tendency to judge the real world of our experience against a self-enclosed and perfect blueprint. Though it is conceived as completely isolated, and without reference to any of the tried and tested value-experiences of mankind, it brings a special kind of emotional and intellectual satisfaction. This tendency is not an invariable feature of man's everyday practical life, even of his long-term, ambitious or exceptional undertakings, but it is always present to some degree, at least as a temptation, when he thinks about changing, improving or constructing things – even when there is no question of political activity on a vast scale. Utopian novels and fantasies are clearly different from social thought expressed discursively and with some definite end in view, but it would still be stupid to deny the historical interpenetration of these two modes of ideological activity. Plato, Campanella, Morelly, Fourier, Shaw and other creators of Utopias were not primarily concerned to entertain their readers. On the other hand, nothing could be clearer than the utopist aspects of Rousseau and Bentham, or even the completely materialist and earth-bound Hobbes. Millenarian fanatics are entirely serious, and also completely utopian. Marx is perfectly justified in talking about 'utopian socialisms' and in distinguishing their kind from his own – though of course he had no idea that his own doctrine, with its 'scientific' toughening and parade of empirical 'objectivity', would give the utopian will its mightiest scope.

An analysis of the utopian mind is, of course, no substitute for the historical exposition and critical appreciation of social ideologies, in their general and locally conditioned meanings. But only an investigation of utopism as such can bring out the implicit *utopian presuppositions* of social ideologies which are in many ways totally inhospitable to cheap dreams of earthly perfection and accomplished bliss, and draw on values and motives quite free of utopism. The fact is that our social thought, our political movements, our governments, are all, in different ways and degrees, shot through with utopism; and this fact is revealed through the study of utopian models of thinking – of 'utopism' as distinct from this or that particular literary Utopia, 'utopism' not in the sense of a unique doctrine or organized party but of a temptation inherent in the human mind. In keeping with the phenomenon, and in continuity with the first (literal or rather literary) sense of 'Utopia', I prefer to use the word 'utopist' – or, better, 'utopian' – for the same practical conceptions, above all social ones, which are rendered in stylized, condensed, disengaged and epigrammatic form in visionary and literary Utopias proper. ('Utopist' suggests a doctrinal position, a definite programme, whereas 'utopian' seems more suited to describe a structural trait or style of thinking.) Among the main characteristics of the utopian mind are belief in a 'perfection' achieved, guaranteed, indestructible, the idea of a hidden key, now at last rediscovered, which opens the door to the solution of many different problems at once, the 'confusion of normativities' (Ruyer) – that is, value monism, and the mirage of an autonomous 'totality' which constitutes a kind of counter-reality to the stained and patched-up structure of customary reality. These motifs reappear in more clear-cut form, unencumbered by strictly scientific interests and workaday tasks, in the plastic forms and visible conceptions of the literary 'Utopias'.

It goes without saying that even in the explicit Utopias, and even more in ideological utopisms, aspects of the utopian mind are mingled with conceptions and motives which - right or wrong, approvable or condemnable – are not in the least dependent on a utopian view of things and retain their own meaning even in these utterly alien surroundings.

This symbiosis of the utopian spirit with ideas and projects which either are or could also be non-utopian does not in the least mean that utopism simply consists in excessive or untimely reformatory zeal, and the importunity of those possessed by it. The utopian mind is not constituted by wild enthusiasms, or even simplistic one-sidedness, any more than by undisciplined imagination, indomitable hopes or sophistical reasoning in the service of emotional prejudice. No, the utopian state of mind will be present, perhaps only in vestigial form, wherever we find the – perhaps unobtrusive and unpolished – signs of the perfectionist illusion, and the idea of a rupture between the given reality of the world and the counter-reality 'set apart', the object of perfectionist infatuation and construction.

2 THE UTOPIAN PRESUPPOSITIONS

It is important that we do not confuse perfectionism with the sustained, concentrated, thoroughgoing and multilateral pursuit of values. Utopia has nothing to do with any sense of values, however acute and exacting. Nor is it constituted by any attitude to goods, possessions or pleasures. Utopism does not necessarily involve greed or concupiscence, the fear of distress or pain, or again, well-wishing, generosity or charity. Nevertheless, together with moral and aesthetic sentiments of all kinds, these things may serve to fill out utopian visions or blueprints, and enhance their appeal both to the plain man and also to subtle and sensitive thinkers. What, then, is the distinguishing mark of perfectionism? Can we conceive of it as a kind of search for perfection *rather than* value, 'the perfect' in *abstraction* from 'the good'? Our answer is that we can, thanks to certain characteristic *illusions* to be found, at least in germ, in everyday practice.

The perfectionist thinker is attracted not so much by outstanding excellence or indisputable foundational values as by objects or conceptions bearing the 'form' – the appearance, sign or pretension – of achieved good, 'all of a piece', without admixture of evil. In other words, the perfectionist looks for objects which not only stand for embodied or realized value but also suggest a necessary and complete union between value and being. In actual fact, hardly any 'perfect' things exist, but there are many models of quasi-perfection which, of their kind, are beyond criticism or correction; the idea of a 'perfect' object in this sense is not quite the same as the idea of a very high value or a maximum of attainable value. Things like logical coherence, mechanical precision, formal correctness (as in the harmonious proportions of the classical style), or projects worked out with almost infallible foresight are incontestably valuable, perhaps very valuable, but they do not imply maximum value or even very high value. Nor does an intense and ambitious pursuit of value have to move in this direction. In some respects and situations 'the perfect' can be aimed at only in the mode of abstract imagination, out of key with the authentic search for values themselves. The perfectionist thinker will make up for this by illusory constructions, relying on the primordial fallacy according to which whatever has the colour of perfection, and gives the idea of a 'best', 'total' and absolutely assured good, is in fact necessarily superior to any alternative value or any rival solution.

This forced postulate of an order of pre-established harmony which can be translated into reality as soon as we have glimpsed it, attended to it and pursued it – or perhaps produced and elaborated it in accordance with its own laws – also entails the (at least virtual) utopian rupture with the real order of things. It is superficial to think that utopism can be characterized by an 'exaggerated' thirst for values, coupled with an 'idealistic' disdain for reality. The truth is that the utopian spirit is fascinated by the idol of a reality which is 'all value', corresponding to the concept of a value-*perfection* automatically incorporating every 'valid' value, including that of the capacity for complete realization. It sets itself against the 'evil' world of reality, *distinct* from the harmonious reality glimpsed in its conception of the identity between being and value; it is no less hostile towards the idea of values which connote imperfection or limitation, as also, in some way, towards experience of realized values as such.

Some perfectionist illusions – necessarily based on metaphysical assumptions though interwoven with the stuff of everyday life – stop short of explicit utopism. These can be defined as expressions of the *forced negation of ineliminable tensions*, as in the confusion of categories (a prominent mark of Utopias themselves); or again, as imaginary and obsessional deductions from a postulated harmony. Their apparent soundness derives from the imperfect and partly accidental, but nevertheless real, convergences among values; and also from the genuine possibility of combining various advantages and producing obvious improvements through intelligent practice and a run of good luck.

Let us take some characteristic examples. The tension between the agent's 'goodness' and his 'good', between the justice and the success of a cause, between 'morality' and 'nature', between 'beauty' and 'utility', and so on, is not absolute. It is in general reduced by the existence of certain 'convergences' which hint at a principle of ultimate unity, without which even the terms of the tension might seem empty of meaning. Moral goodness tends to evoke the approval and acknowledgement of others, and to produce a quiet conscience, which are part of our good. Even in itself it implies a positive attitude to man's good, and above all compassion for others' misfortune: complete indifference towards extra-moral good and evil is incompatible, if not with all virtue, at least with goodness in a moral sense. In general, the ineliminable 'tension' between value demands and the resistance offered by 'brute' reality can sometimes be briefly overcome in limited practical contexts. It is quite often feasible to aim for practical 'solutions' that are satisfactory from all points of view, and success is not uncommon. But the perfectionist illusion twists this original convergence of values (essentially limited, incomplete, fragile and tenuous) into the magic abstraction of a law of nature; it transmutes this possibility of 'best possible solutions' into a gratuitous postulate of their universal and permanent availability. It aspires to a global resolution of tensions, at least in some particular respect or other.

This is the origin of those maxims of false moralism like 'morality guarantees happiness' (or health, or success in life), 'a just cause must triumph', 'spiritual weapons are bound to prevail over material ones', 'goodness is an irresistible force', 'the moral must be beautiful', 'true virtue manifests itself in all aspects of morality', 'all misfortune is the wages of sin', or 'virtue is in itself efficacious and fruitful'. Compare the corresponding sophisms from the naturalist, historicist and immoralist camps, such as 'what is natural is good', 'morality is being true to oneself', 'spontaneity is the expression of moral sovereignty', 'historical success decides the value of an opinion or a cause', 'if it does no harm to anyone it cannot be immoral', 'morality is a function of utility', 'genius (or the artist, or collective interest) is above the law', 'the criminal is sick', and many more. Certainly there is a real difference between the moralist and the immoralist emphases. But perfectionist attitudes, ambiguous or wavering between the two poles, are equally present in both (this also goes for the optimist and nihilist, activist and quietist, futurist or progressivist, and 'presentist', retrograde or 'extra-temporal' aspects of utopism).

In his longing to overcome or conceal at any price the classic scissures which characterize human being, the perfectionist necessarily tends to become less sensitive to values in their essential diversity. He preaches an artificially constructed 'moral principle' from which he pretends to 'deduce' the goodness of an action or the obligation arising in a situation, thereby disregarding the duality between man whole and entire (however virtuous) and man as moral agent confronted with a norm. Thence arises that *negation of conscience* so characteristic of utopist visions and their image of man automatically good, thanks to a refashioning of human nature by the spirit of human planning and the permeation of the recesses of man's soul by the magic of institutions; without this man must be hemmed in by the barriers of 'objectivation' or chafe under the 'inhibitions' or 'alienations' which circumscribe his spontaneity. Again, the perfectionist tries to free life from the integral role of chance, or practical uncertainty; he demands, and tends illusorily to anticipate, a practical assurance assimilated to theoretical knowledge, since this has decoded the laws of the future, and its calculus is infallible. The uselessness of conscience is thus accompanied by the *utopian negation of practice*, or of individual prudence. It will be replaced by human 'providence', instituted by the pre-utopian creator of the utopian world.

The perfectionist approach, then, is poles apart from mere exaggeration or excess in the keen pursuit of some kind of goods, or an acute and exacting sense of values, or a passionate and even obsessive love for a cherished object or an exalted end. It is of a totally different order. It will burst out, for example, in a special taste for conceptions and undertakings which seem to combine in themselves very varied attractions and advantages; or in the tendency to engage in an enterprise that is banal or common as such, but in a way which seems to surround it with mysterious meanings surpassing its usual significance, suggesting illusory promises and arbitrary perspectives; or again, it will serve to nourish projects whose success could be interpreted as the accomplishment of a quasi-logical, even cosmic, necessity.

If social utopism, whose actual causes are as diverse as those of any other historical phenomenon, cannot be simply represented as a new step in the dialectic of perfectionist ideas, it nevertheless answers to this description in respect of the mentality controlling it. The passage from the perfectionist attitude, which is diffuse and atemporal, to social Utopia, located in history, somehow expresses *the illusion of passing from illusion to reality* along the line of perfectionism.

3 SOCIAL UTOPISM

There is an 'intelligible', if not logically necessary, step from perfectionism to social utopism, which we may reconstruct as follows. Suppose, first, that the idea of a perfect reality is accepted; it follows that the perfecting of reality is a real possibility, and that whoever has the secret of it may manage his affairs perfectly. Suppose now that in the light of the facts, and a critical examination of the crass illusions it employs to give itself psychological credence, this idea about the nature of things is shown up as gratuitous and totally false. This partial undeception still leaves the essential idea intact, and the next step will be the creation of a task: man must, on a global scale, *create a reality fundamentally 'other'*, corresponding to and expressly modelled on the perfectionist idea.

Though in fact it entangles its devotees more hopelessly in illusion, social utopism thus marks, from one point of view, an advance towards an activist 'realism' born of disillusion. This disillusion is itself illusory, since it implies a devaluation of *actual* reality which is as false as its perfectionist interpretation, and stems from the same inability to conceive of any value except in terms of perfection. By affirming the possibility of replacing the actual world with a 'really' perfect one, social utopism advances and strengthens the initial illusion. In every case it protects itself by an illusion less immediately refutable by everyday experience; it gains a reprieve from confronting the unchangeable data of the human condition. The new sphere of unreason it opens up is attained by a new advance of reason. To think about realizing an impossible (even contradictory) dream of happiness is somehow more 'realistic' than remaining simply stuck in the dream; it is to issue a *challenge* in the face of reality. So the perfectionist illusion, chastened in respect of its artless – or rather, implicit – belief, but not of the deep-rooted attitude which sustains it, gives birth to the utopian *will*. This might be formulated as follows: *To confirm the system by imposing it*, or: 'To prove perfection by realizing it'.

The discovery of 'the *Social*' as a central theme of human existence was to some extent anticipated by Greek thinkers, especially Plato. Its characteristic salience in 'modern' thought is directly linked to the utopian mind. There can be no doubt of its intellectual and moral importance; nor can it be maintained that the rational and critical analysis of social institutions, or the elucidation of the framework of conditions they imply for individual thought, must be based on illusion. Modern progress is, by and large, real progress, and we have no better reason to assert that it *would have* taken place without the help of utopian *hubris* than we have to show that it *could not have been* brought about without the distortions this alliance has produced. But it is certain that the 'social' outlook of the modern age – theoretical and practical, economic and political, progressive and (reactively) backward-looking – has been mortgaged up to the hilt, and diverted from its legitimate ends by the original perfectionist and utopist overestimation of social structures. These have been seen both as amenable to human purposes and as themselves embodying 'the' will of 'man' – a determining principle of human existence taken as a whole. There is nothing illogical about an analytical and conceptual study of the world of social relations, a concern to remedy tangible injustices and absurdities in their confined reality and without extending the concept *ad infinitum*, or research into improvements in the standard of living at those points where desire is strongest and counter-indications are fewest. These things are entirely thinkable, and have often been acted on – effectively if unspectacularly, but without false hopes, illusory pretensions and monstrous desires for the 'self-redemption' of man at the cost of his denaturing and the rupture of his self-identity.

So when I speak of the *idol of 'the Social'*, I have the ideological line in mind, and am not making any obscurantist, quietist or amoralist point. This idol is the corollary of perfectionism, and the categorial instrument of the will arbitrarily to refashion human reality.

Man is himself and his setting in the world; above all, his social setting. This transcends him and does not depend on him, although it leaves him a certain limited freedom to build his own personal world, and is thereby modified in its turn, usually to an infinitesimal degree but occasionally in just perceptible fashion. But the possibility of collective action, where there are high metaphysical pretensions, seems to alter and even reverse this law of the human condition. Were man to understand and organize himself as '*unique subject*', could he not attain to a completely new sovereignty, become the *author* of his setting, including the facts of his own nature outside his conscious will? Could he not raise himself above the distressing harshness of scissures, oppositions, clashes and discordances which issue from the divided and contingent character of non-utopian human being; the harshness of deficiencies and dissatisfactions, which result from man's 'abandoned' state and, at the same time, engender 'false needs'; the harshness of necessary disciplines which confine his pure spontaneity, and come from his not being a self-regulating and self-contained agent but one confronted by 'alterity' as by a 'fact' to a great extent alien and opaque, and potentially hostile? Could he not raise himself above transgression, morals and the pangs of conscience, be established in his primordial and integral 'goodness', purified by an inner harmony relieved of the things that made him 'sin' – competition, fear, malice in respect of alien interests, licentiousness stirred up by taboos and by suspicions of his own nature – and liberated henceforth from every rule which is not the luminous expression of his own nature, 'rational' and 'sensible', all in one? Could he not finally raise himself above the need for uncertain predictions and fallible decisions, in the midst of a world which encircles him and evades his control?

But if the illusion of living here and now in an essentially harmonious world, to which the individual can happily adapt himself provided he exercises a wise discretion, has proved untenable, the idea that he could – even with a band of co-religionists – somehow make good the world's imperfection by his own action is so chimerical that it cannot possibly be entertained. It is no less so if he now thinks of his being as *identical* with his social being, with a society-'person' who reproduces and embodies him instead of being a 'setting' which bruises and confines him; if, that is, he understands himself as a function of his social being with no remainder, and refers to it all the aspects, problems and shortcomings of his own being. Here we have the birth of 'the idol of the Social', by which I mean not a presumptuous state authority incongruously demanding adoration, or an overblown dogma of economic socialism or political egalitarianism, but a *conception of man* as ontological social unity, ruptured or refashioned, of which all the facts, qualities and fortunes of individual lives are simply a function, even an epiphenomenon.

The classic literary Utopias, which represent experimental play seemingly devoid of utopian will, leave out this stage, thanks to imagination's licence to please without responsibility. But the depiction of what men *are* in a fictional existence only serves to indicate, tentatively and indirectly (with a stamp of frivolity which suits this mode of allusive thought), what man in reality *could and ought to be*. But Utopia is in fact an 'individual' and arbitrary community located outside any social setting, cut off from the outside world, and indifferent or hostile towards 'society'. These somehow *asocial* characteristics merely translate into the language of achieved perfection a pretension to universalism and a view of man as he exists in social reality. The utopian chapel standing apart from the world and sheltered from its influences is not an asylum for fugitives but prefigures the one world made perfect, the body of tomorrow's divinity.

Apart from rationalist and abstractionist perfectionism linked with the literary flourishes of constructive Utopia, there is another source of social utopism – the millenarian tradition. This is a version of the sectarian form of religious experience, and heralds the 'conspiratorial' mode of political organization, whose heroic and monstrous greatness bursts forth in Marxism–Leninism. This supremely vigorous force, the main theme of our epoch, presents a striking analogy with the isolation device characteristic of utopias in the original sense. The millenarian dream of setting up on this earth a material 'kingdom of heaven' as *this other and unique* reality – perfect as such and owing nothing to any tricks of organizational genius – is social from the start; it necessarily and directly engages the will, despite the important differences between this conception of the human will and that of constructive rationalists long exposed to Enlightenment thinking. The millenarian devotion to a 'numinous' force beyond man's calculating reason survives, scientifically disguised, in historiolatry, which serves to distinguish the Marxist–Leninist type of humanism from what Marx called 'utopist' socialisms. In fact Marx's utopism, though he brushes aside with disdain the idyllic detailed representations of the perfect society of the future readily set forth by the makers of literary and fantastic Utopias, brings to Utopia not only a serious and stubborn determination to realize it, but also an intrinsic dimension of supreme importance: the para-religious belief in the *necessity* of the perfect order of things. The full human Reality, which is Society, the unique subject, in which everything human is founded and expressed, *must* come. Then the individual will be completely free and all-powerful because he will be purified from all scissure between himself and society, and hence from all the divisions which rend him in his virtually pre-human, pre-historical and unreal condition of yesterday and today.

To end these remarks on social utopism, let me add two caveats to ward off any puerile misunderstanding:

(a) No form of social utopism, as existing reality and active force in history, could be 'deduced' or 'reconstructed' in the terms of a pure dialectic of ideas, or even those of a descriptive analysis of some conceivable mental structure. For example, the 'full flowering' (or the 'culmination') 'of social utopism' does not in the least *define* Communism, and would certainly not allow us to guess some of its salient and essential traits.

(b) Again, the historical evolution of social utopism in general, and its especially emphatic presence in certain societies and at certain times, cannot possibly be understood as the simple effect of an original cause, susceptible of neat definition and itself bearing an unambiguously utopian sign. The analysis of the chains of concepts, together with their affective charge, which constitute the utopian mind seems to me indispensable for a *sociology* of utopism, but could not replace or be confused with it.

4 THE UTOPIAN CONTRADICTION

It has been noted that the number of people who leave, or try to leave, the countries making up the Communist empire to take refuge in the more imperfect world which we are pleased to call 'free', considerably exceeds that of those who leave their countries in the opposite direction. But those who have studied the constructions of literary Utopia (sometimes with sympathy and admiration) have often noted something even more important from the theoretical point of view. The level of contentment of the inhabitants of Utopia is equivocal; but the literary utopists, expecting this, instinctively provide elaborate measures, more or less severe, for preventing the corruption of utopian obedience and virtue by the allurements of the non-utopian environment, or by the weeds which, it seems, continue to burgeon in the depths of the human heart. Liberty of opinion and the freedom to criticize do not flourish any more spectacularly in versions of Utopia than in the hard and austere reality of Soviet Russia. It has been said that no utopia would ever tolerate '*utopists*'; no 'citizen' of a utopia would ever be allowed to play with the thought of a *rival* utopian conception, or even the demands of values considered false and empty in *his own* community – in the spirit of its rulers and its creator. Utopian institutions and the psychological workings of the individual actions which depend on them can, *a priori*, function only if they function '*perfectly*', or with perfect accuracy; every individual lapse, every irruption of the unforeseen, would threaten to bring on the collapse of the entire system. The uniformity of joyful spontaneity presupposes a foundation of comprehensive and seamless artificiality.

I therefore venture to maintain that Utopia suffers from an *utterly fundamental contradiction*. It promises to do away with fetters and frictions, and to heal wounds. None of this is conceivable without the creation of a new scissure, paramount and absolutely permanent. No mere traditional practices, which can clearly die down and disappear, are at issue here, but human spontaneity itself, which is supposed *both* to be established in power and *also* to be excluded. This novel and utterly strained polarity, which cannot be avowed yet must be proclaimed, an object of shame as of pride, leaves its imprint on every aspect of a so-called 'integrated' life. 'Realist' critics of utopism miscalculate in their insinuation that utopian joys are 'easy to conceive but hard, if not impossible, to realize'. This is irrelevant. It is, in fact, easy to imagine a utopian ideal, but impossible to think it through to the end without contradiction, however inscrutable one's ratiocinations. If we are to believe the Catholic writer G. Möbus, the literal meaning of

Utopia, 'a country nowhere', shows an ironical intention in the mind of its creator, Thomas More. The martyred chancellor by no means identified himself with his character Hythloday, spokesman of the utopian society. He wanted to show, on the one hand, that unbelievers, rational and virtuous after their fashion, were capable of setting up a social practice superior in some respects to that of the bad Christians and pseudo-Christians of Europe; and, on the other hand, that this fantasy of non-Christian perfection, a work of insubstantial and irresponsible speculative construction, is sullied with rank impurities and cannot in general stand up. Utopia depends on nothingness, its place is 'nowhere'. This would accord with the dull and anaemic atmosphere of More's utopian picture, emphasized by Raymond Ruyer. The obvious blemishes in utopist projects which have been put into practice no doubt include accidental features. But they primarily indicate something that cannot be realized *because* it *cannot be conceived* in serious, intellectually responsible, fashion – despite the imagination the project can kindle and the determined will it can excite.

Utopian man is man seduced, swayed, hypnotized by the idol of absolute perfection; he adores and serves what he does not desire, wants what opposes his needs, worships what bears no relation to his authentic experiences and appreciations. Abandoned to utopist ecstasy, he neither loves nor hates what he pursues; his object is a pretentious promissory abstraction, whose emotional lure, though powerful, is insulated from the full structure of human affectivity. Quasi-utopian man of the modern age in its most characteristic manifestations is man blunted by being the bearer of a sovereign will released from all constraint: man cut in two – tyrant and slave – in the name of his unity, mirror or substitute for divinity. Today's man, in his standard form, is enslaved by the supreme and unique ideal of having or being able to have whatever he wants, without wanting anything of his own choice, without knowing what he wants, dreaming of pure availability rather than of individual things defined, designed, given, lost, venerated, wished for or coveted. The cult of the machine and the mania for speed are eloquent symbols of this.

'Objectivation' and 'alienation' are the key to the utopian contra-diction. (These Marxist concepts actually originate in Romanticism and pre-Marxist Naturalism.) A 'normal' inhabitant of the civilized world – a world of much harshness and opacity, of many obstacles and contingencies – finds himself confronted by a vast multiform universe of 'validities in themselves': of values, norms, laws, obligations, statutes and institutional requirements. (All this resembles a new and difficult tract of country, which demands much experience, study, tact, good manners and self-mastery before it affords the settler a tolerable and perhaps satisfactory existence.) He cannot meet his needs, pursue his ends, or secure for himself the decencies of life, without being guided by, respecting and employing these 'mysterious' intermediaries, these 'powers' become autonomous, these 'objectivations' evolved from human needs but not immediately or exactly translatable into the language of human needs. This endlessly repeated experience of limitation, this necessity of submission to massive 'facts' and impersonal 'dignities', the renunciations and patience (divided attention, absence of intuitive unity) demanded by a life thus framed in a complex of orders – all this offends our taste for perfection and unity, our instinct for domination and our penchant for ease.

The utopist project is, then, to render objectivations transparent, to lead them back to their source in 'pure' humanity, to dissolve them in human intelligibility, direct and unitary.

The only possible outcome of this simplification is a tissue of forced, arbitrary and monomaniac interpretations, coupled with a system of total power for regulating the ensemble of human lives which make up the social unit; for only thus can 'the human' pure and simple at least seem to *be raised above objective autonomies and norms*. The process certainly strips objectivations – those ponderous ghosts of the institutional and the artificial – of their more distinctively 'objective' elements – of measures, rules, validities and directives which do not come from any human will, individual or collective (they are 'found', discovered, interpreted and adjusted to concrete situations by human reason and feeling, not invented or created by man, and they support as much as confine his moral being). But by the same token, they become infinitely more crushing.

Objectivations are resented as an 'alienation'. This word puts a keener stress on the transitory frailty of the individual in the midst of social forces that are 'alien' to him – social authorities whose will cannot be seen to emanate from his own, and whose actions are not an expression of his own agency. But once there is only *a single* public will, a will that is not simply 'political', governmental and administrative but constituted by faith in the transformatory ideology, and claiming to command not only the external actions of individuals but also their wills, motives and existential depths, alienation will seem to be in the process of being 'overcome' at the very moment when it is *pushed to the extreme*. (Compare the *'total alienation'* of the individual will of the 'citizen' in the *Contrat Social*, the guarantee that he can rely on 'obeying nobody but himself'.) The rapture both imposes and suggests identification; that is, it evokes in the subject a sensation – ghostly, unreal, delusive and uncertain, but all the same sometimes intoxicating – of his own liberty and power 'by extension', of his own reality regained.

Moreover, this psychological and pseudo-logical stratagem relies on certain palpable and indubitable material guarantees. The utopian movement or power supports, pursues or secures the abolition of certain injustices or hardships, the increase of economic well-being or cultural opportunities. These will be taken as clear signs that its aims are universally desirable; the subject can easily take them as expressions of his own will, and that of all his fellow-citizens (bar the malicious and benighted). But this does nothing to change the super-alienation inherent in Utopia, and inseparable from its basic law. For it is conceived as a *world set apart from the ordinary world*, cut off from mankind (with all its historical variations), determined by a particular idea out of touch with the many separate instincts, intuitions and valuations of man; a world ruled directly and arbitrarily, with no limiting principles derived from the nature of things, by a mind and a will which are single and utterly particular, human and superhuman at the same time. Despite the presence of satisfactions rooted in real needs and in the habitual patterns of human thought and will, this new sense of alienation, with its notes of discomfort, terror, nightmare and atrophy of the soul, is bound to persist. It will sometimes even manifest itself in the aggravations of a unique and crushing tension, required by the logic of the situation. For any relaxation of tension would encourage the spectre of 'normalization', and mean the suicide of Utopia and a return to extra-utopian frameworks (modified, perhaps, by the deposit of institutional and psychic changes wrought by the utopian regime).

The utopian protagonists of the struggle against alienations *cannot want* alienation to disappear in reality; the logic of their undertaking compels them to contradict themselves on this ultimate and decisive point. The more successful they are, the more they are condemned to Sisyphaean labour. In brief, the dream of putting an end to alienation *must* produce it to an extreme degree, because it signifies the will to impose on the fundamental structure of man's relations with things, his fellows, his past and all that has helped to form his mental categories precisely *what is most alien to him*. Pascal said: 'He who would make an angel will make a beast' – a precious anti-utopian half-truth. One might add that he who wants to cleanse 'the profane' from all embarrassing and constraining ingredients of the 'sacred' will destroy the autonomy of the 'profane' and also subject man to so much pressure from the ubiquitous 'sacred' (in a sociological sense) that his life will be engulfed rather than simply penetrated, enhanced and reorientated. Thoroughbred utopism does not just aim to realize an idea of 'perfection'; it aims to give birth thereby to *the* authentic reality, to definitive and real 'reality', so to speak; this is why any reductionist metaphysics, insisting on a clean disjunction between what is 'only appearance' and a reality other than the 'phenomenal' world, encourages the formation of the utopian mind. The Platonic utopia of the *Republic* is, in a way, the *topos ouranios* [heavenly place] of the 'ideas' which are the 'true' reality behind things, constructed in embodied form by the sage who has been able to gain the co-operation of the wielders of power. The central theme of Marxism – to install man in his 'full reality' stripped of 'objectivations', impersonal 'fetishes', 'superstructures' which mask the human reality of economic practice, and so on – reproduces this same structure on a clearly very different plane, and one may find in it other avatars with a spiritualist or materialist sign, with more or less explicit emphasis on political action, and, inevitably, running counter to the constitution of the real world.

Utopists have often been reproached with a readiness to sacrifice man present and living – today's and tomorrow's generations, with their interests, values, rights and ways of life – for a human perfection, indeterminate and uncertain, projected into an obscure future. In fact, 'constructing the future' at the price of present sacrifices is a corollary of man's temporal continuity, and an integral

dimension of the meaning of life (though utopian high tension –
with its prospect of blissful freedom from tension - degrades this
relation to the point of absurdity, since the sole meaning of my life
could not consist in its serving only to ensure the joyful perfection
of beings as yet unborn but merely abstractly envisaged. The
subordination and the rupture of continuity contradict each other).
But the absurdity of the utopian conception of temporal succession
in an inverted sense has also been noted, albeit less commonly.
A group of 'imperfect' and 'prehistoric' planners, formed and
encumbered by the defective legacy of the non-utopian past, claims
to install itself as free and omnipotent creator of the 'perfect' Man
of the future, the citizen of Utopia; the superior is to be consciously
and scientifically conditioned and enclosed in its happy automatism
by the inferior, who has emerged from the darkness of the world of
imperfection; man who is more than man, puppet of a pre-existent
determining will here below, from the stock of a less than human
humanity!

Strictly speaking, this formula does not exactly apply to Marxist–Leninist utopism, which rejects the idle elaboration of the
lineaments of the future society, and undoubtedly implies an
aspect of robust pragmatic realism, a compounding with empirical
reality. But in fact it constitutes much the most powerful form
of the utopian will, of Utopia's expropriation of reality, and
merely signals a change of emphasis. We pass from the genre of
exploratory imagination to that of an iron determination to mould
the future with the help of a power-apparatus free of all inhibition,
in accordance with unalterable axioms and the sanctified categories
of unyielding doctrine. Its technical and instrumental flexibility, its
'tactical elasticity', cannot in any way admit of any fundamental
pliancy. Here the utopian contradiction is not so much between
the beatific mirage of total spontaneous harmony and the petty
regimentation of everyday life (obligatory meals in common, and
all kinds of ceremonies redolent of comic opera, over which the
classic utopists and their admirers enthused); rather, it is between
this same mirage of a future buzzing with human activity untainted
by violence – this is the 'reign of man over things' which must
replace the 'reign of man over man' – and the universal terror,
'permanent revolution', the atmosphere of a tyranny which *sets
out to be* extraordinary. Apart from its 'technical' function, terror

is above all the *sign of the survival of the state of emergency* as opposed to the worldly and dispersed 'normality' of extra-utopian society. At the same time, it is the magic and 'surreal' sign that Utopia, not yet attained but always just over the horizon, *is 'realized' here and now in another sense* – namely, that utopism occupies the territory whence the original act of revolution has swept away the non-utopian world, and that the 'evolution' controlled by the utopian will can no longer deviate from the path which must lead to the final accomplishment of Utopia as *sole* reality.

But the utopian dream of unity cannot extend its parasitic mode of existence over 'imperfect' reality. The duality established between it and this malleable yet stubborn reality, as vulnerable as it is indestructible, is the very kernel of its mentality, and the condition of its being able to get a hold on reality and modify it. Were 'organized violence' to appear to be entering its final stage of 'vanishing away', Utopia itself would collapse. Its life depends on the diminished or hidden presence of the tensions it is called to keep back and to mask. In order that totalitarianism may keep alive its proper *raison d'être*, it is constrained to uphold, to engrave on the minds it represents and directs, the unshapely and opaque existence of non-utopian human reality, and the anti-utopian opponents it strives to overcome and claims to eliminate. Social utopism will have left its imprint on reality; it has proved itself capable of bringing about a mighty historical transformation. But however titanic its endeavours, it cannot bring about a metaphysical change in man. Man cannot replace himself by a being superior to himself, carved in human material after a human conception; what is more, although he can dedicate and sacrifice himself for this presumptuous goal, so alien to his own life-goals, he can only will it in opposition to his concrete pursuit of values.

5 UTOPISMS

Corresponding to the indeterminate number of 'Utopias', to which a new specimen, differing in many respects from its predecessors, could always be added, there exists a no less essential plurality of 'utopisms' – that is, of historical and typological realizations of the utopian mind. For example, any wide-ranging utopism tends to inspire some form of political totalitarianism. But in the first place, the utopian mind may not be wide-ranging, but confine itself to a perfectionist mania bearing on a restricted material or a particular set of ideas. Secondly, the emergence of political totalitarianism is not a simple corollary of the utopian mind, but also depends on certain objective conditions. Finally, as is well known, clearly distinct types of totalitarianism are possible thanks to the necessity for concrete determination of the perfectionist abstractions. In other words, the idols which spur the utopian will to irrupt into the reality of existing historical forces, and the scales of values acknowledged by the societies or social circles concerned, must be identified. We find here another manifestation of the utopian contradiction. The utopian island cannot complete its mission except by finally engulfing the human universe; the new being it represents is in principle incompatible with its insertion into the non-utopian world; at the same time, it cannot yet abandon its insular peculiarity, the foundation of its identity as Utopia.

Because the utopian mind is monist, theoretical, anti-traditional, and in love with construction and planning, and thus hostile to 'given' reality and 'common sense', to a sense of limitations and equilibrium, it is bound to be potentially subversive and, most probably, of the 'Left'. But there are complications. There are no logically rigorous relations either between extremism and the 'Left', or between utopism and extremism. (In the first case, although Fascism and Nazism developed in partial opposition to conservative doctrines, they had more affinity with traditional conservatism and rightist nationalism than with any other political groupings; in the second, non-utopian motives, resulting from temperament or circumstances, may curb extremist zeal, and partially but distinctively utopian spirits may be timid or fastidious.) Besides, *in relation to the world produced or planned by Utopia*, the utopian mind displays a kind of rigid and authoritarian conservatism hostile to all criticism and frightened by any spontaneous thought of reform. Plato's *Republic*, the first and most celebrated of the great classic Utopias, despite its reckless abstract constructions and its mechanist and socialist aspects, is stamped with a 'rightist' sign because of its hostility towards democracy, or competitive egalitarianism, and its pseudo-restorative archaism. By contrast, the ideologies and programmes of the 'Left', though rarely without some dependence on utopian thought-patterns and enthusiasms, may reveal an anti-utopian dominant in their attempts to bestow compensatory advantages on the weak, limit the scope of privilege, watch over the exercise of social power in the light of rational and moral criteria which are open to public examination and discussion.

Certainly leftist utopism is utopism in its primordial shape, most likely to be authentic and efficacious. For tradition and continuity are the major anti-utopian forces; moral codes in the full sense (quite independent of actual power *hic et nunc*) are themselves traditional, and the formation and exercise of discursive reason and individual conscience both depend on traditions and the capacity for detachment which is engendered by social stability. What we might call rightist Utopia could also be called reactionary, or again 'interpretative', since it denotes a kind of return to a species of perfectionism fixated on an illusory interpretation of existing, or long past, reality. It is, therefore, a kind of counterfeit Utopia, and can neither command the fervour nor approach the audacity, thoroughness and universal note of 'true' utopism. Besides, reactionary Utopia is largely pseudo-traditionalist, falsifying the tradition by which it claims to be inspired and squeezing it into the mould of an artificial, simplistic and rigid pattern; moreover, it idolizes a distant past, arbitrarily selected, and in this way becomes itself a participant in the subversive mode of *breaking continuity*. But even subversive utopism itself usually has some backward-looking elements – myths of a golden age before the fatal scissures intervened, of the 'noble savage' not yet spoiled by the incongruities of historical contingency or soiled by the tacky deposits of civilization; of bygone democracies, or a universal vocation to manual work.

Only a very brief glance can be cast here on the varieties and the problem of '*limited utopism*'. In general the term is applied to illusions of 'departmental' perfection, concerning a limited sphere of objects or activities (by contrast with the human condition as a whole), or to highly pretentious systems, self-enclosed, symmetrical, with a look of 'definitive satisfactoriness', provided such conceptions are of a kind to determine choices and suggest directives for action. Examples include (a) the economic fetishes of 'automatic equilibrium' ensured by the free play of market forces, or, by contrast, of the planned economy as guarantee of general well-being; (b) the doctrine of the perfect state constitution, guarantee of the real goodness of things; (c) medical monomanias and other gospels of pseudo-science; (d) blinkered and literal adherence to arbitrary yet plausible sets of 'rules of life' or 'words of wisdom'. Besides this there is a whole range of concepts with a strongly emotional slant, not in themselves utopian (or only ambiguously so), which have been elaborated and made into a cult by thinkers tainted with utopism and utopian ways of thinking. 'Peace', 'progress', 'personality', 'nationality', 'the organization of relations between persons and institutional functions in a framework of moral norms' – each of these stands for a genuine well-known possibility, crowned with a halo of authentic and lofty values; but the 'ideological' life makes these into a set of utopian and virtually self-contradictory concepts such as 'pacifism', 'progressivism' (or 'belief in progress'), 'national self-determination' or fetishistic phrases with a utopian ring like 'the Rights of Man', 'democracy' ['*la* démocratie'], and 'social justice' ['*la* justice sociale'].

Limited, 'departmental' or 'partial' Utopia may be distinct from total Utopia, but it still *insinuates* a perspective of total 'perfection', and the general utopian conception of human being. In the main it is not so much its intrinsic aim (achievable or not) as the ideological attitude, the atmosphere of half-hidden hopes and pretensions in which it pursues it, which betrays the presence of illusion at war with reality, and the utopism eager to replace it with a 'new' reality rather than improve it. The constitutive trait of utopism is not the passion to implant value in reality or to develop its profusion of values, but a delight in confusing them and the mirage of an identity between value and reality, first to be postulated and then to be created once and for all; it is not even a disordered and one-sided relentlessness but, rather, the compelling idea of an order at variance with the given order of creation.

(Translated by Francis Dunlop)

EDITOR'S NOTE
The original paper, 'La Mentalité Utopienne' (*La Table Ronde* [Paris], 153, September 1960, pp. 62–84), had a bibliography. This will be found at the end of the present volume, supplemented by other works used by Kolnai for his Utopia project.

Utopia and Alienation

Utopia can be defined as life without alienation. The contradiction this entails is the gravest kind of contradiction proper to a utopia-ridden society.

Alienation means man's being confronted with what is not himself: the landscape of alterity which constitutes his world – indeed, defines world as such. In especial, it means human alterity, that is, the non-existence of '*Man*', and man's dependence on human reality that is not the expression of *his* mind and will; moreover, and above all, not the expression of any self-identical and unitary human essence and will (with which he might identify himself). Dimensions of alterity are:

(i)   objective categories and their inexorable, opaque autonomy (e.g. money, scarcity, values, rights, laws, obligations, taboos, the physical, the supersensible);

(ii)   works of man 'given' not only to the subject but to the society of which he is a member (e.g. towns, districts, institutions, traditions);

(iii)   the essential distinctness and precarious harmony between actual human wills; the impossibility of 'democracy' proper; spontaneous 'general will' as a mere limiting case;

(iv)   the caducity of the individual life and the transitoriness of self;

(v)   the very fact of conscience;

(vi)   the problematicity of practice;

(vii)   the contingency of the social process (including history) and its elusion of tests of justice and rational order.

Alienation is reality: *selfhood in its limitation*. It involves pressure, sobriety and resignation. Not human pursuits as such, but human pursuits to a large extent are of necessity aimed at a smoothing out and damping down of alienation. Thus: love, fight, curiosity, understanding, virtue, possessions, rank, equalization, conquest, adaptation, ordering, institutions, rationalization, planning, fraternities, levels of equality and identity. Likewise, a religious interpretation and integration of life. But alienation also constitutes a fount of pleasure, thrill, happiness, vitality, a sense of being alive, a 'sense of being in the world'. It belongs to a normal, balanced and vigorous life not only to reduce some alienations but also lustily and affirmatively to experience alienation and the tension of self and spontaneity with the solid opposition emanating from the world.

There is, however, a (virtually) utopian *temper* (or state of mind) hypersensitive to alienation, and there are historical (crisis) situations in which alienation forces itself upon men's attention (some significant men's, shall we say) as an unbearable burden. These may be situations of homelessness and uprooting, the emergence of new powers, laws, points of view, standards and thing-autonomies, which tower above men's lives as frightening ghosts and impress their minds with an experience of the meaninglessness of things, of life and the world. Hence a terrain favourable for the rise of Utopias, 'flight from the world', and a yearning for subversion as a new vehicle of meaning. Naturally, there are other important conditions: factors facilitating mob actions; possibilities of expansion; a sense of incongruity between the unsatisfactoriness of present existence and its containing peculiar promises of satisfaction (e.g. productivity, the wealth of the wealthy, science); the predominance of emptiness and spiritual (perhaps with material) starvation over the more palpable and sobering pains of crude anarchy and rabid tyranny (which, like massive bodily injuries, are hardly stimulating for the utopian state of mind and rather calculated to arouse common-sense reactions).

Alienation was discovered by Rousseau, Hegel, Feuerbach, Marx, Kierkegaard, Nietzsche, twentieth century irrationalism and fascism (Sorel, Hitler, down to Marrero's 'intimate power') under the impact of such events and circumstances as the establishment of 'civilization' in a strict and emphatic sense (enlightened absolutism, centralization and formalization); the Industrial Revolution (which characteristically is *not* a centrally planned political revolution proper); the loss of a transcendent meaning of life; the threatening ghost of *accomplished order*; the survival of social hierarchy in a climate of 'self-evident' atomistic equality; the discrepancy between harmonistic economics and socioeconomic facts; the emergence of money as a spectral monistic all-determinant of social relations; trade crises and unemployment; the fictitiousness (to a large extent) of constitutionalism and the functional rule of politicians; the unintelligible character of Party and later of trade-union 'bureaucracy'; the machine age; the unreality of the speculative metaphysical systems (in particular Hegel's, with its comprehensive pretensions).

Utopia, the volitive dream of spontaneity, harmony, and self-realization in a universe of 'Man', is directed against alienation as such, by contrast with an endeavour to correct alienative processes at single salient points: against a world of health and disease as distinct from the attempt to remedy urgent diseases. Rather than trying to modify human conditions, it aims at the impossible creation of 'Man' (compare socialism as against a correction of property distribution, planning as against intervention at key points, abolition as against regulation and control of privilege). By 'impossible' I mean an impossibility verging on the analytic (going against human nature or, more critically put, 'the basic constitution of man', which precludes the actualized existence of 'Man'). Instead of endeavouring to relativize hyper-autonomous objectivations and apparently extra-human quasi absolutes, it tends to replace them with a unitary and all-embracing Absolute, an identical and direct expression of man's mind and will. It thus introduces a new form of alienation, an unheard-of super-alienation; not that this is the express content of its programme, but as the sign and effect of its logical absurdity, negation of reality tied to its descent upon reality, and incurable self-contradiction.

It is clear that a real sense of alienation does exist in normal social life, and that utopianism brings with it one kind of sense of *non*-alienation or 'restoration of man to self'. Otherwise, it could not have sprung up and become a lasting force. It is from here that we should approach Totalitarianism. Utopia, like evil (that is, sin), arises from the context of ordinary human motives and ultimately settles down in the texture of reality, which it has helped to mould. Its evilness resides between its origins and its enduring effects; in its central substance, not in its pre-natal germs or its residual survival. Put differently: in its subsistence *as* utopian concept and endeavour, representing an eccentric, perverse and contradictory scheme of counter-reality at war with reality.

It is this last proposition that expresses the character of Utopia as *super-alienation*; all domination of reality by the utopian idol places man in a medium utterly divorced from (though, in its contents, not altogether unrelated to) his everyday concerns, traditional categories and spontaneous self-activity. In the real world, man is confronted (in various ways and measures) with the ineliminable ghostly aspects of the non-ghostly familiar universe; in the utopian atmosphere or regime, he is at the mercy of a ghost-world. For the lunatic tints of the normal world has been substituted the lunatic asylum as the exclusive universe.

Tolerably normal man, in circumstances of reasonable normality, *feels at home in the midst of alienation.* This is the salient point. He is not a *mere* plaything of meaningless and impenetrable, uncanny and sinister forces, but an agent, reminded again and again of his weakness, fragility, ignorance and other limitations, but lodged in his habitual kinship with his environment (in the widest sense) and the traditions which made him (i.e. from whose framework he has grown towards, and in, freedom) and on which he somehow freely reacts. He is, within limits, in a position to try conclusions with what is hostile to his essence or concerns, and compresses his free space. He may play off one set of alien forces surrounding him against another. His sense of alienation is assuaged by virtue of the very fact that he experiences alienness not simply 'between himself and the world' but within the world. As against stridently alien forces, he may rely upon the effectiveness of other, more familiar and more friendly ones. All this splitness and order in manifoldness is part of his homeland and the constitution of his mind, and in such a sense he is at one with the world: his own normal consciousness being worldly. It is only a concourse of exceptional conditions, inner and outer, personal and social, including factors like an exceptional rate of social change, which evokes a sense of unbearable, overwhelming alienness, powerlessness, homelessness and isolation.

Utopia enters with an emphasis of millenarian hope grafted on despair; concentrating, exaggerating and pushing to excess the experience of alienation (instead of dissolving it in parts and mitigating it at other points) with an anti-mundane experience of radical oneness, fusion, harmony, and made-to-order homelikeness. It converts the world into a lunatic asylum; very well, by the same token it converts the world into 'one house', if not 'one hall'. The magic concept stands as a consolatory upper storey of mental existence against mere reality proper, disorderly and oppressive reality teeming with alienations; or, having *become* reality in a totalitarian movement and then in a totalitarian regime, it stands as true and self-fulfilling reality as against residual, fixational, obsolescent, fragmentary and doomed failure-reality. No doubt it is in fact unrealizable; it cannot even be *willed* to be realized precisely because it goes against the fundamental laws of human reality (individuation and its primary implications; object-knowledge and the alienness that implies: 'ob-jectum') and is defined by its character of goal, movement, alienness from the real world, and un-spontaneity as a guarantee of everything being subordinated to the paramount aim and forced into the rhythm of the 'march'. Utopia realized collapses as Utopia; the utopian experience is tied to a double world, the utopian super-world and the ordinary world of concerns, the existence of which must therefore be preserved (and whose most evident – though in part arbitrarily selected – contents must even receive a special cult, not only for tactical reasons but for the essential reason of keeping alive a sense of sameness between the two strata, and of the process as self-fulfilment and self-integration). If *monism is thus a reality*, it is *dependent for its life on dualism*; a fearful and formidable reality indeed, it is dependent on emphasizing its character as an appearance distinct from and antithetic to reality. This is symbolized by 'the Party', 'the *Kreml*', the various trappings of Asiatic tyranny, the 'nightly tribunal' of Plato's *Laws*, secret 'justice', the sense of omnipresent peril mingled with blind faith in invincibility, mystical materialism, and so on. The mankind in spontaneous control of life, the mankind of harmonic selves and all-pervading social unity, released from shackles and autonomous collective entities and taboos ... would amount to a new contradiction: a *non-utopian mankind* busy setting up new concrete objectivations and returning to the reality of multiple alienations. This must be avoided at all costs; the fanatical utopian will is a victim of its utopianism, and cannot but avoid achieving what it is committed to achieve, though with febrile emphasis incessantly achieving all kinds of things materially connected with its unfulfillable central aim.

Now what if there *is* a 'utopian mankind' deriving satisfaction from this monolithic, all-of-a-piece self-alienation, and *preferring* it to the mundane common sense experience of alienation? Which feels *at home* in the totalitarian hell? Why not?

It is impossible to forbid anyone to feel happy under utopian government, just as it is impossible to forbid a masochist to enjoy maltreatment and humiliation. It is also impossible to deny that satisfactions of this kind exist. No utopian regime could be established and survive if it did not respond to certain mass aspirations, and did not actually procure satisfaction to a great number of people. The utopian type of super-alienation is not assimilable to a vulgar error capable of direct and unequivocal rectification. What we have to say against it is the following:

(i)   It is evil as a fiction, a monstrous lie, a misrepresentation of reality. It pretends mendaciously to do away with alienation, and pretends that it is possible to eliminate alienation.

(ii) By the same token, it perpetuates itself as a transition towards a goal which is inaccessible and which it refuses to achieve. It is perhaps the only system of consciously willed and issue-less anarchy (cf. Arendt: not the leader's *command* but the leader's *will* is supreme: the object is more to enrapture than to force the will of the individual).

(iii) It in fact appeals only to a more or less exceptionally perverted type of man. Human nature is changeable in many ways, but its fundamental data are ineradicable. The subjects of utopian regimes are not and cannot become, as a rule, happy. Utopianism is proved to breed isolation, increased selfishness and cynicism, and so on. Prolonged utopian domination is likely to land in a destructive crisis, owing to the necessary adaptation to reality and loss of magic accompanying its realization.

(iv) But supposing it did succeed in breeding a generalized species of utopian mankind, the horrible sacrifices required would suffice to outweigh its justification; present and continuous human concerns would be not served but contravened by that endeavour.

(v)   Indeed, herein lies the climax of alienation: the subjection of man's concerns, not to a world of restraints, restrictions, necessities, scarcities, laws, value demands, and so on, which claim to confront and control, not to supplant them (in fact, to modify, guide, educate and in many ways serve them), but to the *concerns of a discontinuously different kind of man* (another species, rather). There is no connecting link except a present coterie of tyrannous cranks and their appeal, not to men as such, but to men in so far as they have developed one aspect of degraded mass-being.

What man wants, what he agrees to, what he accepts, what he is satisfied with – these matters are extremely complex. It is only on certain presuppositions and in certain types of situation – on certain scales of comparison – that it is possible to distinguish unequivocally between volitive affirmation and negation: acceptance and rejection. Thus, many Communists are not true Utopians but disgusted with other parties, or mistake Communism for a harbinger of justice; again, many adherents (or at any rate, loyal subjects) of a Communist regime take this position from conservatism and fear of destructive consequences in case of its tottering.

There is undoubtedly such a thing as 'false consciousness' [*unwirkliche Gesinnung*], though this is a dangerous concept which it is very tempting to misuse.

What Utopia overcomes – or, rather, does not overcome but does in fact suppress to a degree and, above all, obscures as an experience – is not the irremovable split in man but his proximate, natural and multiform splitness, at the price of working the deepest imaginable cleavage in him: not a world of corresponding entities surrounding his self but his subjugation by an imaginary and partly present but ghost-like and parasitical 'self' not his self; and this in a sense incomparably further extended than in the case of such regulative powers as Law, Conscience, 'Superego', Divinity or Christ, which essentially fall short of claiming to constitute his self *in place of* his self.

EDITOR'S NOTE

This paper is undated, but was probably written in the early sixties. It seems to be referred to in Kolnai's 'running notes' for the continuation of Chapter III of *The Utopian Mind*.

The Utopian Negation of Fundamental and Ineliminable Distinctions

1 PRACTICE AND ACTUAL EXTRINSIC SUCCESS

There is a utopian delusion that man can be free from frustration, suffering, the endurance of contradictions, risks and failures: that, given 'perfect' prudence and virtue (in short, an appropriate practice), he is assured of results.

It has a progressive and revolutionary bent: man (the individual as such) here and now cannot make his practice victoriously and fruitfully valid; but *Man* is essentially destined to attain such a status, which is tantamount to his self-realization.

This delusion has Greek and Christian – and, generally, religious – roots. Utopia is secularized religion: where 'secularized' means *both* falsified, distorted, devalued, caricatured *and* 'translated into full reality', 'brought down to earth', 'taken seriously'. Religion and idealistic philosophy – including moralism – places in man's hands an ambiguous IOU, an insolvent title to riches, which he insists on realizing in the progressive-revolutionary attitude.

The progressive and the revolutionary (chiliastic) aspects are alternative modes of approaching reality in the spirit of utopia. They fuse in Marxism–Leninism, where we find presuppositions of Progress (which in Leninism becomes postulate and *task*) and assurance of the direction of 'evolution'; anticipation of the formal structure of fulfilment; and guarantee of the presence of the new world by virtue of political totality.

More particular and more modest manifestations of this delusion are the presupposition that all (grave) evils are avoidable, so that whenever one happens it is somebody's fault, that in a mystical way all evils that befall man are punishments for sins committed, the idea of the 'verdict of history' (chance does not exist in important and public matters); that 'we' are free to 'forge our destiny' and to 'determine the future'; even the stoical idea that the 'sage', though not lord over his outward fate, is not significantly touched by it and is omnipotent, at least in the sense of being the only source of his own happiness.

Historicist fatalism (Hegel, Marx) is utopian as a circuitous pretension to *total mastery* of fate, projected into the future (self-realization: task and certainty) but anticipated in the form of present understanding of necessity (and faith in the possibility of real coincidence of necessity and freedom).

Though it is apparently a denial of human freedom (and *de facto*, aiming at annihilation of the freedom of the individual), historicist fatalism is true utopian practicism, far more pretentious than direct, first-order, utopia referred to the individual or even to the state ('administrative' Socialism) by virtue of the mystical totality it portends, and of its essentially unverifiable validity. To create human reality anew is a 'solution' entirely transcending the scope of ordinary practicism and organizationalism.

2 PRACTICE AND ITS SPECULATIVE-TECHNICAL APPARATUS

Utopianism substitutes knowledge of facts, intellectual certainty and mechanical efficiency for practice proper. In other words, it reduces man's estimative and prudential functions to scientific clearness, unequivocality and pre-established control of 'means'.

'Ends' are taken for granted, as an absolute constant. Man is not to elaborate his ends *in vivo* [in practical life], while dealing with means. Commensuration involves no decisions, it being a matter of comparing two quantities. 'Choice' is as irrelevant as it is between a correct and an incorrect sum.

There is standardization of needs as opposed to standards of conduct. Practical error occurs in the sense of miscalculations only – wholly reducible to speculative error. Hence the moral emphasis or collateral of practice proper is undermined: man cannot misjudge, partly from moral infirmity, what he really and enduringly wants (though this is really the essence of practical error: by no means identical with immorality, but quite different from erroneous beliefs about causal efficacy and inefficacy or external states of fact).

This delusion is necessarily related to levelling and tyranny on the one hand, to the mirage of human omnipotence on the other. For, of course, the well-nigh ineffable and unjudgeable character of true personal practice, while affirming the rational freedom (self-governance) of man, precludes the guarantee of success – its evidence and testability.

We can dispose of and rule over stones more perfectly than we can command bread. Only – stones are stones, not bread. Synthetic 'psyche' is pliantly accessible to science – because it is *not* the soul of man.

The whole modern problem of culture and education issues from this misconception. All goods tend to lose value – to become mere shadows of goods – owing to the assumption of illegitimate sovereignty over their administration. The more unlimited our disposal of them seems, the less they have the substance of goods.

The rationalist-utopian negation of practice leads to immoralism, for man as a practical being (exercising prudence) is a quasi-moral being by contrast to man as a mere subject of desires and claims, a mere beneficiary of catering and enjoyer of security and possessions. Practice means not, indeed, man's subjection to standards of (his own) value and to a higher claim upon him, but the necessity of man to seek his good (the good *for* him) by taste, choice, discrimination and judgement, which is an approximation and complement of morality. The negation of the distinction between practice and its speculative-technical presuppositions is not identical to the reduction of morality to practice, but aligned with and complementary to it.

Utopia is a *gnostic* attitude – esoteric-ecstatic, 'sapiential' (Greek origins) or modern scientistic. Estimative judgement can be 'bought beforehand' – in tins, as it were. Whereas in reality the life of the pure speculative intellect, including the merely technical, requires the life of practical intelligence; for practical life is centrally the life of the mind, and its atrophy must paralyse the rest.

The tendency to a speculative interpretation of practice essentially implies reduction of the speculative – of knowledge itself – to the patterns of mechanistic science, precisely because our knowledge of human character and situations arises largely in the practical context, and is bound up inseparably with estimative functions. Here as elsewhere, the utopian mirage of perfection through full perspicuity makes for narrowing-down of the object-world of human intelligence, and for blunting human sensibilities.

The ultimate motive of this aberration (as of others) is not, of course, specifically 'modern' but timeless and ever-present and, of course, eminently practical; in short, it is practical impatience. For, so far as it is possible and relevant, the speculative-technical handling of practical problems is most efficacious; in reference to causal relations there exists a possibility of cogent evidence and conviction which is *essentially* impossible in the properly practical context – more so even than in the moral, for on the ethical plane there is at least a skeleton of fixed principles. But practice proper is the most elusive and personal of things. In all practical arguments we instinctively try to clarify and settle in our favour such speculative questions as are implied. (Practical argument proper is not impossible, but is never in itself cogent; it consists chiefly in warning our interlocutor about *possibilities*: 'You think you very much want this, but before long you will regret having given up that other good for its sake'.) Still, the line of the rationalist-reductionist temptation *is* specifically Cartesian, mathematistic and mechanistic, and thus far modern. Its Christian background is fascination with a very high good: *value-free knowledge* (the neutral, non-emotive approach) and its unique reliability. The way for this was prepared by the Christian – anti-heathen – *devaluation of 'the World'*.

3 PRACTICE AND MORALITY

Nevertheless, the logical nerve of Utopia seems to me to consist not so much in the confusion of practice and its speculative-technical conditioning as in the confusion of practice and morality – between the good of the agent and the goodness of the agent, between his pursuit of what is good for him and his choice between right and wrong, between prudence and conscience, between possessions and being (as bearers of value), between human happiness and human quality.

For even practice 'served ready' (on the collective's behalf) fits into the agent's own practical perspective – at least ideally, as being of the same genus: it overemphasizes the serviceableness of the means and, with it, the constancy, evidence and tangibility of the end, but does not interfere with the fundamental categories of value and modes of value-experience. It amounts to indirect atrophy of the soul by expropriation of its intimate function, but not to express destruction of the soul proper. This is the object of the utopian war waged against conscience – that is, moral experience and its claim and mode of obligation; for which Utopia substitutes calculatory prudence within the framework and conditions of a world moralized wholesale and *a priori*.

The overstrung, ambiguous and dangerous – but, rightly interpreted, ethically deep and fruitful – dictum of St Augustine, 'Love and then do what thou wilt', is modified, in utopian thought, into 'Do what thou wilt, provision being taken for what thou wilt being the right thing'. This, of course, is capable of significant variations – of classic variants of interpretation.

It may oscillate between an *immoralist* and a *perfectionist* emphasis. The former is concretely predominant, but could not subsist without the background tinge of the latter. Pure naturalist reduction of morality to practice needs the complementary assurance of ecstatic perfectionism, the moralistic fetishes of justice (as the structural principle of a re-created world), equality, universal solidarity and identity of will. In Rousseau's general will the core of the whole pattern is present. Rousseau is halfway between Mandevillean liberalism (objective regulation making selfishness an extrinsic but infallible instrument of the public good) and chiliastic anarchism (man is *all* good, once he is emancipated from the fetters of contingency, wants, cleavage into groups, division and limitation). Marxism–Leninism adds the assurance of the historical conditions of this emancipation: the purposeful activity of the proletarian class movement, an appropriate new ethics and a reshaping of human nature, simultaneously and interactively with the creation (ordained to the self-creation) of a new *objective* world of *Man*, beyond the distinction of practice and morality.

But this basic aspect of utopianism is not all modern either, nor all emancipationist, at least in the modern Cartesian, rationalist and formalist, *tabula rasa* sense.

Its *Christian* roots are (i) the love-ethic inimical to Law; (ii) the clerical substitution for moral standards of the interests of the Church, an embodiment of sanctity; (iii) the express immoralism and quietism of Luther; (iv) the Calvinist emphasis on the rationally ordered will as a direct expression or prolongation of the Divine Will in the 'elect'; (v) The sectarian renewal of the ethic of love and community over and above the world. (In (ii) and (iv), we find an obvious reflection of *Judaism*: a specified human reality, possessing a privileged contact with God, becomes a principle of morality in place of the intrinsically thematic moral conscience.)

Its *Pagan* roots are: (i) the cult of the sage; (ii) the Platonic aesthetics of the City-state as a falsification of ethics; (iii) the Aristotelian confusion of prudence and morality. In Greek consciousness, the root confusion between 'good for me' and 'my being good' is central.

But, as Greek immoralism is pre-ethical rather than post-ethical, all these forms of aberration remain partly potential, and balanced by some recognition of intrinsic morals. The utopian non-distinction of morality and practice is linked, in its full unfolding, to the modern trend of emancipation and equalization, with the splendour of mathematical science and the 'logicization' of history at its core.

From these immense discoveries arise the specific antagonisms (i) between the relative opaqueness and rational challengeableness of moral obligation and the evidence of mathematical truth, now on a large scale applicable to the promotion of practical ends; and (ii) between the definitiveness and the essentially limited spatio-temporal perspective of moral obligation and the theme of history, with its alleged finality as an imaginable cynosure of conduct. Now, the non-identity of practice and morality constitutes, as it were, the central stigma of man's irremovable defectiveness and limitation – despite the implied possibility of righteous conduct – and thus the central target of utopian enmity. Recall, in this context, the substantiveness and thematic primacy of evil, which in the traditional or common-sense outlook is strictly ineliminable and an element of every life, in its full sense implying guilt for everybody. The ineliminableness of evil as a proximate and living theme is the same thing as the ineliminableness of conscience as a reality.

The utopian conception is directed centrally against conscience – not so much because conscience is the bulwark of personal freedom and an obstacle to collective regimentation as because sin-conscious man cannot believe in the utopian aim and in the redemption of man through mental enlightenment or a set of institutions which would *make* him good simply through his naturally and spontaneously seeking his own good. Utopia – that is, life sanctified as of a piece – is incompatible with the *dualism* of goods and the good, of practice and morality, of prudence and conscience, of will-wholeness and will-direction.

Virtue-ethics is a pre-utopian scheme *par excellence*. It is utopian in that it aims at circumventing conscience and repentance; at reducing morality to a matter of the spontaneous 'appetite'. But (apart from the fact that, in Aristotle, the status of justice is in this regard ambiguous) it is non-utopian in that it ties virtue to prudence and, therefore, personal deliberation (though all this has something ungenuine and aestheticizing about it) and interprets virtue as a product of personal education and slow acquisition, without visualizing it as universal. Virtue, in Aristotle, seems to come about from an unconscious repeated practice of right not at first morally motivated. The pre-utopian naturalism of 'virtue' and also its limits – what separates it from true utopia – are expressed in the formula about 'virtue as a second nature'. Morality proper – that is, a well-ordered conscience and obedience paid to it – is *not* a second nature (however strongly anchored in the agent's nature, and however easily practised as a rule), for moral man *does not 'live out' himself*; but utopian perfectionism understands the good not as man's 'second' nature but as his nature pure and simple. The Aristotelian conception makes of man the inmate of an institute of gymnastics, subject principally to training; the utopian-perfectionist conception, rather, makes of him the inmate of a nursery – fully conditioned but fully sovereign, good without effort and discipline, spontaneously self-realizing and entirely in harmony with the community.

But is it utopian, or self-defeating, to wish to help man to be moral (i.e. to do right) by the logic of the institutions in which he is set; to make it easy rather than difficult for him to be moral; to permeate his nature with (intrinsic) morality rather than make it necessary for him to sustain a hard and frequent struggle with his nature? Obviously not; otherwise it would be a good thing to put men in the way of temptation. On the reasonable assumption that the dualism cannot be altogether eliminated without destroying morality and spoiling practice with it, why not allow this as an ideal, to be approximated, even though not attained? Where is the line to be drawn beyond which such an endeavour would appear immoral rather than moral, pointless rather than useful?

Certainly the opposite aim – a maximum of conscientious thematic morality; rejecting a 'penetration of the appetite' as 'mere sub-morality' – is altogether mistaken. In fact, it is *itself utopian or pre-utopian*. It is one way to liberation from the consciousness of man's frailty and imperfection: the bearer of 'pure' morality in us, the 'intelligible ego', identified with infallible conscience, embodies an actual and perfect moral will, a sanctified human entity. 'Empirical' humanity, hopeless anyhow, is dismissed, but over and above it towers *another human nature*, which is 'good in itself'. This is Kant's 'noumenal' self and Rousseau's 'citizen'; 'sublated' in Hegel's self-realization of the Idea and sanctified State (via Fichte's Great or Universal Ego) and in Marx's deeper and more concrete vision of the birth of a thoroughly 'valid', spontaneously perfect, supra-moral, humanity.

There is a definite harking back in Marx (and Feuerbach) to Aristotelian naturalism: the liberal-Kantian-Rousseauian *split* between man-spiritual and man-empirical (not to be confused with the *real* split, expressed in the experience of right and wrong) is discarded, and a kind of 'virtue' – that is, the intrinsic rectification of human nature as a whole – is put in the place of split-conscious thematic morality. But there is an enormous difference between Aristotle and Marx. Though both have a primarily and unduly *political* conception of virtue, Aristotle has in view a 'second' nature of man which really means a *good character* to be obtained laboriously (and uncertainly) in every person as such, with the essentially imperfect general human nature subsisting as its background and undergrowth, whereas Marx means a re-creation, by social institutions as moulded and conditioned by history, of the nature of mankind as such, to be realized not in quasi exceptional elite individuals but wholesale, automatically, and on a plane of actual universality. Thus human existence is, in a sense, to emerge from the 'dissipation' of space and time into a unified and integral status of all-selfhood and all-validity, above any inhibitions and any categories of right and wrong: Utopia proper, of which Aristotle would never have dreamed, although his 'virtuous man' (and the Greek 'sophos' [wise man] in general) certainly bears a utopian connotation. Still, Aristotelian man remains in a non-utopian mode in that he is *placed in 'the world'* altogether, confronted with the universal condition of man's weakness, imperfection and dividedness – whereas the entelechy of the Marxian vision is a man who – in the Christian phrase, but in a very different sense – 'has overcome the world'. Morality is meant to be absorbed in practice: there is something Aristotelian and Thomist, reminiscent also of Nietzsche and the existentialists, about Marxism's insistence on *not* delineating beforehand the picture of the *Zukunftsstaat* (future state), which will be organized in freedom by a different sort of human nature and consciousness. For it means that moral demands are in themselves meaningless, and that in Communist society man will create his own world not by conforming to any moral claim but by *pure practice*, which precisely is outside the reach of moral imperatives and of control by a consciousness not itself. This is the Christian fantasy of unjudgeableness taken seriously, integrally and atheistically.

It is not, of course, utopian or objectionable to further the penetration of man's will and its supporting appetites by morality, and to make it easier rather than more difficult for man to do right and to shun wrong. In fact, the intrinsic (intuitive, intentional) conception of morality is strictly incompatible with the emphasis of pure conscientiousness and the dichotomy between the so-called 'mass of inclinations' and the one abstract and homogeneous rational will. The manifoldness of moral emphases and values must imply penetration and intermediate positions between formal thematic morality and dispositions which 'happen to be good' (such as an innate normal sexual instinct). The proper balance between 'inurement' to temptation and the removal of strong, staple temptations, and so on, cannot be determined in a wholly general fashion. How far social institutions could be refashioned so as to evoke an intrinsically 'moral' rather than favour an 'immoral' practice on the part of individuals is also a very complex problem incapable of a once-and-for-all solution. Though their subject-matter is moral, questions of this kind are practical rather than 'moral', or subject to moral norms.

What *is* utopian and profoundly immoral is the programme of discarding conscientious and thematic in favour of an automatic and prefabricated (habitual and infra-emphatic) morality; and this tendency can be active not only in ambitious political conceptions but in the details of everyday educational activities. For instance, the method of obtaining 'intrinsically good' behaviour through non-moral means, including false practical arguments, and omitting to acquaint the pupil with the necessity of observing moral rules *as such*. Virtue ethics in this exquisite sense means the exclusion of the most important single virtue: the habit of being prepared, if need be, to act against one's appetites or inclinations as well as against one's interests.

In other words, the utopian attitude consists not in cultivating and orientating practice as such, in convergence with moral demands, but in postulating, expressly or operationally, the supersession of moral demands by the immanent 'perfection' of practice, as if man could be 'simply good' and live righteously (at any rate, successfully, happily and self-sufficiently) without awareness of the *tension* between what he feels like doing and what he ought to do.

It is of central importance to note that man lives morally mainly by what may briefly be called 'moral sentiments' – the sense of objectivity and justice, the capacity to put oneself in the other fellow's place, compassion, the horror of falsehood or of dissipation, and so on – which are *neither* the abstract sense of duty, reverence for the Law or obedience to the Divine Will, *nor* primary spontaneous appetites; in fact we may well *feel* vividly, 'in our very bones', the moral necessity of acting in a certain way and, at the same time, the pull of countervailing pleasures or interests. No doubt, the better a man is morally the more he will tend to do right by sheer inclination, spontaneous desire, or indeed the immanent governance of practice: the last, because the thought of doing wrong would make him unhappy, and upset his practical balance, thus devaluing whatever pleasure or advantage he might draw therefrom.

But such a state of consciousness presupposes thematic morality – that is, an awareness of the radical insufficiency of the immanent practical governance of conduct. He will usually do right easily – which does mean greater goodness – but without any emphatic *in*distinction between right and wrong, and not without a marginal thought of having to and being ready to do right even were it not easy, or in some hypothetical situation in which it *wouldn't* be easy. The state of conscience of such a person will differ qualitatively from that of a person who likewise does right easily, but who at the same time suffers from the delusion of perfection, and believes that what he does easily or by a reflective confrontation of his tastes and interests *is* the right thing *eo ipso*. The first type of man is reliable, the second is not; moreover, on many of us the first will produce, with his ingrained righteousness, an admirable, the second, with his false angelicism, a disgusting impression; and Utopia, in this context, means preference for the second type, in the belief that his 'morphological perfection' really means moral perfection.

4 IMPLICIT AND THEMATIC MORALITY

This has been dealt with above by implication; but one point of view should be subjoined. All utopian and subversive mentality creates a new type of cleavage in the human mind in place of the dividedness it is intent on doing away with. The utopian dreamer or planner of a 'seamless' world is out to reduce all morality to *implicit* morality (men so situated, conditioned and educated that they cannot sin, and will do right by following their appetites and planning the details of their joint lives). But at the same time this monistic obsession itself, in the utopian mind, corresponds to the attitude of an exclusively thematic morality, and is usually associated with some arbitrary ethical postulate ('the elimination of social justice' – whatever that is; 'the creation of true community'; 'the elimination of conventional lies'; 'the creation of a complex conspectus and conscious management of the concerns of mankind') installed in absolute rulership over life, riding roughshod over all other values or desiderata, moral and practical. A short-circuited theme of perfect moralization, then, links up here with the programme of driving all concrete moral themes, with the tensions they imply, out of the texture of men's lives. The regime of revolutionary tyranny is only a projection, on the plane of concrete moral organization, of the *logic* inherent in the utopian mind: the polarity of an extreme moral thematicism which that mind assumes as its own norm, and a total materialization and functionalization of the moral theme in the human mind-to-be which that mind presumes to 'create'.

5 LEVELS AND MODALITIES OF VALUE

The utopian mind has this in common with Kantian or formalist ethics – that, the emphasis being on a perfect and perfectly dominant will rather than on the manifold criteria and dimensions of value, the appreciation of different degrees, levels and modalities (ethical, aesthetic, intellectual …) tends to disappear. (This implies postulatory perfectionism, puritanism, pedantic negation of *parvitas materiae* [material insignificance]; claims that pleasure must be divine service and vice versa, that the highest art is guaranteed by the perfection of the *mind* we may primarily experience as 'truth' or 'justice', etc.) But there is a difference. The totalitarian monism of the utopian attitude is only *announced* in the Kantian-formalist conception, which is inimical to the intrinsic manifoldness of values but not to division as such; its ethic is monomaniac but strictly at variance with a metaphysical monism of value; the split between the intelligible and the empirical self is an inadequate but emphatic barrier against ecstatic monism. But there *is* complete agreement – betraying the half-hidden totalitarian bent of Kant's moral as of Rousseau's civic formalism – as regards the strictly monistic conception of moral value, which is identified with thematically moral intention (Rousseau: intention on behalf of the community) as such, and therefore cannot be specified by the type of objects (purposes and situations) meant in an action.

6 CENTRES OF PRACTICAL REFERENCE: THE INDIVIDUAL AND THE COMMON GOOD

Again, Kant and Rousseau identify the 'moral' or 'civic' (that is, morally valid) will with a universal or general will. The difference is that the universal will derives from pure rationality – in an Averroistic mode, as it were: pure reason can only be the *same* reason, whose-ever reason it is - whereas the general will, a conception less radical from a qualitative point of view, derives from a social act of juridical self-commitment, as contrasted to a self-constitution *qua* 'real' self. The Rousseauian scheme is less crazy than the Kantian in that it more openly reposes on a fiction of identity; Kant's suggests a metaphysical essence of man actually identical in all men, though in general submerged under their individually different empirical egos. Practically, Rousseau points more dangerously to a realization of Utopia, the general will being embodied in the Jacobin leadership. But neither Kantian nor Rousseauian rationalism crosses the ultimate utopian threshold of a mirage of actual identity of the intelligible with the empirical man, and correspondingly, of Individual and Society. This is what Communism aims at, with the instrument of dialectical materialism and 'interpreting a world *through* changing it' at its disposal.

Under the Communist dispensation, morality is *eo ipso* non-existent − in the sense of conscience − because personal practice, properly speaking, is doomed; there shall be only one indissoluble unity of human practice (the practice of mankind) which, of course, is *en bloc* equivalent to morality. The deeper metaphysical sense of the Individual–Society Identity is that Man is meant to be identical with the world: this anthropo-pantheism is expressed by Marxian materialism but also by Comte's divinity of mankind, by personified Evolution and Heidegger's personified *das Dasein*, notwithstanding its pessimistic and blind, impersonal note. Man is no longer *in* the world but *his own world* all in all. Once more, Ou-topia.

EDITOR'S NOTE

This self-contained extract from 'Copybook I' (see Editor's Introduction, p. xxx) was probably composed in 1956. A certain amount of rewriting was necessary to convert notes into reasonably continuous text, and some slight omissions have also been made.

Life without Utopia

Estoy, luego soy
('Not to be somewhere is not to be')

A SOME FORMAL PRINCIPLES OF THE ANTI-UTOPIAN ATTITUDE

1 Regard for the future in continuity with the present only.

2 Potential change confined to limited points or a conjunction of quasi isolated points only. ('Point' has not necessarily, of course, a local sense.)

3 Express emphasis on maintained continuity in regard to institutional frameworks and symbols: reforms, however deep-cutting, to be conceived in the broader context of an intention of maintenance.

4 Morally inspired reforms to appeal to permanent standards, not constitute moral innovations.

5 The *particular* reference of a plan of reform (an organization, action or improvement) not to be fictitiously *identified* with 'the interest of the whole' but only brought in connection therewith.

6 Thematic primacy of the negative: incisive reforms not justified except as response to a 'pressing need' – anxiety to get rid of a definite evil vividly resented as such.

7 The elimination of an evil not to be interpreted as a phase in the 'emancipation *from evil*': express awareness of the danger of new evils.

8 Intrinsic limitation of the range of competence and 'mission' of governmental power: notwithstanding its dignity and importance (and the falseness of its reductive liberal conception) it is only *one* of the forces of civilization and centres of power in society, and a merely secondary agent of the shaping of personal life.

9 No human factors, agencies, authorities or powers are morally sovereign incarnations of value; there is no such thing as

an all-uniting Centre of Consciousness. All must expressly submit to external standards not of their own creation.

10 Terms like 'liberty', 'happiness' and 'rights' (likewise 'glory', 'popular will', 'culture', etc.) always to be used with express reservations and qualifications – campaigns, propaganda, reforms, and so on, to be expressly and conspicuously *removed* from the aura of perfectionist and omnipotential illusions.

11 Conjoint emphasis on existing good and the difficulty of its preservation, and on continually emerging special tasks.

12 Stimulating men's pride in seeing through and despising utopian delusions.

B   HOW CAN WE LIVE WITHOUT UTOPIA?

It is impossible to live without Utopia, just as it is impossible to live without evil: that is, it is impossible to eliminate the utopian attitude altogether. To make 'life without Utopia' *depend* on this would itself be utopian.

But to try to purify one's thought and will from utopism is perfectly possible, just as it is possible to seek the good and fight against evil. One must;

- take account of utopian influences and bar the road to them in forming one's conceptions and projects;
- live in awareness of the utopian peril (with its pseudo-realist disguises);
- formulate and cultivate (a) an expressly anti-utopist will, and (b) non-utopian types of practical activity, both moral and reformatory;
- combine intense and even radical evaluative attitudes with a many-sided awareness of uncertainty, and the necessarily mixed character of both their hoped-for and their probable results.

A list of anti-utopian axioms must take into account:

- moral imperatives and the primacy of the negative;
- the finitude and plurality of our value-references;

- the special courage needed to face imperfection;
- habits of detachment and openness;
- adjustment to reality and resistance to historicism;
- maintenance of self-distance while keeping open the sources of primordial energy . . . .

Anti-utopism must be simultaneously:

- from below: an appeal to primitive vitality, to the senses, to the instinct of propriety, to well-rooted traditions;
- from the side: an appeal to pluralism, the sense of contingency, limits, balance, moderation, compromise, awareness of one's being inserted in time;
- from above: education for a high level of awareness, but not beyond the range of human capacity, as required for firm convictions and sustained, vital and concentrated willing without the help (rather, founded on the exclusion) of utopian narcotics.

How can religious ties help in this? They provide an antidote against the depressing effect of terrestrial uncertainties, and help to render ineffective the mirage of false practical certitude. In addition, the religious dimension may reinforce the sense of the *given*, the full acceptance of the Real as such, as against the infantilism of omnipotence and its cheap fantasies of man the 'creator' ('unique subject', 'general will'). The Christian sense of personalism, of non-unifiable identities, of 'dividism', equilibrium and insurmountable preponderances.

EDITOR'S NOTE
Kolnai's Spanish motto comes from a projected table of contents closely related to the one mentioned in my note at the end of The Utopian Mind, Chapter III.

'Some formal principles' comes from 'Copybook II' (see Editor's Introduction, p. xxx), and probably dates from 1956. 'How can we live without Utopia?' (my translation) probably dates from late 1959 to early 1960, and constitutes most of a very short paper in French entitled '*L'Utopie et la réalité sociale*'.

Notes

INTRODUCTION

1 See Adam Ferguson, *An Essay in the History of Civil Society* (1767), IV, 1.

2 See Michael Oakeshott, *Rationalism in Politics, and Other Essays*, London: Methuen, 1962.

3 See Hannah Arendt, *The Origins of Totalitarianism*, New York: Harcourt Brace, 1951. Revised edn, New York: Meridian Books, 1958.

4 On these points, Kolnai's analyses are very close, though he could not have known them, to those developed by Alain Besançon in his great work *Les origines intellectuelles du léninisme* (Paris: Calmann-Lévy, 1977), English translation *The Rise of the Gulag*.

5 See Sir Karl Popper, *The Poverty of Historicism*, London: Routledge & Kegan Paul, 1957; also 'Towards a Rational Theory of Tradition', in *Rationalist Annals*, London, 1948.

6 See Michael Oakeshott, *On Human Conduct*, Oxford University Press, 1975; also *Rationalism in Politics*.

7 Kolnai wrote a noteworthy review of *Rationalism in Politics*: see *Philosophy*, XL, 1965, pp. 263–4.

8 [Ed.: Pierre Manent could not have known that some of Kolnai's plans for the book show that he intended to deal at length with this topic, though he never actually did so.]

9 [Ed.: Kolnai himself pointed, incidentally, to the utopian aspects of Hobbes. See the translation of 'La Mentalité utopienne' in this volume, p. 155.]

EDITOR'S INTRODUCTION

1 *Der ethische Wert und die Wirklichkeit*, Freiburg im Breisgau: Herder, 1927.

2 'Die Ideologie des sozialen Fortschritts' and 'Kritik des sozialen Fortschritts', *Der deutsche Volkswirt*, I, 30, 22 April 1927, pp. 933–6; I, 31, 29 April 1927, pp. 965–9.

3 'Uber das Mystische', *Imago*, VII, 1, 1921, pp. 40–70.

4 Hence his instinctive affinity with G.K. Chesterton.

5 See also *The Utopian Mind*, I, 6.
6 *The Thomist*, October 1944, pp. 429–57.
7 *Cité Libre*, Montreal, 13, 1955, pp. 9–20.
8 *Philosophy*, XXXV, 1960, pp. 234–54.
9 *La Table Ronde*, September 1960, pp. 62–84.
10 These were printed in the posthumous collection: Aurel Kolnai, *Ethics, Value and Reality*, London: The Athlone Press, 1977, pp. 63–122.
11 *Philosophy*, XL, 1965, pp. 68–71.
12 *Philosophy*, XXXVII, 1962, pp. 368–9.
13 Unpublished letter to Salvador Pons, 20 October 1956 (in Spanish).
14 Unpublished letter to D.Z. Phillips, 2 February 1970.
15 The paper is also related to Kolnai's war on Existentialism.
16 During the last years of his life he became exhausted from the sheer weight of his winter clothing.
17 See also the passage quoted above, p. xxxii.

The Utopian Mind

CHAPTER 1
(For full references to some of the books mentioned, see the Bibliography in this volume.)

1 Talmon (1952), p. 255.
2 Ibid., p. 253.
3 It is according to this trivial usage that the saying 'The utopias of today are the realities of tomorrow' is confirmed (as often as not) by experience. This defence of utopianism will be fully discussed below (II, 2, iii).
4 There is a slightly utopian ring about the 'United States of America' (compared to 'Mexico' or 'Canada') as a name for a nation, and a vastly more explicit utopian flavour about the 'Union of Soviet Socialist Republics' or 'the Soviet nation'.
5 *Uchronie*: coined by the French philosopher Charles Renouvier in 1876.
6 Compare Walter Besant's delightful counter-Utopia *The Revolt of Man*.
7 Criminals, styled 'atavistic survivals', likewise incur medical treatment in Bellamy's *Looking Backward* (from the year 2000).
8 Renan's old-age fantasy *Dialogues philosophiques*; Stapledon's *Last and First Men*.

9 [Ed.: On the connection between 'literary' utopias and 'serious' utopian works, see also the first section of The Utopian Mentality below.]

10 [Ed.: Compare II, 6, iv; also the two short fragments entitled Life without Utopia.]

11 Plato proposes adoption by the 'guardian class' of the myth that its members are 'born to rule' by virtue of their distinctive make-up, their nature being 'composed of gold'. Again, the young people whom the magistrates, for eugenic reasons, bar from marriage should be made to believe that their rejection was due simply to blind luck: their names were not among those drawn in the pairing lottery. Such devices of conscious and cold-blooded imposture, though freely used by subversive totalitarianism as well, are more inherently characteristic of its regressive sub-species; the chimera of 'perfection' is not genuinely believed here but, rather, fostered as a means to ensure stability. (Compare the nationalist forgeries, in eighteenth-century Scotland and nineteenth-century Bohemia and Hungary, of ancient literary documents.) Plato, however, expects *later generations* of his 'guardian class' actually to *believe* the myth of their golden substance, which falls in entirely with the logic of utopian 'perfection': the 'perfect' happiness, harmony and self-satisfaction of mankind necessarily connote a trait of idiocy, which the visionary *creators* of utopian perfection reserve for its fortunate products.

12 Pacifistic Utopias may similarly bifurcate into a conception of 'world harmony' based on 'national self-determination' and the massive unitarism of the 'World State'.

13 [Ed.: A *'phalanstère'* is a self-sufficient social unit, and features in utopian treatises by Charles Fourier published in 1808, 1822 and 1829.]

14 The *Men like Gods* of H.G. Wells are not, of course, hampered, thwarted or driven to work by anything like penal severities, the threat of starvation, or a vexatious education seeking to enforce moral discipline. But is not such a state of things likely to breed an abundance of idlers, which may hardly be conducive to the public weal or provide an altogether beautiful sight? By no means: there will be few idlers or none, for idlers would 'find no lovers' – the high tone of a perfect society ensuring that 'no one loves those who lack energy and distinction'.

15 Quoted in Talmon (1952), p. 53. All the following quotations from Rousseau, Robespierre, Saint-Just, Babeuf and Mably are from Talmon's book.

16 Ibid., p. 114.
17 Ibid., p. 42. Virtue, as traditionally understood, means a stable habit
    in man of obeying the dictate of his enlightened and informed
    conscience; a 'second nature', perhaps, but distinct from and
    superimposed upon his 'first nature' – not substituted for it –
    of whose 'sinful' tendencies he remains aware, should he even,
    conformably to the Aristotelian formula, 'do the good with
    pleasure'. [Ed: For a discussion of the 'attenuated utopianism' in
    the Aristotelian ethics of 'virtue' and of 'prudence', see The Utopian
    Negation of Fundamental and Ineliminable Distinctions below.]
18 Talmon (1952), p. 84.
19 Ibid., p. 39.
20 Ibid., p. 37.
21 A primary tendency to radical egalitarianism is proper to Utopia,
    seeing its horror of distinctions and diversities (which harbour the
    germs of dissensions, frontiers and haphazard compromises: that
    is, a finite, contingent and imperfect existence). A 'single Mind'
    of society, in which all individual minds are 'fused', would best
    accord with an *identical* state of perfection for all: the '*pantisocracy*'
    of the late-eighteenth-century radicals; Rousseau's *volonté générale*
    [general will]; Bentham's 'omnicompetent legislature' as an organ
    of everybody's 'balance of happiness'. Yet, Identity rather than
    Equality as such being the keyword of the utopian conception,
    it will secondarily reveal an option for possible inequalities with
    a functional position in the life of the social 'Whole', *regulated
    by central authority* and cleansed from the counter-aspects, the
    ambiguities and the lability which attach to inequality in liberal
    society or to the pre-liberal 'Tory' conception of inequality. (Cf.
    Wells's 'Samurais', or the artificially bred Greek-lettered castes in
    Huxley's *Brave New World*.)
22 I do not, however, admit that utopianism is a mere product,
    reflection or vital requisite of industrial civilization: see the passage
    from Talmon (1952), p. 255, quoted above in section 2 (p.7).
23 Talmon (1952), p. 61.
24 Ibid., p. 195.
25 *Troilus and Cressida*, Act I Scene iii.
26 I trust I am making it clear enough that what I mean is *not* that
    reality as such is 'good', or that good is what is 'according to nature'.
    Rather, I mean the very opposite: that reality as such and the good
    as such are not *and cannot be made* identical, and that we can, should
    and must work for the realization of values and the erasure of evils,
    but that we cannot do so or even form a relevant *conception* of doing

so except in the framework of *given* reality, the matrix of existent good on the one hand and (as a whole) unalterably defective on the other. Where exactly the boundary lies between 'nature' and the simple 'factual' data of life I do not know; but if by 'nature' is meant the ensemble of the relatively constant features of human existence, I would venture to say not, indeed, that good is defined by conformity to and evil by opposition to nature, but that the good can be fruitfully pursued – more, can only be validly thought – only in consonance with nature, and that disregard for nature constitutes one pre-eminent form of evil.

27 '*Tension* with imperfection' – implying an acceptance, not of any specified imperfection (let alone of all) but of the fact of imperfection, and therewith, *in concreto*, of many specified imperfections, existing and not able to be tackled in a given context, or foreseen as an accompaniment of reformatory actions. Burke's ingenious defence of 'prescription and prejudice' expresses (and sometimes slightly overstates) this insight; so does Grillparzer's Emperor Rudolph in *Ein Bruderzwist im Hause Habsburg*, standing for conservative wisdom as against the clerical dictatorship represented by his brother Ferdinand and the pro-liberal progressivism of his brother Matthias:

> May Matthias rule, then. And may he come to feel that cavilling is easy and supercilious criticism deceptive - playing as they are with blithe possibilities – while action is difficult, as a reality which must tune in with the orbit of realities. He will discover that human statutes necessarily bear in them an admixture of the unreasonable, seeing that they are made for men, the children of irrationality.

Or again, concerning monarchical power:

> Do you think it was in the hope of seeing a galaxy of great rulers arise that hereditary right was established in the State? Not at all: only because a Centre is necessary round which all that is good and right may gather, withstanding things false and evil – for that reason alone did men plant the seed of a harvest, in the dubious realm of the future, which at times has proved to be rich, and at other times mediocre.

28 Its deceptiveness lies mainly in the false semblance that the abstract and general concept of 'perfection' or 'supreme value' actually encloses, involves and represents the goods and perfections, as known from their genuine experience and diversified pursuit, in their immense variety.

29 Talmon (1952), p. 87.
30 The Marxian myth of the 'class struggle' (linked to the silly and venomous Marxian caricature of 'class society') is often superficially criticized as a piece of 'coarse-grained naturalism' or a 'gospel of hatred' on a par with polemical and particularist nationalism or racism. In fact, it has no meaning or motive except as a 'dialectical' preamble to the 'eirenic' utopia of the 'classless society' of Man restored to perfect unity.

CHAPTER 2

1 The reference is to Knittermeyer (1949).
2 See note 1.
3 Jacob Burckhardt, *Judgements on History and Historians*, trans. Harry Zohn, London: Allen & Unwin, 1959, p. 214.
4 [Ed.: All these short philosophical quotations were used as chapter-mottoes in Kolnai's doctoral thesis (Aurel Kolnai, *Der ethische Wert und die Wirklichkeit*, Freiburg im Breisgau: Herder, 1927).]
5 Utopian and anti-utopian moods may alternate in one man's mind. Michael Vörösmarty, possibly the finest Hungarian poet, celebrated the fourth centenary of the invention of the printing-press in his poem 'To the memory of Gutenberg' (1836), a majestic, enthusiastic and amazingly precise and complete vision of the social-revolutionary Utopia: Gutenberg's triumph will be consummated only on the day when the postulates of Enlightenment, Social Equality, Universal Peace with the elimination of all violence, Universal Direct Democracy and Universal Justice according to the uniform conception of Mankind shall have been fulfilled. (Technological marvels and boundless abundance alone are – strangely enough, in this context – forgotten.) Yet, chastened by the disappointing outcome and aftermath of the 1848–9 revolutions, the selfsame Vörösmarty was to write in the grandest of his poems, 'The Old Gipsy' (1854), this magnificent anti-utopian strophe – not without an echo of formal and historicist utopian expectations:

> Let the blind star, this miserable earth,
> Toss in the whirlpool of its bitter broth;
> Of filth and frenzy and delusion's fury
> Let it be cleansed in the dire tempest's wrath.
> Above the flood, from out the plumbless dark,
> Enshrining a new world, rise, Noah's ark!

6 Cf. in English 'the common good', 'common courtesy', 'common decency', 'common sense', on the one side; yet 'common' as a synonym of 'vulgar' on the other, and the neutral 'common occurrence'. In German, *ordentlich* means 'orderly' or 'neat' and sometimes 'decent' or 'regular', while *ordinär*, the same word as 'ordinary', is colloquial for 'offensively vulgar', 'dishonestly mean' or sometimes 'flashily or noisily pretentious'.

7 [Ed.: This chapter was written in late 1958 and the first half of 1959.]

8 See section 2, i of this chapter.

9 See section 4, ii of this chapter.

10 [Ed.: The 'Running Notes' for Chapter IV (Chapter III of this edition) referred to in the Editor's Introduction imply that it was to have dealt further with the theme of wanting, and refer to a 'separate sheet'. A small sheet answering this description reads as follows:

> We don't know why we want this, why we want that. Certainly there are connections, end-and-means schemas, convergences, and 'intelligible' desiring, preferring and deciding within established horizons of practice; there are constants in no apparent need of justification, and justifications in their terms. But the plurality and contingency of our needs and desires, and in their framework, of our choices, is irreducible. This canvas is further shot through with alternances and contrasts as well as with standard inter-individual and intergroup divergences, so much so that incongruity is ineliminable and a sense of contradiction arises, the more so as we tend loosely to express our singular maxims of action or decision in universal terms.
>
> *Utopia* means redemption from this 'disorder' (i.e. order interwoven with disorder and dependent on it) at the price of a set of *standard contradictions*, the centre of which are 'wanting *above all* something one doesn't *want*', 'creating reality outside the acceptance of reality', and 'dissociation destined to ensure unity'. Thereto corresponds the linking of Identity with the rupture of identity, and anonymous (non-identifiable as to its wielder) yet genuine (unitary and unlimited) tyranny.

11 See section 5, i of this chapter.

12 [Ed.: But cf. Life without Utopia in this volume.]

Other Papers

THE MORAL THEME IN POLITICAL DIVISION

1 For the partly non-relativist character of Marxist ethics and its having some points in common with ordinary morality, see H.B. Acton, *The Illusion of the Epoch* (1955), pp. 195 ff.

2 The distinction roughly corresponds to that between teleological and deontological concepts; cf. P.H. Nowell-Smith, *Ethics* (Penguin Books, 1954), pp. 224 f. I hold that 'ideals', however great their moral significance may be, are as essentially distinct from universal moral obligations as are 'interests' or 'tastes'; but the point cannot be argued further here.

3 Cf. W.B. Gallie, 'Liberal Morality and Socialist Morality' in *Philosophy, Politics and Society* (ed. Peter Laslett, 1956), pp. 116–33. In this most penetrating essay, the author's opinion – with which I disagree – that political ideologies with a partly antithetic moral emphasis mean 'different moralities' is not unequivocally sustained.

4 Contrast, in classic political literature, such authors as Filmer (or even Aquinas and Hooker) with the aristocratic and libertarian rightism of Tocqueville or, today, B. de Jouvenel in *Power* (English edn. 1948).

5 Cf. de Jouvenel's conception of liberty as being primarily a possession, a position, and a personal character ('Liberty's Aristocratic Roots', in *Power*, pp. 270–87).

6 For research of this kind, see H.J. Eysenck, *The Psychology of Politics* (1954), *passim*, especially as regards statistical enquiries into possible connections between political attitudes and types of temperament.

7 The formula was coined by G.K. Chesterton, writing, in that context, as an equalitarian social reformer in opposition to the cult of success and strength.

8 Often emphasized by Charles Maurras; see, for example, *Mes idées politiques* (1937), p. 55.

9 Cf. Karl Mannheim, 'Conservative Thought' in *Essays on Sociology and Social Psychology* (1953), p. 88; and his distinction between direct, spontaneous 'psychological' traditionalism and modern 'ideological' conservatism, pp. 94 ff.

10 See Raymond Aron's distinction of realistic, critical conservatism, nostalgic traditionalism, and Fascism, in Part I, 'De la Droite', of *Espoir et peur du siècle* (1957), p. 38 and *passim*. Cf. also his logical refutation of traditionalism, p. 98, and his demarcation of realistic conservatism not only from the socialist faith in planning but also from the rightist liberal dogma of the market economy, p. 72.

11 Cf. the theory of a Christian Toryism, affirming the social necessity

of class and status but reluctant to interpret social in terms of intrinsic superiority, as set out by Christopher Hollis in *Dr. Johnson* (1928), pp. 9 ff.

12 For the morally positive effect that may be produced by state compulsion, see J.D. Mabbott, *The State and the Citizen* (1948), pp. 66–70.

13 The Marxian prophecy, writes Michael Polanyi in *The Logic of Liberty* (1951), pp. 105 ff., 'required from its disciples no other belief than that in the force of bodily appetites and yet at the same time satisfied their most extravagant moral hopes'.

14 On 'rights' in the strong and in the weak sense, see D. Daiches Raphael, *Moral Judgment* (1955), p. 47.

15 Ibid.

16 Bentham's idea of the 'Panopticon' (cf. Elie Halévy, *The Growth of Philosophic Radicalism*, English edn 1928, pp. 82 ff.), the architectural symbol of a completely perspicuous society, expresses the vision of all human affairs lying open to one governmental Reason. Given a society so ordered that the self-interest of everybody coincides with the general interest (pp. 404–9), public Reason and Will are to represent the reason and wills of all. This is expressed in the postulate that the legislature, the representative organ of all adult citizens, shall be 'omnicompetent'; any checks or restraints on its competence would 'contradict the Greatest Happiness Principle' by disrupting the all-embracing conspectus and calculation of utility (ibid.).

17 For a peculiarly incisive criticism of this conception, and of all ideals of a single 'ethos' informing Society, see Claude Sutton, *Farewell to Rousseau* (1936); e.g. on p. 213: 'We assert . . . that a man cannot be a good citizen if he only feels himself obliged to do what *everyone* else feels to be obligatory for *everyone*.'

18 'Il faut que la clarté du dedans et la clarté du dehors se confondent et pénètrent et que l'homme . . . *ne discerne plus dans la réalité nouvelle* ce que jadis il appelait *de noms en apparence contraires* l'idéal et le réel.' ['Internal clarity and external clarity must mingle and interpenetrate, and man must . . . *cease to distinguish in the new reality* between what he once called "the ideal" and what he once, *using an apparently contrary term*, called "the real".'] From a speech by Jean Jaurès, quoted in *Almanach Hachette*, 1908 (emphasis added).

19 As a 'non-millenarian' leftist, distrustful of human perfectibility, Raymond Aron (*Espoir et peur du siècle*, pp. 97 f.) names 'Alain', who, in the 1920s and 1930s was the outstanding philosopher of French radicalism. He might have added the name of Julien Benda. We might further instance the rationalist K.R. Popper

in this country, and the Lutheran divine Reinhold Niebuhr in the USA.

20 Cf. in Ulysses' speech on the destruction of 'degree' and its consequences (*Troilus and Cressida*, I, iii), the lines (emphasis added):

> Force should be right; or rather, right and wrong,
> Between whose *endless jar* justice resides,
> Should lose their names, and so should justice too.

21 Cf. in the famous passage: 'But the age of chivalry is gone . . .' in Burke's *Reflections on the Revolution in France*, the actual use of 'illusion' as a *pro*-word (a usage current in Spanish:

> All the pleasing illusions, which made power gentle and obedience liberal . . . are to be dissolved by this new conquering empire of light and reason. All the decent drapery of life is to be rudely torn off. All the superadded ideas, furnished from the wardrobe of moral imagination, which the heart owns, and the understanding ratifies, as necessary to cover the defects of our naked, shivering nature, and to raise it to dignity . . . are to be exploded . . . . On this new scheme of things, a king is but a man, a queen is but a woman . . . (Everyman's edn, p. 74)

22 The logical impossibility of finding 'a formula of overall distributive justice' – this presumption necessarily involving 'indifference to the immediate obligations of commutative justice' (p. 163) – is exposed with unparalleled clearness and cogency in Chapter 9 of B. de Jouvenel, *Sovereignty* (English edn 1958). At the same time, the author devotes to the problem of 'social justice' a very much more positive, painstaking, sincere and intelligent attention than is usual with rightist thinkers.

Bibliography

The basis of this booklist is a bibliography attached to 'La Mentalité utopienne' ('The Utopian Mentality'). I have added to it the works referred to in *The Utopian Mind* and other works studied in detail by Kolnai or mentioned by him as important in relation to his project. It also includes the 'literary' Utopias, including 'anti-Utopias' mentioned by him, but excludes 'serious' utopian writing, such as works by Plato, Rousseau or Marx.

Acton, H.B., *The Illusion of the Epoch*, London: Cohen & West, 1955.

Arendt, Hannah, *The Origins of Totalitarianism*, New York: Meridian Books edn, 1958.

Arendt, Hannah, *The Human Condition*, Chicago: University of Chicago Press, 1958.

Aron, Raymond, *L'Opium des intellectuels*, Paris: Calmann-Lévy, 1955.

Aron, Raymond, *Espoir et peur du siècle*, Paris: Calmann-Lévy, 1957.

Babbitt, Irving, *Democracy and Leadership*, Boston, MA: Houghton Mifflin, 1924.

Baroja, Pio, *Desde la Última Vuelta del Camino* (Memoirs, vol. I), Madrid, 1950.

Benn, S.I. and Peters, R.S., *Social Principles and the Democratic State*, London: Allen & Unwin, 1959.

Berneri, Marie-Louise, *Journey through Utopia*, London: Routledge & Kegan Paul, 1950.

Burckhardt, Jacob, *Judgements on History and Historians*, trans. Harry Zohn, London: Allen & Unwin, 1959.

Cochin, Augustin, *Les Sociétés de pensée et la démocratie*, Paris: Librairie Plon, 1921.

Cohn, Norman, *The Pursuit of the Millennium*, London: Secker & Warburg, 1957.

Delvaille, Jules, *Essai sur l'histoire de l'idée de progrès jusqu'à la fin du XVIIIᵉ siècle*, Paris: Alcan, 1910.

Doren, Alfred, *Wunschräume und Wunschzeiten*, Hamburg: Warburg, 1925.

Dubos, René, *Mirage of Health: Utopias, Progress and Biological Change*, London: Allen & Unwin, 1960.

Folch, Gallart, *Alejandro: el ocaso de una gran utopía*, Buenos Aires, 1941.

Freyer, Hans, *Die politische Insel: eine Geschichte der Utopien von Plato bis zur Gegenwart*, Leipzig: Bibliographisches Institut, 1936.

Freyer, Hans, *Theorie des gegenwärtigen Zeitalters*, Stuttgart: Deutsche Verlags-Anstalt, 1956.

Gallie, W.B., 'Liberal Morality and Socialist Morality', in *Philosophy, Politics and Society*, ed. Peter Laslett, Oxford: Blackwell, 1956.

Gomperz, Heinrich, *Die Wissenschaft und die Tat*, Vienna: Gerold, 1934.

Halévy, Elie, *The Growth of Philosophic Radicalism*, London: Faber & Faber, 1952.

Hayek, F.A., *The Counterrevolution of Science*, Glencoe, Illinois: Free Press, 1952.

Hollis, Christopher, *Dr. Johnson*, London: Gollancz, 1928.

Imaz, Eugenio, *Topía y Utopía*, Madrid, 1947.

de Jouvenel, Bertrand, *Power*, London: Hutchinson, 1948

de Jouvenel, Bertrand, *Sovereignty*, Cambridge: Cambridge University Press, 1958.

Jünger, Ernst, *Strahlungen*, Tübingen: Heliopolis, 1949.

Kirk, Russell, *The Conservative Mind*, London: Faber & Faber, 1954.

[Kirchenheim] Anon., *Schlaraffia Politica*, Leipzig: Grunow, 1892.

Knittermeyer, Hinrich, *Jacob Burckhardt*, Stuttgart: Hirsel, 1949.

Little, J.M.D., *A Critique of Welfare Economics*, Oxford: OUP, 1950.

Mabbott, J.B., *The State and the Citizen*, London: Hutchinson, 1948.

Mannheim, Karl, *Ideology and Utopia*, London: Routledge & Kegan Paul, 1936.

Mannheim, Karl, *Man and Society in an Age of Reconstruction*, London: Routledge & Kegan Paul, 1940.

Mannheim, Karl, 'Conservative Thought', in *Essays on Sociology and Social Psychology*, London: Routledge & Kegan Paul, 1953.

Matthias, L.L., *Die Entdeckung Amerikas Anno 1953*, Hamburg: Rowohlt, 1953.

Möbus, Gerhard, *Politik des Heiligen: Geist und Gesetz der Utopia des Thomas Morus*, Berlin: Morus Verlag, 1953.

Morente, Manuel G., *Ensayos sobre el progreso*, Madrid: Revista de Occidente, 1945.

Myrdal, Gunnar, *The Political Element in the Development of Economic Theory*, London: Routledge & Kegan Paul, 1953.

Niebuhr, Reinhold, *The Irony of American History*, London: Nisbet, 1952.

Oakeshott, Michael, *Rationalism in Politics*, London: Methuen, 1962.

Ortega y Gasset, José, *La rebelión de las mases*, Madrid: Revista de Occidente, 1930.

Parkin, Charles, *The Moral Basis of Burke's Political Thought*, Cambridge: Cambridge University Press, 1956.

Polanyi, Michael, *The Logic of Liberty*, London: Routledge & Kegan Paul, 1951.

Polanyi, Michael, *Personal Knowledge*, London: Routledge & Kegan Paul, 1958.

Popper, K.R., *The Open Society and its Enemies*, London: Routledge & Sons, 1945.

Popper, K.R., 'Towards a Rational Theory of Tradition', *Rationalist Annals*, London, 1948.

Popper, K.R., *The Poverty of Historicism*, London: Routledge & Kegan Paul, 1957.

Quabbe, Georg, *Das letzte Reich: Wandel und Wesen der Utopie*, Leipzig: Meiner, 1933.

Raphael, D.D., *Moral Judgement*, London: Allen & Unwin, 1955.

Röpke, Wilhelm, *Die Gesellschaftskrise der Gegenwart*, Zürich: Eugen Rentsch Verlag, 1942.

Ruyer, Raymond, *L'Utopie et les utopies*, Paris: Presses Universitaires de France, 1950.

Sutton, Claude, *Farewell to Rousseau*, London: Christophers, 1936.

Talmon, J.L., *The Origins of Totalitarian Democracy*, London: Secker & Warburg, 1952.

Talmon, J.L., *Political Messianism: the Romantic Phase*, London: Secker & Warburg, 1960.

Tillich, Paul, *Politische Bedeutung der Utopie im Leben der Völker*, Berlin: Gebrüder Weiss, 1951.

Tuveson, Ernest Lee, *Millennium and Utopia: A Study in the Background of the Idea of Progress*, New York: Harper Torch edn, 1964.

Voigt, F.E., *Unto Caesar*, London: Constable, 1938.

LITERARY WORKS

1 Utopias
Bellamy, Edward, *Looking Backward*, 1888.
de Bergerac, Cyrano, *L'autre Monde*, 1638.
Butler, Samuel, *Erewhon*, 1872.

Cabet, Etienne, *Icarie*, 1840.
Campanella, Tommaso, *City of the Sun*, c.1602.

Foigny, Gabriel (pseudonym), *Jacques Sadeur: Aventures dans la découverte et le voyage de la terre Australe*, Paris: Charles Osmont, 1705.

Goethe, Wilhelm Meister's *Years of Travel*, 1821–9.
Goetz, Bruno, *Das Reich ohne Raum*, Potsdam: Gustav Kiepenheuer, 1919.

Haldane, J.B.S., *The Last Judgement*.

Lamartine, Alphonse, *Utopie*, 1837 (a poem).
Lytton, Bulwer, *The Coming Race*, 1871.

More, Thomas, *Utopia*, 1516 (French trans. 1550, English trans. 1551).
Morelly, *Basiliade*, Paris: Société de Libre, 1753.
Morris, William, *News from Nowhere*, 1890.

Renan, Ernest, *Dialogues et Fragments Philosophiques*, Paris: Calmann-Lévy, 1876.

Shaw, Bernard, *Back to Methuselah*, 1921.
Skinner, B.F., *Walden Two*, New York: Macmillan, 1948.
Stapledon, Olaf, *Last and First Men*, 1930 (Penguin edn 1963).

Wells, H.G., *Men like Gods*, 1923.

2 Anti-Utopias
Besant, Walter, *The Revolt of Man*, Edinburgh: Blackwood, 1882.
Borchardt, Herrmann, *The Conspiracy of the Carpenters*, New York: Simon & Schuster, 1943.

Huxley, Aldous, *Brave New World*, London: Chatto & Windus, 1932.

Lewis, C.S., *That Hideous Strength*, London: The Bodley Head, 1945.

Orwell, George, *Nineteen Eighty-four*, London: Secker & Warburg, 1949.

Index

Also Published by Athlone

Anti-Oedipus
Capitalism and Schizophrenia
GILLES DELEUZE AND
FÉLIX GUATTARI
Preface by Michel Foucault
'a major philosophical work' Fredric
Jameson, *Yale University*
0 485 30018 4   pb

A Thousand Plateaus
GILLES DELEUZE AND
FÉLIX GUATTARI
'a rare and remarkable book' *TLS*
0 485 11335 X   hb
0 485 12058 5   pb

Cinema I
The Movement-Image
GILLES DELEUZE
'brilliant observations on the works
of particular directors and individual
works.' *Theatre Journal*
0 485 12081 X   pb

Cinema II
The Time-Image
GILLES DELEUZE
Analyses the representation of
time in film.
0 485 11359 7   hb
0 485 12070 4   pb

Dialogues
GILLES DELEUZE AND CLAIRE
PARNET
Examination of Deleuze's
philosophical pluralism.
0 485 11333 3   hb

Foucault
GILLES DELEUZE
Examination of Foucault's principal
themes – knowledge, power and the
nature of subjectivity.
0 485 11345 7   hb

Kant's Critical Philosophy
GILLES DELEUZE
'written with a breadth of vision and
an eye for significant particular points
which are both remarkable' W H
Walsh, *THES*
0 485 11249 3   hb
0 485 12101 8   pb

Logic of Sense
GILLES DELEUZE
Deleuze seeks to determine the status
of meaning and meaninglessness
through a series of enquiries
with language, games, sexuality,
schizophrenia and literature.
0 485 30063 X   hb

Nietzsche and Philosophy
GILLES DELEUZE
'an extremely rich and systematic
reading of Nietzsche' Ronald
Beiner, *THES*
0 485 11233 7   hb
0 485 12053 4   pb

The Fold: Leibniz and the
Baroque
GILLES DELEUZE
The book embodies an original way
of understanding major intellectual
and artistic movements, employing
the Baroque as a theoretical tool to
analyse contemporary works of art
and the so-called modern condition.
0 485 11421 6   hb
0 485 12087 9   pb

Difference and Repetition
GILLES DELEUZE
A brilliant exposition of the critique
of identity.
0 485 11360 0   hb
0 485 12102 6   pb

Also Published by Athlone

Nietzsche and Metaphor
SARAH KOFMAN
Provides an unusual reading of
Nietzsche's ideas and an incisive
method for investigating his style.
0 485 11422 4   hb
0 485 12098 4   pb

Nietzsche: The Body and Culture
ERIC BLONDEL
'very exciting' Bernard Williams,
University of Cambridge
0 485 11391 0   hb

On Nietzsche
GEORGES BATAILLE
Bataille's profound, life-long
engagement with Nietzsche seen in a
context of modern European thought
and philosophy.
0 485 30068 0   hb

The Tragic Philosopher:
Friedrich Nietzsche
F.A. LEA
The classic account of Nietzsche's
thought, first published in 1957, is
now available in paperback.
'grievously underrated' Michael
Tanner *TLS* (1989)
'illuminating' Edwin Muir
0 485 12095 X   pb

**Difficult Freedom: Essays on
Judaism**
EMMANUEL LEVINAS
An important contribution to the
growing debate about the nature
and significance of religion within
philosophy.
0 485 11379 1   hb

**Beyond the Verse: Talmudic
Readings and Lectures**
EMMANUEL LEVINAS
Further essays from 1969 to 1980,
treating specific Jewish questions
of doctrine, exegesis, religious
philosophy.
0 485 11430 5   hb

In the Time of the Nations
EMMANUEL LEVINAS
Levinas considers Judaism's uncertain
relationship with European culture
since the Enlightenment.
0 485 11449 6   hb

Outside the Subject
EMMANUEL LEVINAS
Levinas engages in critical dialogue
with important contemporary
Continental intellectuals including
Martin Buber, Franz Rosenzweig,
Jean Wahl and Merleau-Ponty, and
takes up major issues of philosophical,
religious and literary concern.
0 485 11412 7   hb
0 485 12097 6   pb

Re-Reading Levinas
BERNASCONI and CRITCHLEY,
eds
Presents essays by thirteen leading
commentators on the work of
Levinas.
0 485 30066 4   hb

**My Life in Germany Before and
After 1933**
KARL LÖWITH
A philosopher's autobiography.
0 485 11414 3   hb
0 485 12109 3   pb

Libidinal Economy
JEAN-FRANÇOIS LYOTARD
A philosophical development of
the Freudian concept of 'libidinal
economy'.
0 485 11420 8   hb
0 485 12083 6   pb

**Redemption and Utopia: Jewish
Libertarian Thought in Central
Europe**
MICHAEL LÖWY
A study in elective affinity.
0 485 11406 2   hb

Also Published by Athlone

Criticism and Truth
ROLAND BARTHES
'an effective introduction, helpful
footnotes ... engaging (and very clear)
foreword to the book.' *Philosophy and
Literature*
0 485 11321 X   hb

Sollers Writer
ROLAND BARTHES
Barthes raises critical issues of central
importance – such as the nature of
narrative, the theory of language, the
problems of traditional realism and
the relationship between literature
and politics.
0 485 11337 6   hb

Death and the Labyrinth
The World of Raymond Roussel
MICHEL FOUCAULT
Major study in literary theory,
criticism and psychology.
0 485 11336 8   hb
0 485 12059 3   pb

The Conflict of Interpretations
Essays in Hermeneutics I
PAUL RICOEUR
Collection of Ricoeur's major essays
on structuralism, psychoanalysis,
hermeneutics and religion.
0 485 30061 3   pb

From Text to Action
Essays in Hermeneutics II
PAUL RICOEUR
Sequel to Ricoeur's earlier volume,
*The Conflict of Interpretations: Essays in
Hermeneutics I*
0 485 30064 8   pb

Violence and Truth
On the Work of René Girard
PAUL DUMOUCHEL, ed
A major collection of essays focusing
upon the critical and interpretative
work of René Girard in advancing a
general theory of culture.
0 485 11329 5   hb

Things Hidden Since the
Foundation of the World
RENÉ GIRARD
'both original and provocative'
Sunday Times
0 485 11307 4   hb

The Scapegoat
RENÉ GIRARD
'an exhilarating book, lucid, concise,
combative, provocative' *Magillis
Literary Annual*
0 485 11306 6   hb

Deceit, Desire and the Novel
RENÉ GIRARD
Offers an interpretation of some basic
cultural problems of our time.
0 485 12067 4   pb

Violence and the Sacred
RENÉ GIRARD
'Crucial reading for anyone interested
in the dynamics of society and
culture' Victor Turner, *Human Nature*
0 485 11341 4   pb

Job: The Victim of his People
RENÉ GIRARD
Girard discusses the question of
sacrifice as the driving force of
culture.
0 485 11304 X   hb

To Double Business Bound
Essays on Literature, Mimesis and
Anthropology
RENÉ GIRARD
An individual desires an object,
not for itself, but because another
individual also desires it. This mimetic
desire, René Girard contends, lies
at the source of all human disorder
and order.
0 485 11343 0   hb